The Crime of the Democrats: Andrew Jackson, Woodrow Wilson, Franklin Roosevelt, Lyndon Johnson, and the Destruction of the Founding Fathers' Dream

Terry L. Koglin

ISBN 979-8-89345-272-3 (paperback)
ISBN 979-8-89345-273-0 (digital)

Copyright © 2024 by Terry L. Koglin

All rights reserved. No part of this publication may be reproduced, distributed, or transmitted in any form or by any means, including photocopying, recording, or other electronic or mechanical methods without the prior written permission of the publisher. For permission requests, solicit the publisher via the address below.

Christian Faith Publishing
832 Park Avenue
Meadville, PA 16335
www.christianfaithpublishing.com

Printed in the United States of America

Abstract

A clear distinction can easily be made between the two major groups contending for control of the government of the United States. This distinction became readily apparent at the very beginning of civil government after the American Revolution and took material form during the debates over ratification of the Constitution. Those who supported ratification became known as Federalists, while those opposing ratification were called Antifederalists. Once ratification of the Constitution was accomplished, the term "Antifederalist" became a pejorative term, and that group, quite large but unable to prevent ratification, chose to become known as Republicans under the leadership of Thomas Jefferson. Jefferson's group was unable to limit the power of the federal government by tortured interpretation of various points contained in the Constitution but was able to make an accommodation with it after taking effective control of the government in the election of 1800. Jefferson and his Republican-Democratic, Republican-Jacksonian-Democrat followers in Congress, and most members of that party since, in the White House and Congress, have been less than respectful of the United States Constitution in spite of being required, per that Constitution, to take an oath of support of it.

Under the leadership of Jefferson and other major Southern slaveholders, the then-named Republican Party's major task was to protect the institution of slavery, which it did successfully until its excesses in that regard led to the Civil War and the complete eradication of slavery shortly thereafter. The term "Republican" had been replaced by Democrat in the party's title during the administration of Andrew Jackson, by which time most Southerners recognized and supported the party's role as the protector of slavery. Ironically, the antislavery group, going under various names and loosely affiliated with the Whig Party organized primarily to oppose Andrew Jackson, eventually chose the word *Republican* for the name of their party, twenty years after its abandonment by the now Democrats. These Democrats, tainted with their disunion attempt, became the minority party after 1860 and remained so for the next seventy years.

The Progressive Movement, originating within the Republican Party around 1900, soon became quite popular and was adopted by the Democratic Party at the same time as the more conservative elements regained control of the Republican Party. The convulsions of the Depression of the 1930s made the Democrats the majority party again, and they immediately ran into opposition from the Supreme Court in their unconstitutional attempts to broaden the powers of the federal government. The Supreme Court's opposition faded after the Democrats received overwhelming support from the public in the election of 1936, in which Roosevelt received his highest percentage of the popular vote. This support continued up to the late twentieth century, when many saw that the liberal policies of the Democrats were unsustainable. The past half century has seen control of the national government passing back and forth between the Democrats and the Republicans, and increasing animosity and lack of ability to form a consensus in government.

Under the Articles of Confederation, the Continental Congress, or the United States in Congress Assembled, was the seat of government with the president as merely the presiding officer. In their proposed plan of government, the delegates to the Constitutional Convention deviated from this distribution of power, maintaining Congress as the seat of government, but delegating more administrative power to the president and adding a nebulously defined court. As revealed in the Federalist Papers,[1] Congress was assumed to be capable of overpowering both the president and the courts, and required restraint. Things did not work out that way, as the House and Senate soon deteriorated to partisan bickering, and most mem-

---

[1] By James Madison, John Jay, and Alexander Hamilton, McLean Edition, 1788, originally published in New York City newspapers.

bers were more concerned about the benefits to their particular state or district than to the good of the nation. Beginning with George Washington, and continuing almost continuously to today, the president assumed the role of leader of the government, including providing leadership to Congress. This book assumes that the presidency is the heart of the government, with the other two branches strictly secondary. The presidents have frequently bypassed the legislative authority of Congress with executive orders and other means, and their role in shaping the Supreme Court has been decisive, particularly with presidents who have served lengthy terms. The presidents have been more or less successful, depending mainly on their own merits, as Congress has usually proven itself to be incompetent to lead, even in legislation alone. Even when controlled by the president's own party, Congress has often been more of a hindrance than a help in promoting the president's legislative agenda.

Comparison is made in this book between Republican presidents and Democrat presidents based on their success at (1) making America great in terms of world prestige and power; (2) improving the quality of life for all Americans; (3) meeting crises, both domestic and international; and (4) overcoming opposition, particularly while president. The forty-six presidents of the United States are ranked in this book according to a numerical rating system based on their influence on the welfare of the United States and its people. Possible ratings range from minus thirty-six (-36) to plus thirty-six (36), with negligible influence rated at 0.0, the maximum possible positive rating at 36.0, and the minimum negative rating at -36.0. The ranked presidents are grouped as follows:

> The Great Presidents: Washington, Lincoln, and Reagan. Ratings: 18.4 to 20.8.
> The Very Good Presidents: Jefferson, John Adams, Polk, Theodore Roosevelt. Ratings: 12.8 to 15.2.
> The Better-than-Average Presidents: Eisenhower, Nixon, Trump, Arthur, McKinley, Taft, Hoover, Coolidge, Ford, Monroe, George

H. W. Bush, John Quincy Adams, Taylor, Hayes. Ratings: 1.6 to 10.8.

The "Average" Presidents (those with a neutral rating of 0.0): Benjamin Harrison, Garfield, William Henry Harrison, Cleveland (First Term).

The Below-Average Presidents: Cleveland (Second Term), Grant, George W. Bush, Harding, Fillmore, Andrew Johnson, Tyler, Van Buren, Carter, Franklin Roosevelt, Truman, Clinton. Ratings: -0.8 to -12.2.

The Poor Presidents: Kennedy, Madison, Wilson, Obama. Ratings: -16.0 to -18.4.

The Bad Presidents: Biden, Lyndon Johnson, Jackson, Buchanan, Pierce. Ratings: -20.2 to -26.0.

Comparison is made between presidents' popularity as measured by election results and their effectiveness as chief executive.

Based on this analysis, it is quickly recognized that, in terms of presidential politics, Republican is good; Democrat is bad. In Congress, the case is not so clear, as each member is free to act according to his own interests and those of his constituents while the spotlight is consistently on the White House. The president is forced to act in the national interest, as he sees it, and is held accountable, by the impeachment process, to the Constitution, by Congress, as they see it, while members of Congress are immune from outside criticism except by the ballot box, which has been proven to be an ineffective remedy for bad government.

Acknowledgements

I received a great many valuable suggestions from Dennis Marchetti of Manchester Center, Vermont, but all ideas, statements, errors, and omissions are my own.

Introduction

The American Revolution was fought primarily to free residents in the thirteen British colonies in North America from the severe restrictions imposed on them by the British government, Parliament, and the King. These restrictions stifled American entrepreneurship by prohibiting most manufactures, severely restraining external trade, and limiting settlement in the West. Freedom, to most Americans, meant the removal of those restrictions. In the beginning, freedom also meant chaos as each former colony pursued its own destiny in typical self-centered fashion, erecting customs barriers and prohibiting certain types of intercourse that allowed the citizens of one state to profit from the labor of citizens of another. While the majority of citizens were willing to accept this state of affairs as long as they were individually able to make the best of the situation, many of the more substantial citizens recognized the shortcomings of the situation in regard to international respect and commerce and sought to make order out of the chaos. It became generally recognized that the Articles of Confederation had to be grossly modified to ensure general prosperity in the United States. The Constitution was developed by the delegates to the Constitutional Convention of 1787, sponsored by Congress, to unify and strengthen the United States so that commercial prosperity became an attainable goal for all. This necessarily gave an advantage to those individuals whose innate abilities and training allowed them to take better advantage of the commercial and legal environment thus provided. The Constitution therefore led directly to the formation of political parties in the United States, as those most suited to prosper in the new environment were opposed by those who preferred to be left alone to make do without regard for larger issues. The "left-aloners" were largely indifferent to the issues at hand and mostly ignored the debates and the votes on the revisions to the Constitution. Only the "suited-to-prospers" took great issue with the revision to the Constitution, and actively supported ratification of the Constitution as presented by the Convention. With little active opposition, their view prevailed. The "suited-to-prospers" were greatly outnumbered by the "left-aloners" as the former became Federalists and the latter became Antifederalists. This split continued, through several permutations to this day, with the Federalists now called Republicans and the Antifederalists becoming Democrats, but now it's the Democrats who want big government on the national level.

George Washington expected and hoped that the president and Congress would work together and develop legislation and policies by common agreement, but this did not work out. Partisan bickering began almost immediately, particularly in Congress where it soon became apparent that there were profound differences of opinion among congressmen, and formal political parties began to develop. These differences eventually spread to the presidency, particularly in contested elections such as in 1800 and 1824. This difficulty was further aggravated by the strong tendency of members of Congress to be more concerned about the welfare of persons in their own state or district, particularly themselves and their friends, than for the country as a whole.

The United States is one of the few federal republics in the world. A federal republic is created by a grouping of sovereign states that give up part of their sovereignty to a central administration. Each federal republic has its own rules as to what part of sovereignty is held by the central power and what part is retained by its constituent states. The original thirteen states that made up the United States of America, having had serious difficulties after achieving independence in 1781, revised how their federal republic would function by ratifying the Constitution, which is the book of rules for their federal government and "the supreme Law of the Land" per Article VI. This was modified immediately by the Bill of Rights but is still a basic truth.

Per the Constitution, in the United States, each state has two members in the Senate, in spite of the smallest state, Rhode Island, having less than one-half of 1% of the area of the largest, Alaska, and the state with the least population, Wyoming, having less than 2% of the population of the state with the largest population, California. In the House of Representatives, where membership is based on population, each state is guaranteed by the Constitution at least one vote in spite of its population (as it happens, even the least populated state as of the 2020 Census, Wyoming, has a sufficient number of residents to entitle it to one representative based on its share of the total population of the United States). In choosing the president, each state has power equal to the sum of its House and Senate representation.

The basic rule of operation for the government of the United States, the Constitution of the United States of America, has been amended several times since its adoption in 1788. It defines the office of the president and provides rules on the selection of the person who is to fill that office. The preamble to the Constitution states: "We the People of the United States, in Order to form a more perfect Union, establish Justice, insure domestic Tranquility, provide for the common defence (sic), promote the general Welfare, and secure the Blessings of Liberty to ourselves and our Posterity, do ordain and establish this CONSTITUTION for the United States of America." The Founding Fathers believed that Congress, the legislature, would be the heart of the government, and most of the details of what the United States government could do and not do were described in the section, Article I, describing Congress.

The president was looked upon as an administrator, with one of his primary duties being to "take care that the laws be faithfully executed." These laws are made by Congress, with the president's only direct input being to veto laws he believes to be inappropriate. Even this input can be overridden by Congress if they can muster enough votes in the House of Representatives and the Senate. According to the Constitution, the president is also head of state, a sort of elected king. The history of countries with elected kings is not very good: Poland, for one, ended up being partitioned out of existence by its neighbors—Prussia, Russia, and Austria—and the Holy Roman emperor was largely impotent in the empire's later existence due to its member states becoming overly strong, and the emperor became largely a figurehead.

The Constitution details in Article II specific tasks to be performed by the president; these can be briefly described as head of state, commander in chief, and executor of the laws. Further details of these duties, per the Constitution, are as follows:

Head of State

- Make treaties
- Appoint ambassadors
- Receive ambassadors

Commander in Chief

- Head of the Army
- Head of the Navy
- Head of the militia when serving the United States
- Commission all officers of the United States

Executor of the Laws

- Require opinions of heads of departments
- Grant reprieves and pardons
- Appoint justices of the Supreme Court
- Appoint other officers not otherwise provided for
- Give Congress information on the State of the Union
- Give recommendations to Congress on necessary measures
- Convene Congress on extraordinary occasions
- Adjourn Congress when House and Senate cannot agree on adjournment
- See to it that the laws are faithfully executed

In addition, the president has the following powers per the Constitution:

- Veto laws of Congress, subject to conditions of override
- Guarantee to each state a Republican form of government
- Protect each state against invasion
- Protect each state against domestic violence, when requested

No additional powers have been granted to the president by any constitutional amendments, except where Congress has been given authority to enact additional legislation, which the president is then required to enforce.

In order to assist the president in the performance of his duties, several cabinet departments have been created, some per specific constitutional requirements, and others in order to comply with acts of Congress. There have been additions, rearrangements, consolidations, and eliminations to the cabinet. At present, it is composed of the following cabinet positions, in approximate chronological order of establishment:

- Secretary of State
- Secretary of the Treasury
- Attorney General
- Secretary of the Interior
- Secretary of Agriculture
- Secretary of Commerce
- Secretary of Labor
- Secretary of Defense (replaced much earlier War and Navy secretaries)
- Secretary of Housing and Urban Development
- Secretary of Transportation
- Secretary of Energy
- Secretary of Health and Human Services
- Secretary of Education
- Secretary of Veterans Affairs
- Secretary of Homeland Security

Several of the above secretaries head departments covering activities not specifically mentioned in the Constitution. In addition, there are many federal agencies not part of any of the above departments, but for which the president is nominally responsible. These extraconstitutional responsibilities are generally considered to be implied powers under the necessary and proper clause of Section 8 of Article I of the Constitution. In addition, many presidents have performed deeds that do not relate to any of the above. Some of these deeds have taken the form of "executive orders," such as Lincoln's Emancipation Proclamation, in which the president unilaterally makes a rule and then enforces it. Debate over the legality of these extraconstitutional duties is the basis for the existence of various libertarian parties and for the "strict constructionist" view of the Constitution and the United States government held by many political conservatives.

Election to the presidency of the United States by the Electoral College is based on a combination of state sovereignty and population, with each state guaranteed at least three votes, but with additional votes allocated to states according to their population. Thus, per the 2020 Census, California has 54 electoral votes while Alaska, Delaware, North Dakota, South Dakota, Vermont, and Wyoming have only three electoral votes. After almost every presidential election, the losing side complains about the unfairness of the Electoral College. The Democrats or their predecessors have lost 30 presidential elections, and the Republicans or their predecessors have lost 30 presidential elections, so the results after 2020 are dead even. If only two-person presidential races are considered, the Democrats could have ground for complaint, as Republicans John Quincy Adams in 1824, Rutherford B. Hayes in 1876, Benjamin Harrison in 1888, George W. Bush in 2000, and Donald Trump in 2016 all won the election while polling fewer popular votes than their major opponents (see Appendix B), while every Democrat who has won the Electoral College has also won at least a plurality of the popular vote.

However, it must be said that in some of these elections, minor candidates who were aligned ideologically with the Republican winner kept the losing Democrat from getting an absolute majority of the popular vote. This was the case in two of the most contentious cases, the election of 1824 and the election of 2016. The loser in 1824, Andrew Jackson, and the loser in 2016, Hillary Clinton, with their adherents, argued loud and long and made the winners' presidencies very difficult but did not have a valid case for complaint. If in a parliamentary system of government, which the United States is not, it is likely the winner or "prime minister" would have been the same person as the one who ended up as president (see page 34). The constitutional rules for choosing the president were not intended by the original framers of the Constitution to be purely democratic, and none of the subsequent amendments to the Constitution except for Numbers 15, 19, 22, 23, 24, and 26 have resulted in a material change to the degree of the democratic nature of the method of choosing the president.

In another example of federalism in the United States, the Constitution, including the means of electing the president, can only be changed by the states, without consideration of population, and three-quarters of the states must agree to the change. Any change in the rules is unlikely, as only a little over half the states are "red," or Republican-leaning, resulting in something like a fifty-fifty split on any partisan question. While less than one-quarter of the states are "blue," or strongly Democrat-leaning, there are several "lavender" states that frequently vote with the blue states, so that the blue percentage can exceed 30%, with several lavender states that are likely to join the blue states in preventing a change in the rules to favor red-state politics. In addition, there are a few "pink" states that often vote with the red states so that the "reds" can assemble a majority but usually do not attain the three-fourths required for a constitutional change. In presidential politics, the true battleground is the "purple" states that almost always decide a presidential election. There are approximately six of these in 2024: Wisconsin, Michigan, Georgia, Arizona, Nevada, and Pennsylvania, in more or less decreasing order of volatility. These states can also be instrumental in passing or not passing a Constitutional Amendment.

The most common complaint is that the president should be selected solely by population, discarding the Electoral College.

There is some validity to this, as only 23 of the states were actually once independent countries or colonies: Delaware, Pennsylvania, New Jersey, Georgia, Connecticut, Massachusetts, Maryland, South Carolina, New Hampshire, Virginia, New York, North Carolina and Rhode Island (the original thirteen), Texas, California and Hawaii and Vermont, Louisiana, Missouri, Florida, Oregon, Utah and Alaska. A few of these states experienced some quasi-independence but, except for Texas, never established themselves as bona fide independent countries. Nineteen states are actually creations of the federal government, so could be considered subservient to it, while the other eight developed somewhat independently but within the authority of the United States. It is questionable whether this change would actually make any difference in the selection, as the Red/Pink State and Blue/Lavender/Purple State populations are fairly equal, and only a handful of presidential elections have had a winner who did not get a plurality of the popular vote, and these were usually very close in the popular vote. The major exception is the election of 1824, in which the winner, John Quincy Adams, got only 31.4% of the popular vote, while one of the losers, Andrew Jackson, got 43.3% of the popular vote. Adams and his ally, Henry Clay, got a total of 63% of the popular vote, but Jackson ignored this fact while crying foul (history repeats itself; Hillary Clinton and her Democratic Party colleagues did the same thing after the 2016 election even though Trump and his political cohorts got 51.2% of the popular vote). As no candidate obtained a majority of the electoral vote in the 1824 election, the House of Representatives, following the Constitution, chose Adams. Jackson and his followers, although they had no valid cause, were quite irate and remained so until Jackson eventually won in 1828.

Originally, the Constitution did not consider the existence of political parties. George Washington considered political parties to be pernicious and a detriment to good government. In the election of president and vice president, the Constitution originally called for the collection of electoral votes from each state, with the person winning the most votes becoming president, provided he had a majority of the total number of votes cast, with the person coming in second becoming vice president. After the election of 1800, when two leading candidates received the same number of electoral votes, forcing the House of Representatives to choose the president, the 12th Amendment was ratified in 1804 so that the president and vice president ran on the same ticket, thus implying the existence of political parties. Since then, the House has only had to choose the president once, in 1824 when several prominent candidates ran as independents. No further constitutional change to the means of electing the president has been made other than preventing restrictions on ex-slaves voting, in 1870 (15th Amendment), giving the right to vote to women, in 1920 (19th Amendment), limiting the number of terms a president can serve, in 1951 (22nd Amendment), giving three electoral votes to the District of Columbia, in 1961 (23rd Amendment), eliminating the poll tax, in 1964 (24th Amendment), and lowering the voting age to 18, in 1971 (26th Amendment). In a definitive nod to federalism, in the case of no candidate receiving a majority of the electoral vote, the House of Representatives chooses the president, with each *state* having one vote, regardless of population or the number of Representatives in Congress.

In the history of the United States, from 1789 to 2024, the government, including both houses of Congress and the Presidency, has been controlled by the Democrats, or their predecessors, 34.8% of the time, while they have controlled the presidency 50.8% of the time. The Republicans have controlled the government 22.0% of the time while controlling the presidency 49.2% of the time. For the remainder, the government was mixed. For the purpose of these computations, John Tyler is considered a Republican as he was elected vice president on the Whig ticket, even though his party loyalty is nonexistent; John Quincy Adams is considered a Republican because he was fully qualified to be a Whig due to his anti-Andrew Jackson stance; and Andrew Johnson is considered a Democrat, for the purpose of this evaluation, being elected Lincoln's vice president as a Democrat under the Union Party banner.

From 1789 to 2024, the federal government has been divided 43.2% of the time, with one party controlling the presidency and the other party controlling one or both houses of Congress. In actuality, there have been five distinct periods in the history of the United States when one party, or no party, has been dominant. From 1789 to 1801, the Federalists (read modern-day Republicans) controlled the government 50% of the time, while ancestors of the present-day Democrats never controlled the government, as it was divided for the remainder of the period. From 1789 to 1801, only Federalists (assuming Washington was a Federalist) sat in the presidency. From 1801 to 1861, the Democrats or their predecessors controlled the government 70% of the time and held the presidency 80% of the time. From 1801 to 1861, the Republicans never controlled the government, but it was mixed 30% of the time. The Republicans held the presidency from 1861 through 1931, 74.3% of the time; the Republicans controlled the government 52.8% of the time. The Democrats controlled the government 8.3% of the time and held the presidency 25.7% of the time from 1861 to 1931. The government was divided 38.9% of the time from 1861 to 1931. From 1931 to 1981, the Democrats controlled the government 62.5% of the time while having a president in office 64% of the time. The Republicans controlled the government only 4.2% of the time from 1931 to 1981, while holding the presidency 36% of the time. The government was divided 33.3% of the time from 1931 to 1981. From 1981 to 2024, the government was mixed, or divided, 77.3% of the time, while the Republicans controlled the government 13.6% of the time and the Democrats controlled the government 9.1% of the time. The Republicans held the presidency 52.4% of the time, and the Democrats held it 47.6% of the time from 1981 to 2024. The presidency has changed parties 27 times since 1789, averaging once every 8.7 years. The House of Representatives has changed 28 times. The Senate has also changed 28 times, but not in sync with the House. This cyclic nature of the government of the United States of America can have several explanations, the discussion of which is beyond the scope of this book.

    Several presidents have had the luxury of holding office for their entire term or terms with a sympathetic Congress. These include John Adams, Thomas Jefferson, James Madison, James Monroe, Andrew Jackson, Martin Van Buren, Abraham Lincoln, William McKinley,

Theodore Roosevelt, Warren Harding, Calvin Coolidge, Franklin Roosevelt, John F. Kennedy, Lyndon Johnson, and Jimmy Carter. This has not necessarily been helpful in securing them entry into the pantheon of the greatest presidents. Only one of these presidents, Abraham Lincoln, is universally recognized as one of our very greatest presidents. Two others, Thomas Jefferson and Theodore Roosevelt, are held in high esteem by most authorities. All the others are rated highly or not so highly depending on who is doing the evaluation.

Most presidents, thirty-one in all, have served at least part of their term while one or both houses of Congress were controlled by the opposite party. This phenomenon started with George Washington and has included every president from Harry Truman to the present except Kennedy, Lyndon Johnson, and Carter. In some cases, such as with Washington and Zachary Taylor, the individual president's personal popularity has outweighed the public's slant in the opposite direction politically. Both Washington and Taylor were war heroes who disdained political parties. Others, such as John Quincy Adams and Herbert Hoover, were overwhelmed by political sea changes that were felt in Congress before their presidential terms were over.

In one very critical aspect, the government of the United States today differs quite substantially from the government devised by the Founding Fathers at the Constitutional Convention of 1787. At that time, it was assumed that Congress, particularly the House of Representatives, would represent the people of the United States at the seat of government. The president was to be aloof from the people, not even directly responsible to them for his election. Today, Congress is held in such poor repute that usually only the news media have a lower approval rating than congresspersons in general. The president is now considered by most citizens as the true representative of all the people and is generally given credit for anything good that comes out of Washington, DC. There is considerable evidence to suggest that, except for "pork barrel" projects, the general perception is correct. For that reason, this book looks primarily to the presidents for its evaluation of the government of the United States.

Chapter 1

The Presidents

The Continental Congress ran the government of the United States from the first active rebellion in 1775, with the president of the Congress merely serving as a chief clerk while all decisions were made by vote, by states. This did not change after the Declaration of Independence. The Constitution was adopted in 1788 with the intention of giving more power to Congress so that it could enforce its decisions and raise funds to pay its expenses. From 1789 to 1861, Congress was still expected to make all important decisions, with the president acting as chief clerk and administrator. A few presidents, such as Andrew Jackson, Thomas Jefferson, and James K. Polk, seized the initiative in a significant way, but they were the exception.

The United States originally was a land of entrepreneurs. Almost every European immigrant into the United States aspired to make an independent living as a farmer, merchant, or tradesman, even the indentured servants who came over as little better than slaves, being referred to as bondsmen or bondswomen for the period of their contracted service. This attitude was reflected in the ratification of the Constitution, which was primarily a document that limited the power of the government to control people's lives. The Constitution left to the states the determination of which citizens participated in the government, and most states limited the franchise to property owners. Suffrage was gradually expanded as more and more people entered the United States, and a larger and larger percentage of the population owned no real property. The choice of the president did not follow this increasing democratization, as even today the president is chosen by the Electoral College, legally free in most states to vote for whomever they wish regardless of the popular vote of their state. Each state has at least three electoral votes regardless of its population so that the existence of the states is critical in the selection of the president.

This book was originally intended as an unbiased, factual evaluation of the government of the United States, based on the performance of each of the 46 presidents. It soon became apparent that an unbiased evaluation of the facts shows that results are not equal. Of the three best, or "great," presidents, all were Republicans or, in the case of George Washington, nonparty but leaning strongly toward the Federalists, who were the "grandfathers" of the modern-day Republicans. Of the four "very good" presidents, two were Democrats or their early equivalent, and two were Republicans or Federalists. Both of the "very good" Democrats had severe shortcomings but, by virtue of their tremendous gains of territory for the United States—the Louisiana Purchase by Thomas Jefferson and victory in the Mexican War by James K. Polk—achieve a high ranking. Of the fourteen "better-than-average" presidents, twelve were Republicans, and only one was a Democrat; and that was James Monroe, who was elected essentially unopposed, as the Federalists were demoralized and unable to field a presidential candidate, and the "Democrats" (called "Republicans" at that time) soon split into two opposing parties, the National Republicans under Henry Clay, represented by John Quincy Adams, and the Democratic Republicans, led by Andrew Jackson.

At the other end of the scale, the five "bad" presidents were Pierce, Buchanan, Jackson, Lyndon Johnson, and Biden, and the four "poor" presidents are Obama, Wilson, Madison, and Kennedy. All nine of these presidents were or are officially Democrats, except for James Madison, who was a member of the "Republican" (pre-1854) party that eventually became the Democrats.

In the middle are four presidents who registered as nonentities: Benjamin Harrison, William Henry Harrison, and James A. Garfield, plus Grover Cleveland in his first administration. Twenty-six presidents, more than half of the total, are ranked either slightly above or slightly below average. All but one of the slightly above-average presidents are Republicans; seven of the twelve slightly below-average presidents are Democrats, although two, John Tyler and Andrew Johnson, were elected as vice presidents on Republican (Union, in 1864) or Whig (pre-modern-day Republican) tickets and succeeded to the presidency upon the death of the ticket leaders. (Table 1-1 summarizes the rating and ranking of the 46 presidents.)

Summarizing, in a feat of near mirror symmetry, eighteen of the twenty-one best presidents were Republicans (or members of predecessor parties), while seventeen of the twenty-one worst presidents were or are Democrats (or members of predecessor parties), if Tyler is included among the Democrats. This is not a coincidence. The present-day Democratic Party grew out of the eighteenth-century Antifederalist party, which opposed ratification of the Constitution, while the present-day Republican Party grew out of the eighteenth-century Federalist Party, which supported ratification of the Constitution. It is true that something of a reversal of roles took place over the middle decades of the twentieth century as the Democrats abandoned their states' rights policy and the Republicans gradually embraced it, calling it federalism. This temporary reversal passed, and the principles that guided the members of the Constitutional Convention are largely those of the present-day Republican Party, while the present-day Democrats mostly favor what could be interpreted as a creative interpretation of the Constitution but is actually a desire to ignore the Constitution. This is in spite of presidents, as well as each Congress member, being required by the Constitution to take an oath of support for it. For example, Democrats continually attempt to pass laws restricting the right of citizens to own weapons and have succeeded in obtaining Supreme Court decisions reducing the right to bear arms to ownership of sporting weapons. Republicans, on the other hand, consistently maintain that the

Second Amendment[2] is absolute. Lawless police states are the most adamant about refusing to allow the populace to possess weapons; nations that most value individual freedom invariably rely on citizen armies for defense. Regarding the First Amendment, Republicans generally take the freedom of press, religion, assembly, and petition literally, while Democrats prefer a popular vote on each issue, as long as the result agrees with their position.

RANKING	PRESIDENT	TOTAL RATING
1	Washington	20.8
2	Lincoln	20.4
3	Reagan	18.4
4	Jefferson	15.2
5	J. Adams	14.4
6	Polk	13.6
7	T. Roosevelt	12.8
8	Eisenhower	10.8
9	Nixon	10.4
10	Trump	8.8
11	Arthur	8.0
12	McKinley	7.4
13	Taft	6.6
14	Hoover	5.8
15	Coolidge	5.6
16	Ford	4.8
17	Monroe	4.4
18	G. H. W. Bush	3.0
19	J. Q. Adams	2.4
20	Taylor	2.0
21	Hayes	1.6

---

[2] A well-regulated militia, being necessary to the security of a free state, the right of the people to keep and bear arms shall not be infringed.

22	B. Harrison	0.0
23	Garfield	0.0
24	W. H. Harrison	0.0
25	Cleveland (1)	0.0
26	Cleveland (2)	-0.8
27	Grant	-1.0
28	G. W. Bush	-2.0
29	Harding	-2.4
30	Fillmore	-3.6
31	A. Johnson	-4.0
32	Tyler	-6.4
33	Van Buren	-8.0
34	Carter	-8.2
35	F. D. Roosevelt	-9.0
36	Truman	-9.8
37	Clinton	-12.2
38	Kennedy	-16.0
39	Madison	-16.2
40	Wilson	-16.6
41	Obama	-18.4
42	Biden	-20.2
43	L. Johnson	-20.4
44	Jackson	-20.4
45	Buchanan	-23.0
46	Pierce	-26.0
	Average =	-1.03

Table 1-1   Presidential Rankings and Ratings

They consistently fight to prevent speech with which they disagree and have succeeded in getting laws passed to prevent speech they label "hate" speech or harmful speech. Thomas Jefferson said that the way to discredit falsehood is to allow it out in the open. In a trend that has been building for some time, the present-day Democrats have been more than adamant about curtailing free speech that does not agree with their worldview.

There are some significant changes in the operation of the federal government that are not the result of constitutional amendments. The members of the Constitutional Convention assumed that Congress would be the heart of the government, making laws and having various powers. The president was assumed to be primarily an administrator of laws passed by Congress and was to be assisted in his role as head of state by the Senate. The president, because he is the representative of all the people, is increasingly looked at as the leader and director of both domestic and foreign policy. Exceptions to this occur occasionally.

The Constitution does not specify how the constitutionality of laws is to be determined. The Antifederalists and their immediate successors attempted to establish the states as the arbiters of the constitutionality of laws, even though this position had the drawback of not making federal laws uniform throughout the United States. The president can use his opinion of constitutionality when he considers a veto, but this can be overridden by Congress. The Supreme Court gradually took over that duty, starting in 1803 with *Marbury vs. Madison*, and is now acknowledged to be the authority on constitutionality. This has increased the power of the president significantly, as that office has sole power of nominating prospective members to the Supreme Court, subject to confirmation by the Senate.

The original political concept for the United States was for a governing committee representing all interests, making decisions based on consensus. While this worked at the beginning from 1776, as the Second Continental Congress expanded into just "Congress" or, more formally, "The United States in Congress Assembled," there were definitely shortcomings. Material support for George Washington's Continental Army was very, very slow in coming, and the various state militias were extremely slow in responding to crises, if they responded at all. It is extremely unlikely that the United States would have survived if France had not, after the British self-inflicted debacle at Saratoga, stepped in with full, open support for the revolutionaries.

After the Treaty of Paris, it soon became obvious to most thoughtful Americans that the loose union established in North America under the Articles of Confederation was inadequate for the needs of the new country. Conflicts and jealousies between states, with no path to resolution, lack of respect internationally, and inadequate means of funding the requirements of Congress, made it evident that a major change had to be made.

Congress took the bold step of establishing a convention of delegates from each of the thirteen essentially independent states that formed the confederacy called the United States. The difficulty of the project was quickly made apparent with the slowness of delegates to appear. Rhode Island never sent any delegates, and the recall by New York of its delegates (although Alexander Hamilton stayed on, on his own authority) ended the official presence of those two states. On top of that, the convention went beyond its mandate by throwing out the Articles of Confederation, rather than revising them, and proposing an entirely new Constitution that went beyond the federal nature of the Articles and interjected new nationalistic concepts into their proposed form of government.

The Constitutional Convention was marked by strenuous, spirited debate over several issues, but it soon became apparent that there were two splits in the delegation, both potentially fatal to the process. The first to demand resolution was the big state–small state divide. All the small states, which meant all, except Virginia, Pennsylvania, and Massachusetts, were perfectly happy with all decisions being made by state votes, each state being equal. This had been the rule throughout the existence of the Continental Congress and continued up through the Constitutional Convention. The large states, led by Virginia, thought that their larger contribution to the wealth of the country entitled them to a larger share in the decision-making process. John Randolph, delegate from Virginia, proposed in detail a truly national government, in which the states would have a minor role in government, and might perhaps be eliminated altogether. His plan called for a national assembly that would represent the people, with representation based on population. The smaller states, led by Connecticut and New Jersey in particular, refused absolutely to give up their equal status. Eventually, a compromise was reached, whereby each state would have equal representation in the Senate, which would have a larger role in the government than the House of Representatives, in which each state would have a delegation the size of which would be based on population. This compromise was essential to the approval of the Constitution and set the tone for government as well as social intercourse for the people of the United States.

As of the 2020 Census, the 12 largest states have 281 electoral votes, more than half; they control the House of Representatives with 257 of 435 Representatives and the Presidency, while the 38 smaller states, 39 including the District of Columbia when adding electoral votes, control the Senate with 76 of 100 votes. Based on the 2022 election, the large states are split, however, with 103 conservative electoral votes and 115 liberal electoral votes, plus 63 neutral votes, so that any given presidential election could go in any direction within these states. The 38 smaller states are also split but are more biased toward the conservative side, with 132 conservative electoral votes and only 80 (83 including the District of Columbia) liberal electoral votes, with 42 neutral or purple votes (see tables 1-2 and 1-3).

2020 PRESIDENTIAL VOTE ELECTORAL VOTES	PER 2020 PRESIDENTIAL VOTE PERCENT TRUMP	RURAL = 50% OF POPULATION IN TOWNS OF LESS THAN 50,000 STATE	POP 2020	PCT URBAN		
3	69.94%	WYOMING	576,851	21.5%	RURAL	RED
5	68.63%	WEST VIRGINIA	1,793,716	0.0%	RURAL	RED
7	65.37%	OKLAHOMA	3,959,353	38.9%	RURAL	RED
3	65.12%	NORTH DAKOTA	779,094	33%	RURAL	RED
4	63.84%	IDAHO	1,839,106	40.3%	RURAL	RED
6	62.40%	ARKANSAS	3,011,524	24.5%	RURAL	RED
8	62.09%	KENTUCKY	4,505,836	31.9%	RURAL	RED
9	62.03%	ALABAMA	5,024,279	25.0%	RURAL	RED
3	61.77%	SOUTH DAKOTA	886,667	30.1%	RURAL	RED

The Crime of the Democrats

11	60.66%	TENNESSEE	6,910,840	34.1%	RURAL	RED
8	58.46%	LOUISIANA	4,657,757	27.4%	RURAL	RED
5	58.24%	NEBRASKA	1,961,504	42.3%	RURAL	RED
6	58.13%	UTAH	3,271,616	59%	URBAN	RED
6	57.60%	MISSISSIPPI	2,961,279	9.5%	RURAL	RED
11	57.03%	INDIANA	6,785,528	33.3%	RURAL	RED
3	56.92%	MONTANA	1,084,225	28.1%	RURAL	RED
10	56.80%	MISSOURI	6,154,913	27.4%	RURAL	RED
6	56.14%	KANSAS	2,937,880	35.0%	RURAL	RED
9	55.11%	SOUTH CAROLINA	5,118,425	11.7%	RURAL	RED
18	53.27%	OHIO	11,799,448	23.5%	RURAL	PINK
6	53.09%	IOWA	3,190,369	29.4%	RURAL	RED
3	52.83%	ALASKA	733,391	39.7%	RURAL	RED
38	52.06%	TEXAS	29,145,505	52.9%	URBAN	RED
29	51.22%	FLORIDA	21,538,187	37.5%	RURAL	RED
15	49.93%	NORTH CAROLINA	10,439,388	32.5%	RURAL	PURPLE
16	49.24%	GEORGIA	10,711,908	20.1%	RURAL	PURPLE
11	49.06%	ARIZONA	7,151,502	72.1%	URBAN	PURPLE
10	48.82%	WISCONSIN	5,893,718	27.0%	RURAL	PURPLE
20	48.69%	PENNSYLVANIA	13,002,700	19.5%	RURAL	PURPLE
16	47.84%	MICHIGAN	10,077,331	31.1%	RURAL	PURPLE
6	47.67%	NEVADA	3,104,614	80.1%	URBAN	PURPLE
4	45.36%	NEW HAMPSHIRE	1,377,529	15.0%	RURAL	LAVENDER
10	45.29%	MINNESOTA	5,706,494	36%	RURAL	LAVENDER
4	44.02%	MAINE	1,362,359	5.0%	RURAL	LAVENDER
13	44.00%	VIRGINIA	8,631,393	53.3%	URBAN	LAVENDER
5	43.50%	NEW MEXICO	2,117,522	41.0%	RURAL	LAVENDER
9	41.90%	COLORADO	5,773,714	57.8%	URBAN	LAVENDER
14	41.40%	NEW JERSEY	9,288,994	24.2%	RURAL	LAVENDER
20	40.55%	ILLINOIS	12,812,508	38.4%	RURAL	BLUE
7	40.37%	OREGON	4,237,256	41%	RURAL	BLUE
3	39.78%	DELAWARE	989,948	7.2%	RURAL	BLUE
7	39.19%	CONNECTICUT	3,605,944	39.4%	RURAL	BLUE
12	38.77%	WASHINGTON	7,705,281	39.6%	RURAL	BLUE
4	38.61%	RHODE ISLAND	1,097,379	39.4%	RURAL	BLUE

29	37.74%	NEW YORK	20,201,249	51.1%	URBAN	BLUE
55	34.32%	CALIFORNIA	39,538,223	70.3%	URBAN	BLUE
4	34.27%	HAWAII	1,455,271	24.1%	RURAL	BLUE
10	32.15%	MARYLAND	6,177,224	27%	RURAL	BLUE
11	32.14%	MASSACHUSETTS	7,029,917	32.3%	RURAL	BLUE
3	30.67%	VERMONT	643,077	0.0%	RURAL	BLUE

Table 1-2   Percent Conservative Population, by State

The tendency of certain large and small states is to agree on a conservative bias, with 246 electoral votes. The small and large liberal states can only muster 191 electoral votes; but if they win over all nine neutral states, with 98 electoral votes, they are, adding the District of Columbia's three votes, in the majority with 292 electoral votes in a presidential contest that requires 538 / 2 + 1 = 270 electoral votes to win. Neither the large nor small states can win on any issue without their liberal and conservative factions joining forces; in addition, the thirty-eight small states would need to add Virginia and New Jersey to their ranks to win a presidential contest. They would have to add Michigan and North Carolina in addition to gain a victory in the House of Representatives.

The second large split at the Constitutional Convention developed over slavery. The southern slave states refused to allow any restriction or aspersions on slavery to be entered into the Constitution, and some delegates from northern states refused to sign any document that did not put restrictions on slavery. Eventually, a compromise was reached that largely gave the game to the southerners, even banning export taxes which would have largely fallen on the southern, or "staple-producing," slave states that produced rice, indigo, and most importantly, tobacco for export. Northerners generally conceded due to the realization that the economic viability of the new country would be seriously compromised without the rice and tobacco exports of the south if Maryland, Virginia, North and South Carolina, and Georgia were to refuse to join the union. Cotton was not an important export commodity until the invention of the cotton gin, which occurred after the Constitution was ratified. Cotton then became "king," further increasing the economic and political leverage of the southern slave states. The slavery split, of course, became obsolete with the Northern victory in the Civil War and the passage of the Thirteenth Amendment to the Constitution, outlawing slavery.

And so, an agreement was reached on a new Constitution. It was understood by all that Congress would be the heart of the new government, with a president responsible for carrying out and enforcing laws passed by Congress, and answerable to it by being subject to impeachment. Congress, on the other hand, was to be untouchable, with neither the president nor the courts able to deny the right of Congress to do as it wished, except for holding their Acts to the Constitution. Later presidents would be able to provide some leadership to Congress, but this was only informal and dependent on the stature of the particular president. In the Constitution, the Supreme Court was not given the explicit authority to reject acts of Congress as unconstitutional but eventually took this responsibility and was finally sustained on all sides in its assumption of the task.

There were many questions on government procedure, including the determination of constitutionality, that were not answered within the Constitution, and most of these were worked out in the first years after ratification.

The major philosophical split at the federal level today is a conflict between conservatives and liberals. It can be expressed as a rural versus urban conflict. See table 1-3, below:

ELECTORAL VOTE 2024	PCT TRUMP 2020	STATE	POP 2020	PCT URBAN	PCT RURAL	STATUS	DESIGNATION
4	68.63%	WEST VIRGINIA	1,793,716	0.0%	100.0%	RURAL	RED
3	30.67%	VERMONT	643,077	0.0%	100.0%	RURAL	BLUE
4	44.02%	MAINE	1,362,359	5.0%	95.0%	RURAL	LAVENDER
3	39.78%	DELAWARE	989,948	7.2%	92.8%	RURAL	BLUE
6	57.60%	MISSISSIPPI	2,961,279	9.5%	90.5%	RURAL	RED
9	55.11%	SOUTH CAROLINA	5,118,425	11.7%	88.3%	RURAL	RED

RURAL = 50% of POPULATION IN TOWNS <50,000

4	45.36%	NEW HAMPSHIRE	1,377,529	15.0%	85.0%	RURAL	LAVENDER
19	48.69%	PENNSYLVANIA	13,002,700	19.5%	80.5%	RURAL	PURPLE
16	49.24%	GEORGIA	10,711,908	20.1%	79.9%	RURAL	PURPLE
3	69.94%	WYOMING	576,851	21.5%	78.5%	RURAL	RED
17	53.27%	OHIO	11,799,448	23.5%	76.5%	RURAL	PINK
4	34.27%	HAWAII	1,455,271	24.1%	75.9%	RURAL	BLUE
14	41.40%	NEW JERSEY	9,288,994	24.2%	75.8%	RURAL	LAVENDER
6	62.40%	ARKANSAS	3,011,524	24.5%	75.5%	RURAL	RED
9	62.03%	ALABAMA	5,024,279	25.0%	75.0%	RURAL	RED
10	32.15%	MARYLAND	6,177,224	27%	73.1%	RURAL	BLUE
10	48.82%	WISCONSIN	5,893,718	27.0%	73.0%	RURAL	PURPLE
8	58.46%	LOUISIANA	4,657,757	27.4%	72.6%	RURAL	RED
10	56.80%	MISSOURI	6,154,913	27.4%	72.6%	RURAL	RED
4	56.92%	MONTANA	1,084,225	28.1%	71.9%	RURAL	RED
6	53.09%	IOWA	3,190,369	29.4%	70.6%	RURAL	RED
3	61.77%	SOUTH DAKOTA	886,667	30.1%	69.9%	RURAL	RED
15	47.84%	MICHIGAN	10,077,331	31.1%	68.9%	RURAL	PURPLE
8	62.09%	KENTUCKY	4,505,836	31.9%	68.1%	RURAL	RED
11	32.14%	MASSACHUSETTS	7,029,917	32.3%	67.7%	RURAL	BLUE
16	49.93%	NORTH CAROLINA	10,439,388	32.5%	67.5%	RURAL	PURPLE
3	65.12%	NORTH DAKOTA	779,094	33%	66.8%	RURAL	RED
11	57.03%	INDIANA	6,785,528	33.3%	66.7%	RURAL	RED
11	60.66%	TENNESSEE	6,910,840	34.1%	65.9%	RURAL	RED
6	56.14%	KANSAS	2,937,880	35.0%	65.0%	RURAL	RED
10	45.29%	MINNESOTA	5,706,494	36%	64.3%	RURAL	LAVENDER
30	51.22%	FLORIDA	21,538,187	37.5%	62.5%	RURAL	RED
19	40.55%	ILLINOIS	12,812,508	38.4%	61.6%	RURAL	BLUE
7	65.37%	OKLAHOMA	3,959,353	38.9%	61.1%	RURAL	RED
7	39.19%	CONNECTICUT	3,605,944	39.4%	60.6%	RURAL	BLUE
4	38.61%	RHODE ISLAND	1,097,379	39.4%	60.6%	RURAL	BLUE
12	38.77%	WASHINGTON	7,705,281	39.6%	60.4%	RURAL	BLUE
3	52.83%	ALASKA	733,391	39.7%	60.3%	RURAL	RED
4	63.84%	IDAHO	1,839,106	40.3%	59.7%	RURAL	RED
5	43.50%	NEW MEXICO	2,117,522	41.0%	59.0%	RURAL	LAVENDER
8	40.37%	OREGON	4,237,256	41%	58.9%	RURAL	BLUE
5	58.24%	NEBRASKA	1,961,504	42.3%	57.7%	RURAL	RED

28	37.74%	NEW YORK	20,201,249	51.1%	48.9%	URBAN	BLUE
40	52.06%	TEXAS	29,145,505	52.9%	47.1%	URBAN	RED
13	44.00%	VIRGINIA	8,631,393	53.3%	46.7%	URBAN	LAVENDER
10	41.90%	COLORADO	5,773,714	57.8%	42.2%	URBAN	LAVENDER
6	58.13%	UTAH	3,271,616	59%	41.5%	URBAN	RED
54	34.32%	CALIFORNIA	39,538,223	70.3%	29.7%	URBAN	BLUE
11	49.06%	ARIZONA	7,151,502	72.1%	27.9%	URBAN	PURPLE
6	47.67%	NEVADA	3,104,614	80.1%	19.9%	URBAN	PURPLE

Table 1-3   Urban vs. Rural Voting Patterns

There are a few exceptions, but in the main, the "red" or conservative states have primarily rural populations, while the "blue" or liberal states are largely urban. In decreasing order of urban population, it looks like this, with Blue being most liberal, Lavender somewhat liberal, Purple noncommittal, Pink somewhat conservative, and Red being most conservative based on the 2020 presidential election results, with some variation due to votes for third-party candidates (see table 1-3). Of the eight states with a majority 2020 urban population of 50,000 or more, five voted for Joseph Biden, while three voted for Donald Trump. Of the 42 states with a majority urban population less than 50,000, 23 voted for Trump and 19 voted for Biden. Personalities or other special factors such as news coverage could have something to do with the vote.

Chapter 2

The Democrat Presidents

From Antifederalist through "Republican" (Jefferson style), Democratic Republican, and finally through Democrat, presidents and politicians in this group have consistently not been enamored of the Constitution. It is appropriate that the two presidents commonly considered the founders of the Democrat Party, Thomas Jefferson and Andrew Jackson, both considered the Constitution an impediment. Jefferson-Jackson Day dinners were once a high point in the political year for ardent Democrats, but the racist and genocidal stance taken by both these patriarchs has dimmed their glorified position somewhat in more recent years. More recent Democrat presidents and the Democratic Party have favored a "nonliteral" interpretation of the Constitution, which is to say, the context of the times allows the Supreme Court to issue decisions that violate the letter of the Constitution. This allows the Democrats to avoid updating the Constitution via the amendment process, in which liberal views are heavily outnumbered and obtaining a vote of three-fourths of the states for a liberalization of the Constitution would be nearly impossible.

The government, including the presidency, was dominated by Virginians in the first decades under the Constitution. Starting with Jefferson, these Virginians adopted a states-rights, antifederal position, the primary purpose of which was to protect the institution of slavery from northern opposition. Jefferson, Madison, Monroe, and Tyler were Virginians, while Jackson and Polk were natives of the Carolinas who had migrated to Tennessee. Two more proslavery Democrat presidents in this era were Franklin Pierce and James Buchanan, both "Doughfaces," a term commonly applied at the time to northerners with southern sympathies. Altogether, the White House was proslavery for 48 of the 60 years from 1800 to 1860. Protection or expansion of slavery was the primary motive behind the Mexican-American War, which added what could have been six additional slave states to the Union. The annexations of Texas and Florida, two slave states, were speedily accomplished, while Wisconsin was delayed, Iowa and California reluctantly accepted, and Oregon and Minnesota put off until it had become obvious that other solutions to the problem of protecting slavery were necessary.

The first "Democrat" president, Thomas Jefferson, did not participate in the Constitutional Convention and later actively undermined it through authorship, with James Madison, of the Virginia and Kentucky Resolutions of 1798–99 that attempted to make a case for the states being the final authority on constitutional issues. But while he thought the Louisiana Purchase was unconstitutional, he proceeded with it anyway, deeming it of extreme importance and being certain that he could get a constitutional amendment of approval for it if necessary. Jefferson feared that a national government would turn monarchist, and he saw Alexander Hamilton, the staunchest of Federalists, as a man with monarchial ambitions. Jefferson may have been right about Hamilton. This fear no doubt played a part in his antifederalist states-rights tendencies. The ironic death of Hamilton at the hands of Jefferson's archenemy, Aaron Burr, did not lessen Jefferson's fears, and he continued his political machinations to prevent any elitists from taking power in the United States government. Jefferson unrealistically expected the United States to permanently become a nation of yeoman farmers. He wanted no urban proletariat, who would be industrial workers, whom he considered despicable. He thought that the nearly unlimited land to the west would allow all people without capital to eventually become self-sufficient small landowners. Unfortunately, most of the land included in the Louisiana Purchase, west of the Mississippi River into the Rocky Mountains, was and is unsuited to small-scale agriculture. For years it was known as the Great American Desert, named so by Stephen Long, one of the early nineteenth-century western explorers. Later on, it became the "Dust Bowl" of the 1930s. The victory for the small farmers, the Homestead Act, passed not by the Democrats, who opposed it for proslavery reasons prior to the Civil War when they controlled Congress, but by the Republicans, who have always been the party of entrepreneurship, large and small scale, worked in limited areas where small-scale farming was practical but, on the whole, was a failure. The 160 acres allocated to each individual under the Homestead Act was much too small to allow for profitable grain farming, even in the 1860s.

Jefferson's true claim to fame, other than the Louisiana Purchase, came prior to his presidency when he was a member of Congress under the Articles of Confederation when he prepared a preliminary Northwest Ordinance in 1784, although it was not adopted. Part of this was included in the Northwest Ordinance of 1787, which was truly a blueprint for the success of the middle class, particularly those small farmers, as the Northwest Ordinance allowed people of modest means to purchase small farms and also banned slavery from the future states of Ohio, Indiana, Illinois, Michigan, and Wisconsin. Jefferson can also be credited as the originator of political parties in the United States, as he actively promoted the development of a political organization to oppose George Washington and the Federalists.

The second "Democrat" president, James Madison, while a key participant in the Constitutional Convention and a signer of that document as well as the primary author of the pro-Constitution Federalist Papers, later came to agree with Jefferson that the federal government had too much power. James Monroe, the third president of this group, oversaw a divided government that was descending into chaos, as states-rights versus federal authority arguments moved to center stage.

The fourth, now officially "Democrat" president, Andrew Jackson, took personal authority over all issues but destroyed the fiscal authority of the federal government by destroying the Second Bank of the United States. Jackson emasculated the Supreme Court by his refusal to enforce their decision in the question of Georgia versus the Cherokee Nation. He further destroyed the integrity of the Supreme Court by appointing a political hack, Roger B. Taney, as Chief Justice. Jackson's Specie Circular, requiring only hard money—i.e., gold, in payment for federal land purchases—eliminated money from the economy, as banknotes became worthless (in truth, most were already almost worthless anyway) and people hoarded what gold and silver coin they had in their possession. Jackson's policies led directly to the worst depression felt by the people of the United States, a catastrophe that came about under his successor and political heir, Martin Van Buren. Survival of the nation under these conditions was in great part due to the higher percentage of the population that was living under survivalist conditions and was able to hunker down for the duration. Barter largely replaced money in the economic system, a condition that would have been intolerable in the twentieth century.

Jackson's anti-bank bias was emulated by many of his Democrat followers, resulting in bank riots, closing of banks, legislation against banks, and outright banning of banks in some state constitutions at the time. It was hard to live without the services that could only be provided by banks, so much under-the-table banking went on by institutions calling themselves insurance companies, canals, or railroads. Marine Insurance of Milwaukee, The Morris Canal and Banking Company of New Jersey, and the Georgia Railroad and Banking Company are prominent antebellum examples.

James K. Polk, the sixth Democrat president, was primarily concerned with preserving the ascendancy of the slave power by annexing the southwestern territory, which he assumed would join the Union as slave states. He was incorrect in this, as all the territory won in the Mexican War became free states, albeit all except California and Nevada did not enter the Union until after the end of the Civil War. "Arizona" was briefly slave territory while the Confederates occupied it for a short time during the Civil War. Ironically, the slave power could have remained, for a longer time, at at least parity in the Senate without resorting to violence. Texas, as a sovereign nation when it entered the Union, was allowed at its choice to split into up to five states. Texas was approximately as large as the entire Northwest Territory, which did produce the five states of Ohio, Indiana, Illinois, Michigan, and Wisconsin, with a little left over. Making five states out of the slave state of Texas would have kept the South in control of the Senate until at least 1860, but the Texans refused the split.

The next two Democrat presidents, Franklin Pierce and James Buchanan, are universally considered the worst, or two of the worst, presidents the United States ever had. Pierce, by approving the Kansas-Nebraska Act that led directly to the Civil War, Buchanan by committing what many historians and political scientists consider treason by helping to arm the seceding southern states prior to the outbreak of the Civil War.

Andrew Johnson, a Democrat elected vice president under the Union Party banner with Abraham Lincoln, the Republican presidential candidate, became president upon Lincoln's assassination. Although none of this was Andrew Johnson's fault, he was never forgiven for any of it and was probably the most universally hated of any president. He mostly followed Lincoln's policies and intentions, particularly in regard to the treatment of the postwar South but was impeached and tried in the Senate, partly because of his lenient treatment of the former Confederacy but also because he was a Democrat, and came as close as any president to being removed from office. He was selected as the vice presidential candidate by the Republicans, in desperation calling themselves the Union Party, because war weariness made it seem certain that the Republicans could not win the 1864 election. As it turned out, Lincoln won rather handily with 55% of the vote, further alienating Johnson from the Republicans in power.

There were no further Democrat presidents until populism became a prevalent political movement. Grover Cleveland, while not a populist, ran for president as a Democrat, accepting Populist, Greenbacker, and anarchist votes in 1884, 1888, and 1892. He won the popular vote each time but lost in the Electoral College to Benjamin Harrison in 1888. His presidency was largely ineffectual, as Congress was at least partially in the hands of the Republicans

The Crime of the Democrats

during his tenure in the White House, and his conservative stance on some issues alienated some Democrat congressmen.

Grover Cleveland was the last Democrat president to subscribe to the entrepreneurial theory of government of the United States. After Cleveland, every Democrat president promised protection for the laboring class against the capitalists who were gradually taking over the economic power in the country. While the Progressive Movement started as an effort of middle-class Republicans to restrict the power of large-scale capitalism of the huge business trusts and large railroad combinations of the late nineteenth century, the Democrats joined in the early twentieth century. The Progressive Movement eventually became frankly socialist, and by the twenty-first century had taken over the Democratic Party. It has become difficult not to associate liberalism and the modern Democratic Party with progressivism, socialism, and even leftist Marxism.

This leftist new order has been developing since the 1960s when even such conservative (at the time) institutions as Time magazine were noting the emergence of the postindustrial state. Liberals and society in general applauded the closing down of "dirty" industry such as steel mills and paper mills, all in the name of environmentalism, while ignoring or even assisting in the simultaneous growth of such industries offshore. There was little or no concern for the workers displaced by such policies, assuming that the brighter ones could learn a new trade or go to college and become white-collar. The less fortunate were expected to be happy to go on permanent welfare.

Woodrow Wilson, the next Democrat president, won office solely due to a personal feud between Theodore Roosevelt and William Howard Taft. Roosevelt, somewhat of a spoiled child and bully, was rejected by the Republican Party as their 1912 presidential candidate in favor of Taft, who was just as much of a progressive as Roosevelt but seemed to be more amenable to conservative arguments. Roosevelt chose to run as a progressive third-party candidate, thus splitting the Republican vote, giving the election to Wilson, who only obtained 45% of the popular vote while winning 435 electoral votes (82%) to Roosevelt's 88 and 8 for Taft. Wilson was a hero of the American Left for decades until it became clear that his progressivism was for whites only. Wilson's chimerical approach to World War I and the peace that followed is the stuff of legend, while his dictatorial domestic policy was only equaled by the Alien and Sedition Acts of a century earlier and Lincoln's Civil War measures. His nationalization of the railroads of the United States nearly destroyed them; ostensibly a war measure, it was in reality payback for railroad labor support. Permission for the president to take over the railroads was included in the Adamson Act, a measure signed by Wilson that avoided a railroad strike by granting most of the demands made by the railroad labor brotherhoods. Wilson was totally incapacitated after suffering a stroke while crossing the country campaigning for support for his WWI peace treaty. He and his staff kept this a secret so that his wife was virtually acting president for the last several months of his second term. The Democratic Party's crushing defeat in the 1920 election represented the public's opinion of Wilson's actions while president.

The tables were completely turned in 1932 when Franklin Delano Roosevelt was elected the next Democrat president. Herbert Hoover received all the blame for the depression that started in 1929, despite his initiation of several recovery measures that were eventually retained and expanded by Roosevelt, who received all the credit for them. Unfortunately, none of these measures really worked, and the economy of the United States did not fully recover from the depression until World War II, when foreign demand for American goods and American military spending caused the economy to boom. Some economists and historians actually blame Roosevelt's more advanced New Deal measures for prolonging the depression by restraining the recovery of the private sector. Keynesian economic theory, that governments can control the economy by controlling the money supply, was eventually proven correct, but the tremendous amount of deficit spending that it took to end the depression was only justified by the necessity of fighting World War II.

Since 1933, the Democrats have based their political success on promising economic well-being to the poorest segment of society; providing this economic aid was financed by increased taxation of the productive members of society and increased government debt. This unsustainable program eventually became the target of an increasingly conservative Republican Party, leading to the extreme political dichotomy of the United States as of 2024.

It can be justifiably said that Franklin Delano Roosevelt not only failed to end the depression, as the massive effort to stop Hitler did that, but he also failed to win World War II. That war was started to prevent the conquest of Poland by a totalitarian regime. In the aftermath of the war, not only Poland but Estonia, Latvia, Lithuania, Czechoslovakia, Hungary, Romania, and Bulgaria were firmly in the grip of the Union of Soviet Socialist Republics, a dictatorship under Joseph Stalin that was every bit as evil as Adolf Hitler's Germany.

Harry S. Truman was one of the most poorly prepared for his job of any president. This is another black mark against Franklin Delano Roosevelt, who should have been aware of his own fragile hold on life and either given Truman some preparation for the job he was going to inherit or picked a better-qualified vice president. Truman not only inherited Roosevelt's job but also was saddled with Roosevelt's advisors and members of the executive department, many of whom were enamored of Joseph Stalin or who shared Roosevelt's foolish belief that Stalin could be handled. Directly, Truman was personally responsible for the outcome of the Potsdam Conference, which officially gave Stalin authority over most of Eastern Europe. Stalin took advantage of this to provide military assistance to allow the communists to take over the governments of many Eastern European countries, including Poland, Romania, Bulgaria, Hungary, Czechoslovakia, and eventually, East Germany.

Second to Truman in being poorly prepared for his job was John F. Kennedy, who very narrowly won the presidency over Richard M. Nixon, the Republican candidate, in the 1960 election. It is possible that Kennedy's election was fraudulent, as there are rumors of illicit activity in the West Virginia Democrat primary of 1960, in which Kennedy effectively knocked Hubert Humphrey out of the race for the Democratic Party's presidential nomination, and then later in the general election when Mayor Richard J. Daley found extra votes who-knows-where to give Kennedy Illinois's electoral votes and the election. Kennedy proceeded to stumble into one disaster after another, including the Bay of Pigs, Vietnam, Berlin, and the Cuban

Missile Crisis. In each of these, Kennedy's handlers were able to keep his image polished, with the help of the liberal press, while United States prestige withered around the world.

Lyndon Johnson took up where Kennedy left off, particularly in Vietnam, which he turned into a colossal quagmire. Johnson was a very crafty politician, who saw that the increasing wealth of the American middle class would likely turn the Republican Party into the majority party in United States politics. Johnson decided to counter that by "buying" the votes of minorities, particularly blacks, with his "Great Society" program that provided unprecedented preferences and entitlement benefits to minorities. Unfortunately, while the votes were gained for the Democrats, little improvement was gained in the lives of minority citizens, and the "race problem" got worse instead of better.

Jimmy Carter, the next Democrat president, was unable to acclimate himself to the Washington establishment and accomplished little during his single term. He was one of the few elected presidents to lose his reelection contest. Carter somewhat anticipated the current left-wing political agenda with his policy of government as the employer of last resort. It took years for the United States Postal Service to gradually come back to some semblance of reality after enduring Carter's "hire anyone and everyone" policy. Carter's policy of printing money to overcome government deficit spending resulted in unsustainable inflation, wreaking havoc on American industry and leading to the "Rust Belt."

William Jefferson Clinton was the first Democrat to declare he was running for president in 1992. Most leading potential candidates for the Democrat nomination had concluded in 1991 that George Herbert Walker Bush was unbeatable and decided to sit out the 1992 election. After Bush suffered a dramatic, steep drop in popularity, Clinton was an easy victor in the 1992 general election despite his apparent lightweight status and his less-than-stellar run as Governor of Arkansas. Clinton made an attempt at resuming and going beyond Carter's policies, but after a stinging defeat for the Democrats in the midterm elections of 1994, he switched from liberal to conservative, or at least neutral, in his proposed policies. After gutting the military and using the peace dividend to balance the budget, he easily won reelection in 1996. In spite of scandal after scandal, he maintained his popularity, with the help of the liberal media, and survived impeachment. Clinton initially propounded the Democrat "Deficits are meaningless" policy with his Treasury Secretary Robert Rubin but was soon brought to heel by the Republican Congress under Newt Gingrich, where deficits were finally eliminated. Each Democrat president since Lyndon Johnson has continued to use the Keynesian method to finance their social programs, including the latest two, Obama and Biden, but have been stopped by Congress going Republican in at least one House during their terms of office.

Barack Obama, another Democrat politician with little in his background to suggest he was qualified for the presidency, won the 2008 presidential election handily. He proceeded to push a liberal domestic policy and what could only be called an anti-American foreign policy and lost the House of Representatives to the Republicans in 2010, and saw Congress go Republican in both the House and Senate in 2014. He won reelection in 2012 mostly because of an indifferent conservative turnout for the Republican presidential nominee, Mitt Romney, similar to what happened in the 2008 presidential election with John McCain as the Republican nominee.

Joseph Biden was a very experienced politician, well aware of the ways of Washington, having served as senator from the State of Delaware for many terms and vice president for two terms under Obama before eventually gaining the nomination as Democrat for president in 2020. Like John Quincy Adams in 1824, the Republican nominee and victor in the 2016 presidential election, Donald J. Trump, was hounded incessantly throughout his term by disgruntled Democrats and the liberal news media, so that he was presumed to be virtually unelectable when he ran for a second term in 2020. Biden received the Democrat nomination and was inaugurated as president, with the Democrats in control of both houses of Congress, in spite of doubts as to Biden's mental condition and other issues. Due to gross increases in inflation, a botched exit from Afghanistan, border issues, and other problems, the Democrats lost control of the House of Representatives in the 2022 congressional election.

Most of the major Democrat presidents, Andrew Jackson, Woodrow Wilson, Franklin Roosevelt, and Lyndon Johnson, have had one thing in common—they have all been demagogues who have been more interested in getting elected than providing for the good of the country. A frequently cited evil of democracy is that the common people, once they realize that they have the power, can vote themselves whatever benefits they want, without regard for the source of the benefits. This allows them to abandon the Puritan work ethic and join the Consumers Movement where consumption is the first priority. This was hinted at by Lyndon Johnson, actually proposed by Jimmy Carter, and attempted by Clinton, Obama, and Biden, at least for some segments of society. Unfortunately, leaders of the Democratic Party, starting with Franklin Roosevelt, took the lead in this unsustainable practice. Starting with various welfare benefits and make-work projects, under the guise of fighting the depression of the 1930s, they buried the Ninth and Tenth Amendments to the Constitution under a flurry of programs that redistributed wealth and began the destruction of the American economy. These programs benefited a small proportion of the citizenry of the United States but were supported by the majority when the fear of economic collapse and chaos overrode other considerations. Once these fears abated, the responsible middle-class citizens ceased blind acquiescence to the leftist agenda until eventually, the Reagan Revolution began the return of the Democrats to the minority party status that they held from the Civil War until the economic crash of 1929. Not until Alexandria Ocasio-Cortez and her colleagues in the "Squad," demagogues of demagogues in Congress, who promoted with partial success a program of free everything for everybody, caught the attention of members of the post–Baby Boom generation who were brought up expecting a free ride for life, did the situation revert to unsustainability. The results of the election of Joseph Biden to the presidency under Democrat auspices have convinced a great many of the people of the United States that this pie-in-the-sky program cannot continue, but it has been institutionalized to such a point that it seems impossible to stop until Western Civilization crumbles under the weight of it.

Chapter 3

The Republican Presidents

The Republicans could be called the Conservative Party, not unlike their counterparts in Canada and Great Britain, with whom they are often in alliance on issues common to their respective countries, such as the rapport between Ronald Reagan and Margaret Thatcher. Heirs, via the Whigs, to the Federalist mantle, the Republicans have generally maintained a strict-constructionist view of the United States Constitution. Throughout the history of the United States, the Republicans and their predecessors have been considered the elitist party by the most partisan Democrats and have wittingly or unwittingly included various exclusive groups such as the American Party, an anti-immigrant, anti-Catholic party of the mid-nineteenth century. The origins of the present Republican Party are in the anti-slavery movement, more particularly in the movement to prevent the spread of slavery. Most members of the Free-Soil Party joined the Republicans as soon as the party was formed, and the Whigs eventually followed.

In spite of being more in tune with the letter of the Constitution, there have been more strong Republican presidents than strong Democrats, but only by a margin of eight to seven. However, there have been more weak Republican presidents than weak Democrats, by a slightly larger margin of nine to seven. Moderates are again more nearly equal, eight Republicans to seven Democrats (counting Tyler). See Appendix D2 for a more detailed picture of strong vs. weak presidents. The Republicans can claim the only completely unelected president, Gerald Ford, helping to give them more weak presidents.

George Washington acted as the disinterested patriotic statesman throughout his career, although his investment in western lands benefited greatly via the independence of the United States. Although not a member of a political party, as such did not officially exist when Washington became president, Washington consistently favored the policies of his Secretary of the Treasury, Alexander Hamilton, over those of Thomas Jefferson, Secretary of State. Some historians claim that Washington was unduly influenced by Hamilton, and Washington's prestige did, in fact, decline late in his presidency as party politics took center stage with Jefferson's withdrawal from the cabinet to become the leader of the "Republican" Party, composed primarily of former Antifederalists. Washington generally followed strict constitutional guidelines in his presidency, although he did establish many precedents that continued in force long after his retirement.

John Adams was the first, and last, official Federalist president. He believed the president was the head of the government and chief of state and expected to be treated accordingly. He ran into difficulties with his Federalist colleagues, who saw Alexander Hamilton as the true leader of the party, and more or less ignored Adams.

In spite of this, Adams continued the work of Washington in establishing the mechanics of the United States government, including providing for a permanent Navy. Adams also improved the international prestige of the United States by his handling of the XYZ affair, successfully resisting French attempts to interfere in the United States government.

John Quincy Adams can be considered the next Federalist, or Whig, or Republican president, although the only national political party at the time was the "Republican" party of Thomas Jefferson, which was in the process of splitting into the short-lived National Republicans and Democratic Republicans. John Quincy Adams is generally regarded as the only National Republican president. Henry Clay, leader of the National Republicans, ran against Andrew Jackson in 1832 in lieu of John Quincy Adams and lost.

William Henry Harrison, the next Republican (of the modern variety) president, elected as a Whig, spent his entire presidency in a sickbed and died before performing any presidential duties other than reading his inauguration speech. He was replaced by his vice president, John Tyler, a former Democrat, who joined the Whigs in protest of Andrew Jackson's imperial policies but reverted to the Democratic Party agenda after becoming president.

Zachary Taylor, the sixth Republican president, was also elected as a Whig and, like William Henry Harrison, was a war hero, which probably helped him get elected. Unfortunately, also like William Henry Harrison, Taylor died in office. He served long enough to make an effort to solve some of the insoluble problems facing the country at the time, but his political naivety was apparent to all, and his proposals, although quite sensible, were not taken seriously by the professional politicians in Washington.

Millard Fillmore, Taylor's vice president, took over for the remainder of Taylor's term but accomplished little as he faced a hostile Democrat Congress throughout his tenure as president.

The next Republican president, Abraham Lincoln, a former Whig who joined the Republican Party after its creation, is almost universally ranked as the best or the second-best of all presidents. In the face of intense opposition, Lincoln solved the slavery dilemma that had severely troubled the nation since its inception. Some authorities blame Lincoln for starting the Civil War, but the slave states' use of secession as the solution to the slavery crisis was clearly unacceptable, and all other efforts at remediation had failed. Lincoln's stated purpose in running for, being elected, and taking office as president was to preserve the Union. Lincoln initially denied any intent to free the slaves of the South but often expressed his opposition to slavery and his belief that it would eventually die out. Lincoln was strongly opposed to the dissolution of the Union, perhaps recognizing the predicament that western farmers would be in if their crops had to be exported through a foreign country should Arkansas and Louisiana, as well as Tennessee and Mississippi, through which the Mississippi River flows on its way to the Gulf of Mexico, be allowed to leave the United States with the rest of the Confederacy. Lincoln eventually decided that emancipation of the slaves was a necessity but was assassinated before he could help push through the Thirteenth Amendment abolishing slavery. This task was left to his vice president, Andrew Johnson, who, although a Democrat, assumed the presidency upon Lincoln's death.

Ulysses S. Grant, the first of a series of post–Civil War Republican presidents, presided over most of the Reconstruction Era. He largely deferred to Congress on most issues, but his prestige as the victor in the Civil War allowed him great influence on the issues of the day.

Rutherford B. Hayes, the tenth Republican president (counting Tyler), was the first to be elected with a majority of the electoral vote but with a minority of the popular vote. Hayes won the electoral vote as the result of a compromise that decided the winner of several disputed electoral votes. Samuel Tilden, the Democratic Party contender, clearly won a majority of the popular vote and possibly would have won the electoral vote if the distribution of the disputed electoral votes had been completely unbiased. Not unlike John Quincy Adams previously, under similar circumstances but perhaps more justifiably, Hayes was hounded throughout his presidency with cries of fraud and served a somewhat unhappy single term.

Not unlike William Henry Harrison, James A. Garfield, the next Republican president, was not in office long enough to make his mark. Shot by a deranged, disappointed office seeker only four months after taking office, Garfield lingered for a little over two months before dying.

Chester Alan Arthur was Garfield's vice president, a compromise candidate from the Stalwart section of the party, whom no one expected to ever become president. Assumed to be a corrupt spoilsman, Arthur surprised everyone by his virtuous presidency, which included the first meaningful steps toward a nonpartisan civil service.

Benjamin Harrison was the grandson of William Henry Harrison, and little more was expected of him than his grandfather accomplished in office. Benjamin Harrison considered it the duty of his office to administer laws passed by Congress; he had neither the desire nor the ability to provide leadership to the legislative branch, which was only briefly controlled by the Republicans during his term. His loss of the popular vote in the election of 1888 did not provide him with any mandate.

William McKinley, the fourteenth Federalist/Whig/Republican president, was considered somewhat spineless by many, including even a few of his closest colleagues. He was fortunate enough to preside over the beginning of an era of unprecedented increase in prosperity, shared by almost the entire population of the United States, from carriers of the "full dinner pail" to the wealthiest of the robber barons. This prosperity was, in fact, largely the result of the economic and governmental policies promulgated by McKinley and his Republican cohorts. The Republican Party remained in control in Washington, except for a brief period, until 1931.

Theodore Roosevelt became the youngest president of the United States in history when William McKinley was assassinated in September 1901. Roosevelt was hardly welcomed into the White House with open arms by the business community, as he was an ardent progressive and soon began "trust-busting," expanding national parks and forests, and performing other acts that truly frightened the economic power groups of the country.

William Howard Taft was elected the sixteenth Republican president in 1908. He continued Roosevelt's progressive policies and even expanded upon them. However, he was a rather colorless chief executive and did not excite the approbation of the masses. Roosevelt had handpicked Taft as his successor but, after four years, decided that Taft was not the man to be trusted to continue Roosevelt's progressive program. Roosevelt challenged Taft for the 1912 Republican nomination for president, but the party leaders decided Roosevelt was too radical and selected Taft as the party's nominee. Roosevelt immediately turned to the progressives, pushed aside their leader, Robert M. La Follette, and became the progressive, or "Bull Moose," party's nominee for president in 1912. This practically guaranteed the election of the Democratic Party's nominee (Woodrow Wilson) by splitting the Republican vote.

Woodrow Wilson, by maneuvering the United States into World War I on the side of the Allies, guaranteed their victory over Germany. He did not realize, or perhaps ignored, the many secret pacts and treaties the Allies had among themselves that never could have been enforced except with the help of the United States in bringing Germany to the peace table, hat in hand. The resulting peace practically guaranteed a continuation of the war as soon as Germany could build up enough strength to resume it. While the people of the United States might not have seen World War II coming, they did see that Wilson was trying, with his Fourteen Points that were a critical part of the Versailles Treaty ending World War I, to force the United States into a leading position as the world policeman to keep the future peace. They resoundingly rejected this role by giving Warren Gamaliel Harding and the Republicans an overwhelming landslide victory in the 1920 presidential election. Harding received 63.8% of the popular vote, the highest percentage ever recorded in a presidential contest. While Harding made some significant positive accomplishments during his short presidency of only two and a half years, he is remembered today almost exclusively for the malfeasance in office of several of his cabinet members.

Calvin Coolidge became the eighteenth Republican president upon the death of Warren Harding but was elected on his own in 1924. Coolidge was extremely popular, particularly among the middle class, as increased industrial and agricultural production provided prosperity for all, except for American farmers, as increased world production combined with reduced worldwide demand meant lower prices for them. Coolidge perhaps saw trouble ahead as the rest of the world slowly got into competition with the United States for the production and supply of goods and services. He chose not to run again for president in 1928. Coolidge has increased in stature over the decades following his presidency.

Herbert Hoover received the Republican nomination for president in 1928 and was an easy victor in the general election. His joy was short-lived, as the stock market crashed less than a year into his presidency, followed by recession and then outright depression. Hoover could not avoid taking the fall for the depression, despite his innovative efforts to mitigate its effects. He received little assistance in his efforts from a hostile Congress and was overwhelmingly defeated in his reelection bid in 1932.

Dwight Eisenhower was solicited by both the Democrats and Republicans as their presidential candidate in 1952. As the great hero of World War II, he was universally admired and believed to be a competent leader. Eisenhower said yes to the Republicans, perhaps because he felt Franklin Roosevelt and Harry Truman were too easily manipulated by Joseph Stalin and did not represent middle America. Eisenhower went on to easy victories in the 1952 and 1956 presidential elections, although the Democrats took over control of both houses of Congress. It would appear that his "I like Ike" popularity was more personal than ideological.

Richard Nixon was Dwight Eisenhower's vice president from 1953 to 1961. He appeared to be a bit more conservative than Eisenhower and was an ardent anti-Communist. He was eventually proved correct in his allegations that Alger Hiss, a Democratic Party hero, was a communist but was never forgiven by liberals for pushing the issue. He had personality issues that became overwhelmingly prominent later in his presidency but successfully overcame them during the 1968 presidential campaign during which he appeared publicly as a carefree, good-humored man about town. He barely defeated Hubert Humphrey in the 1968 election, due partly to the third-party candidacy of George Wallace, who took the votes of many of the more conservative citizens but may have helped Nixon look more middle-of-the-road.

The resignation of Richard Nixon gave the presidency to Gerald Ford, who was appointed to the office of vice president after the resignation of Spiro Agnew, who was elected with Richard Nixon in 1972. Ford thus became the only completely nonelected president of the United States. Ford was initially quite popular, but his pardoning of Richard Nixon and the sliding of the country into an economic recession, combined with several gaffes of large and small moment, brought his popularity to an end, and he was one of the few sitting presidents to lose his reelection bid.

In spite of, or perhaps because of, being governor of California, ex-actor Ronald Reagan was not taken seriously as a presidential candidate in 1976 or early in the 1980 campaign. However, he surprised everyone in 1980 with a massive defeat of the incumbent, Jimmy

Carter. Reagan went on to achieve immense popularity as president, and in his reelection campaign of 1984, he came as close as anyone since James Monroe in 1820 to winning 100% of the electoral vote.

George Herbert Walker Bush, after being severely critical of Ronald Reagan during the primary campaign in 1980, went on to be his running mate on the Republican ticket in both 1980 and 1984. Bush had an extremely high approval rating as he began his presidency and after the "Shock and Awe" of Desert Storm but was one of the most unpopular presidents ever by the time of the 1992 election. He lost the support of conservatives by raising taxes after he said he wouldn't (actually, he said "No new taxes"), and he antagonized liberals with a less-than-heartfelt approach to poor relief. He also came off as weak in several critical situations, and the "wimp factor" became an issue.

George Walker Bush, the son of George Herbert Walker Bush, became the twenty-fifth Republican president while winning fewer popular votes than his opponent, Al Gore, in the 2000 presidential election. Florida's defective ballots in the presidential election forced the decision on who won Florida's 2000 electoral vote to the United States Supreme Court. The court, with seven Republican-appointed justices and only two Democrat-appointed judges, declared Bush the winner. Democrats cried foul, but there was no possible appeal.

Donald Trump won the Electoral College while his Democrat opponent (Hillary Rodham Clinton in this case) received more popular votes. Clinton did not receive a majority of the popular vote, but this did not prevent her and the Democratic Party from crying foul throughout Trump's first term; beginning, in October 2019, impeachment proceedings. Such activities have gone on since before Trump was inaugurated. The Democrat-controlled House of Representatives twice voted to impeach the president and brought charges in the Senate, where Trump was acquitted. In the meantime, Trump effectively used executive orders and what few laws were passed to accomplish much of his pronounced agenda, and the country was on a continuous prosperity ride until a viral pandemic arrived in late winter.

The Constitution of the United States of America was written, transmitted to Congress, and ratified by people of the business class who demanded stability in their government and protection and security in their financial affairs. They became labeled "Federalists" because of their support for the Constitution, although the term is really a misnomer. Their attitude was more nationalist, as their primary goal was to provide for a strong national government. Federalism was forced upon them during the ratification of the Bill of Rights, the primary purpose of which was to limit the power of the national government, and without the promise of which the Constitution would not have been ratified. The Bill of Rights remains a primary political topic to this day, as people demand their rights and one party or another tries to minimize one or more of those rights.

Republican presidents have largely adhered to the principles of the Federalists, although with increasing democracy they have largely been required to "play to the crowd" to win an election.

Chapter 4

Ranking the Presidents

In many countries, the government's chief executive is chosen by the legislature in a parliamentary type of government. As long as that chief executive has a party that controls the legislature, he or she usually remains in office. In the United States, the chief executive, the president, is chosen wholly independently from the legislature and, as discussed above, frequently is at odds with the legislature, which may be controlled by a political party other than that of the president. The means of choosing the president of the United States is somewhat convoluted, very indirect, and not particularly democratic. Electors from each state gather to cast their votes for president in the Electoral College, and these votes are counted by the president of the Senate. The winner of a majority of the votes cast wins. Each state gets two electoral votes plus one elector for each member it has in the House of Representatives. There are an additional three votes for the District of Columbia. The total number of electors is set by law at 538, so to win the presidency, a candidate must collect at least 270 votes in the Electoral College. It is important to realize that each elector can vote for whomever they wish; there is no federal law mandating that they vote for the winner of any election, although some states require their electors to do so. In practice, the electors are strongly pressured by convention to vote for the winner of a state's popular vote for president. In most states, it is winner takes all, but a few smaller states require their electors to be split to reflect the popular vote. There was a movement at one time for a constitutional amendment to have the electors of each state proportioned based on the popular vote, but this effort failed.

The Constitution is very clear on the duties of the president. In accordance with Article II, "Before he enters on the Execution of his Office, he shall take the following Oath or Affirmation: 'I do solemnly swear (or affirm) that I will faithfully execute the Office of President of the United States, and will to the best of my Ability, preserve, protect and defend the Constitution of the United States.'" The Constitution requires that the president is commander in chief of the armed forces of the United States and the militia when called into federal service. The president may require the opinion in writing of any of the principal officers of the government of the United States and may grant reprieves and pardons, but not in cases of impeachment. The president may make treaties with sovereign nations but must have the concurrence of two-thirds of the Senate. The president, with the concurrence of the Senate, appoints ambassadors, Supreme Court justices, and other officers of the United States. The president is required to inform Congress of the State of the Union on a regular basis. The president receives ambassadors and other public ministers. The president is to "take care that the laws be faithfully executed." The president commissions all officers (military) of the United States. The above constitutes the entire constitutional duties of the president. No amendment to the Constitution to date has altered these duties.

Rating the president on how he or she performs his or her constitutional duties is very difficult, as the details of the above duties are rather complicated and can be open to interpretation. There is also the question of implied powers. And finally, the laws as passed by Congress can, in some cases, be somewhat ambiguous and contradictory. This book rates the presidents of the United States based on four factors: (1) Did they help enhance American greatness? (2) Did the quality of life of the American people improve under their presidency? (3) Did they rise to the occasion when a crisis arose? (4) How much did they succeed in overcoming opposition to doing their jobs? Other minor factors or special cases arose, which modified the rating in some cases. In order to quantitatively rank the presidents, each of the four primary factors is given a weight, and each president is given a rating of minus 100% to plus 100% on how they fared in each category. There are objective criteria, such as real growth in gross national product, increase in national wealth, increase in population, increase in size of territory, which could be used to rate presidents, but as all these could be the result of factors beyond a president's control, or even contrary to a president's intentions, they are not explicitly used here. Subjective evaluations are used almost exclusively in preparing these ratings. Some accomplishments are attributed to a particular president to a greater or lesser degree, even though he may have had little or no influence on them. Some accomplishments were the results of a particularly effective secretary of state or events outside the control of the government in Washington but are here given as credit to the president at the time unless he was actively working against such accomplishments. Efforts to accomplish certain goals are considered, even though the goal in question may not have been reached.

The weights:

1) Enhance American Greatness   10
2) Improving Quality of Life   8
3) Meeting Crises   10
4) Overcoming Opposition   8

The total potential maximum score is thus 36.0. There is no "curve" or other weighting mechanism, and the scores are not comparative, so it is potentially possible that every president could get a perfect score of 36.0, or any or all presidents could be above or below the 50% score of 0.0. A score of 0.0 is considered neutral, although a president may achieve an overall score of 0.0 while having higher scores in one or more categories and lower scores in other categories. As it happens, purely by coincidence, in this ranking, twenty-one presidents received an above-average score of more than 0.0, and twenty-one presidents received an overall score of less than 0.0. Of the four presidents who received a "neutral" score of 0.0, two received scores of 0% in all categories. These scores were given to James Garfield and William Henry Harrison, who both died shortly into their first terms as president. Their scores were used as the basis for the scores of the other presidents, as they were considered to be "neutral," not having any significant records upon which to base negative or positive assessments. This basis differentiates the proposed ranking from all other presidential evaluations that have been mentioned and evaluated in this study, which typically ignore Garfield and the first Harrison or give them low scores despite their not having done anything "bad" as president, equating them to such bad presidents as Franklin Pierce and James Buchanan and the almost universally disliked Andrew Johnson. Other rankings, judging by their results, rate presidents primarily on the increase in democracy or inclusiveness during their terms. These factors are not considered in this ranking, as they are not part of the president's constitutional duties and are a factor of society as a whole, and the individual president's personality, and are not likely to be driven by a president's activities or exhortations.

Popularity is not a factor in the ratings developed here; personality does not enter into the mix except as it may weigh into a president's ability to lead others into his point of view. The majority of modern historians appear to be more interested in star power than in effectiveness when ranking the presidents, and the more common rankings that have been published and have appeared on television or other media appear to reflect this. They do not, as a rule, refer to this quality as popularity but use the phrase "ability to inspire," or something similar, and consistently give it high influence in their rankings. The mainstream rankings also tend to favor "Robin Hood" types, who, simplistically speaking, favor taxing the rich to support the poor. Considering that it is estimated that 78% of Americans live paycheck to paycheck,[3] although not all these people, by any means, are in poverty, popularity and the Robin Hood image can be synonymous. Of nine Robin Hood presidents (Jefferson, Jackson, Theodore Roosevelt, Wilson, Franklin Delano Roosevelt, Truman,

---

[3] Per CareerBuilder.com (2017), cited by CBS News and *Forbes* Magazine.

Lyndon Johnson, Clinton, and Obama, but deferring on Biden), all are in the top 18 of the composite or aggregate mainstream poll, while all are in the bottom 25 of the libertarian ranking. All, notably, are Democrats except for Theodore Roosevelt, who some say was a closet Democrat. This ranking has two in the top ten (Jefferson and Theodore Roosevelt) and the others in the bottom eleven. The Robin Hood syndrome reached a peak with the liberal concept of the postindustrial state, where the middle class would be taxed to support all those who lost means of self-support as manufacturing jobs left the United States for Latin America and Asia. Unfortunately for the liberals, most blue-collar types prefer jobs to welfare, resulting in such phenomena as the "Reagan Revolution," the Republican "Contract with America," and the Trump victory in 2016. The middle class, or bourgeoisie, has always been considered the enemy by the lower classes, who believe themselves to be exploited by merchants and others. The upper classes, the true wealthy, have frequently in history energized the lower classes against the bourgeoisie to protect themselves from inroads into their positions of power.

A third factor, and perhaps the most important in ranking, which seems to be a major one for historians, is the willingness to usurp constitutional powers. The most activist presidents are consistently at the top of mainstream presidential rankings and also at the top of popularity rankings, as the president is generally considered the representative in Washington of the people, while Congress is generally considered the tool of special interests and lobbyists. The ten most active presidents—Theodore Roosevelt, Wilson, Lincoln, Franklin Delano Roosevelt, Kennedy, Lyndon Johnson, Jefferson, Jackson, Polk, and Truman—all, except for Polk, are at the top of most presidential popularity polls. The ten least active presidents—William Henry Harrison, Benjamin Harrison, Garfield, Buchanan, Fillmore, Coolidge, Harding, Arthur, Grant, and Andrew Johnson—are consistently at the bottom of the popularity polls. This is confirmed, in a way, as the libertarians, who are usually the most adamant strict-constructionists regarding the Constitution and most restrictive on the scope of the president's duties, consistently favor the least-popular presidents. Executive orders are a mark of activist presidents but are beyond the scope of this book.

Several mainstream presidential rankings were evaluated. The different mainstream rankings tend to agree on ranking the more popular presidents but differ more widely with unpopular presidents. The ranking spread for the more popular presidents, such as Washington, Jefferson, Lincoln, and Franklin Delano Roosevelt, were 3, 4, 2, and 2, respectively. For Andrew Johnson, the spread in ranking was 26 when measuring from best to worst, the largest range of any president. Herbert Hoover and Martin Van Buren, two very unpopular presidents who had the misfortune to serve during the onset of depressions, both had ranking spreads of 19 best to worst. Ronald Reagan and George W. Bush each had mainstream ranges of 20. In most mainstream evaluations, William Henry Harrison and James A. Garfield are excluded as many felt their terms were too short to be evaluated, and Grover Cleveland's two nonconsecutive terms were combined in one for ranking purposes, even though Cleveland's first and second terms had different results, such as his Supreme Court picks.

The most popular presidents were in the top ten in terms of composite rankings from the 21 sources cited: Lincoln, Franklin Delano Roosevelt, Washington, Theodore Roosevelt, Jefferson, Truman, Wilson, Eisenhower, Jackson, and Kennedy. This ranking only includes five of these in their top ten: Washington, Lincoln, Jefferson, Theodore Roosevelt, and Eisenhower. In a more radical stance, the libertarian Ivan Eland, in his book *Recarving Rushmore*,[4] rates 42 presidents on "peace, prosperity, and liberty." He ranks Grover Cleveland once, combining his two nonconsecutive terms into one ranking, much like most other rankings. Eland does not evaluate the brief presidencies of William Henry Harrison and James A. Garfield, nor does he evaluate Donald Trump and Joseph Biden, who had not yet been elected in 2014. His ranking of "presidential

---

[4] *Recarving Rushmore, Ranking the Presidents on Peace, Prosperity, and Liberty* (Oakland: Independent Institute 2014).

success" has in his top ten only Washington and Eisenhower of the popular presidents listed above.

Eland's top four presidential successes are all among the least-popular presidents. In order: John Tyler, Grover Cleveland, Martin Van Buren, and Rutherford B. Hayes. The Libertarian philosophy zeroes in on strict constructionism as far as the Constitution is concerned. The president, in their point of view, is only there for his explicitly enumerated constitutional responsibilities, overlooking the nebulous clause in Article II Section 3: "He shall...recommend to their (Congress') Consideration such Measures as he shall judge necessary and expedient," and must look to Congress for all initiatives. Eland's top four presidents were unpopular with the public and had no or little support in Congress, even among their own party, so were unable to accomplish much beyond at least a part of their bare minimum constitutional duties.

This ranking and Eland's Libertarian ranking allow zero credit for generating enthusiasm among one's constituents. Eland sets much more restrictive goals for the president than does this ranking. On the other hand, historians and pundits seem to like to see a president who takes the initiative and pushes his agenda, particularly if it is popular with the public, and wins Congress to his side, or goes around Congress as long as he has strong support among the public. Some detailed comparisons between different rankings are in later chapters and in Appendices D and E. The latest rankings are compared in table 4-1. C-SPAN is a cable network concentrating on live presentations of government and government-related public events. Siena is a Roman Catholic University that sponsors an evaluation of the presidents a short time after each new president takes office.

The generally very low opinion most members of the public have for Congress (except for their own congressperson, who usually gets reelected) gives the president some leeway to go beyond the Constitution in pursuing his agenda as long as his public opinion poll numbers are higher than those of Congress, which is usually the case.

The Constitution leaves to the states some of the details on electing presidents, although there are several clauses and a few amendments that provide some restrictions. Originally, the electors were chosen primarily by the state legislatures. New states that entered the union tended to be more democratic, choosing the electors by the popular vote of a substantial percentage of the population. Eventually, the older states were more or less forced by popular pressure to follow the same procedures, so that by the election of 1824, the popular vote became a major factor in presidential elections.

This Ranking	Eland[5]	C-Span[6] (2021)	Siena (2022)[7]
1 Washington	7	2	3
2 Lincoln	29	1	2
3 Reagan	35	9	18
4 Jefferson	26	7	5
5 Adams, J.	22	15	16
6 Polk	38	18	15
7 Roosevelt, T.	21	4	4
8 Eisenhower	9	5	6
9 Nixon	30	31	28
10 Trump	NR	41	43
11 Arthur	5	30	33
12 McKinley	39	14	22
13 Taft	20	23	25
14 Hoover	18	36	37
15 Coolidge	10	24	32
16 Ford	16	28	30
17 Monroe	25	12	12
18 Bush, G. H. W.	33	21	20
19 Adams, J. Q.	12	17	17
20 Taylor	13	35	36

---

[5] Eland from *Recarving Rushmore* Table 2, Peace, Prosperity, and Liberty.
[6] C-Span from a survey of historians.
[7] Siena College.

21 Hayes	4	33	31
22 Harrison, B.	15	32	34
23 Garfield	NR	27	27
24 Harrison, W. H.	NR	40	40
25 Cleveland 1st T.	2	25	26
26 Cleveland 2nd T.	2	25	26
27 Grant	19	20	21
28 Bush, G. W.	37	29	35
29 Harding	6	37	42
30 Fillmore	14	38	38
31 Johnson, A.	17	43	45
32 Tyler	1	39	39
33 Van Buren	3	34	29
34 Carter	8	26	24
35 Roosevelt, F. D.	31	3	1
36 Truman	40	6	7
37 Clinton	11	19	14
38 Kennedy	36	8	9
39 Madison	28	16	10
40 Wilson	41	13	13
41 Obama	34	10	11
42 Biden	NR	NR	19
43 Johnson, L.	32	11	8
44 Jackson	27	22	23
45 Buchanan	23	44	44
46 Pierce	24	42	41

Table 4-1 Comparison of This Ranking with Libertarian, Liberal Rankings

The party identifications usually associated with presidents are modern-day Democrat or Republican. All earlier major-party identifications led to one or the other of these. Therein lies a major source of confusion when discussing party politics in the United States. When political parties were first formed on a national level in the United States, the more conservative party chose the name "Federalist," in keeping with their nationalistic goals of increased power in the central government through the Constitution. People more concerned with maintaining states' rights and preventing the growth of an omnipotent central government that would likely favor large financial interests were labeled "Antifederalists." After the Antifederalists were somewhat forced by events to accept the Constitution, the term "Antifederalist" was no longer appropriate, so they chose a new name, "Republican," in keeping with their enthusiasm for things French (after the French Revolution of 1789 and the First Republic), where the word originated.[8] They briefly became Democratic Republicans, then dropped the word "Republican" during Andrew Jackson's presidency and became simply "Democrats."

These Democrats maintained their states-rights position in spite of being led by the strongly nationalist Andrew Jackson. Unfortunately, the Whigs, the party with nationalist intentions, although formed mainly to obstruct the imperialist Andrew Jackson, no longer had a valid name after the retirement of Jackson from politics and did not represent many of the people who opposed the Democrat Party in the 1850s. When a new party was formed in 1854 in Ripon, Wisconsin, combining most of the Whigs with opponents of the extension of slavery who had partially organized as the Free-Soil Party, the perfectly good name of "Republican" was resurrected.

---

[8] William Wordsworth expressed it thusly: "Bliss it was in that Dawn to be alive." Others were equally pleased to see the downfall of the French monarchy, absolute under Louis XIV and nearly so under the guillotined Louis XVI, and they had no sympathy for the aristocracy which was nearly wiped out by the guillotine. A few slowed their congratulations when the general populace began being executed *en masse* during the Terror. The *Republique* meant *liberte, egalite, fraternite*, or so they thought. Some American "Republicans" kept up their enthusiasm for things French, but even Thomas Jefferson eventually had had enough when Napoleon took over.

Some presidents were associated with third parties before or after their presidencies but were identified with a major party while president.

Previous major parties and their modern equivalents are as follows:

Federalist	becomes	Republican (R) (1854–present)
Antifederalist	becomes	Democrat (D)
Republican (1792–1828)	becomes	Democrat (D)
Democratic Republican	becomes	Democrat (D) or Republican (R) in 1 case, John Quincy Adams, via the short-lived National Republicans
National Republican	becomes	Republican (R)
Jacksonian	becomes	Democrat (D)
Whig	becomes	Republican (R)

The demise of the Federalist Party did not immediately result in the creation of a new party that represented the views of those persons who had called themselves Federalists. The Federalist Party remained in existence after 1800, until about 1828, although it did not put up a candidate for president after 1816. The victory of the Antifederalist-Jeffersonian, Republican-Democratic, Republican-Jacksonian-Democrats was so complete that after 1800 they were the overwhelmingly dominant political force in the presidency and Congress until the Civil War. Eventually, in opposition to the regal presidency of Andrew Jackson, the Whig Party was organized, modeled after the British Whig Party that was primarily, at least originally, interested in opposing the power of the king.

For a period of approximately eight years, from about 1820 to 1828, there was only one major political party in the United States, the "Republicans," founded by Thomas Jefferson in the very late eighteenth century to combat Alexander Hamilton's Federalists. Needless to say, this name, "Republican," would be a point of confusion regarding politics in the United States between 1788 and 1850 if it had not been largely ignored by most historians, who generally use the name "Democratic Republican" although it was not invented until the 1820s, when the "Republican" Party split into Democratic Republicans (to become Democrats) and National Republicans (to become Whigs). These earlier "Republicans" were former Antifederalists who decided to change their party's name after the Constitution was adopted. They are the party of Thomas Jefferson, and thus the predecessors of the Democratic Party, and definitely not associated with the modern Republican Party, which got its start in the 1850s, long after the early "Republicans" became Democrats. The majority of the early "Republicans" became, briefly, Democratic Republicans, and then, when Jackson was president, became officially Democrats. Some say that the second Republican Party did, however, take its name consciously from the first "Republican" Party, in recognition of Thomas Jefferson's role in making the United States a great democracy.

Both major political parties in the United States changed not only their names but also their purpose as time went on. Originally, the Antifederalist-Republicans were the party of the self-sufficient small farmers, who saw no need for government oversight and had small amounts of cash available to pay taxes; this made them very resistant to big government. Two hundred years later, the Democratic Party is very much the party of big government, promoting high taxes and high government expenditures at the national level and very little discretion at the state government level. The Federalists originally favored control of the economy at the national level with minimal discretion allowed by the state governments, and high federal taxes to pay for national public works such as canals and railroads, and a quasi-governmental national banking system. Today's Republican Party generally avoids national funding of public works projects, although exceptions are made, and encourages greater flexibility and responsibility in most areas at the state government level.

Locofocos, Barnburners, Free-Soilers, and the 1850s American Party never elected a president, in spite of some persons who became president having been at one time before or after their presidency affiliated with these party labels. Nor did any of the later third parties, such as Greenbackers and Populists, and more modern-day third parties, Socialist, Green, Libertarian, et al., produce any presidents. Former president Millard Fillmore, running in 1856 under the American (Know-Nothing) Party ticket, won 8 electoral votes and may have thrown the election to James Buchanan. Robert La Follette, a former Republican running for president as a Progressive in 1924, won the twelve electoral votes of his home state of Wisconsin, and the Progressive Party continues in existence to this day. Strom Thurmond, in 1948, won thirty-nine electoral votes as the "States Rights Democratic Party" candidate for president. This "party" ran no other candidates, and its members mostly returned to their roots in the national Democratic Party after the 1948 election.

The Progressive Party mentioned above has had a resurgence in recent years as millennials and others have called for increased redistribution of wealth, to the point of resuscitating the "soak the rich" policies advocated by some prior to World War II. This is somewhat ironic as the Progressive Party originated as a movement within the Republican Party to protect the middle class, including small-business entrepreneur types, against the depredations of "robber barons" such as John D. Rockefeller. The progressive movement quickly became general, with both Republican and Democrat politicians in the early twentieth century jumping on the bandwagon. When it became an independent party, in the election of 1912, it came in second in the popular vote nationwide. The progressive movement moved rather quickly to the left, and one of the originators of the movement, Robert M. La Follette, reconstituted the Progressive Party after World War I as a frankly socialistic organization, which it remains today.

To clarify, there have always been only two major political parties in the United States, each primarily representing a specific group of people, although their stated political philosophies have evolved over time, particularly for what is now known as the Democratic Party. For a brief period in the prosperous 1950s and early 1960s, little differentiated the two parties, but throughout most of United States history, they have been bitterly opposed. This was especially true from Andrew Jackson's time up to the Civil War and has been more pronounced recently as the two major parties have developed conflicting philosophies.

The Federalists of the eighteenth century advocated for a stronger national government, particularly in financial matters, at the expense of the states. They then transformed into the Whigs, who supported strong central government influence on the economy, particularly through internal improvements, a national bank, and restrictive tariffs, but with limitations on the president's central power. This shift primarily responded to Andrew Jackson's many unconstitutional actions; he sincerely (and correctly) believed he had the support of the masses in anything he chose to do. When the Whigs, along with the Free-Soil Party and the American Party, joined the Republican Party of 1856, they adopted a stronger nationalist stance against the states-rights southern Democrats, mainly to prevent the expansion of slavery into the territories and possibly into the free states. Modern Republicans reverted to a more states-rights stance in the twentieth century, opposing the extension of New Deal–type programs into areas believed to be the domain of the states per the Constitution.

The Antifederalists quickly renamed themselves "Republicans" and, under Thomas Jefferson's leadership, advocated for farmers, the country's predominant economic group. They naturally opposed the merchants and bankers at the core of the Federalist Party's membership. These Republicans became essentially the only national political party in the United States after the War of 1812, facing only token Federalist opposition in the presidential election of 1816. The Federalists did not nominate a presidential candidate in 1820 or 1824, leaving the field to the "Republicans." These "Republicans" split due to ideological differences into National Republicans and Democratic Republicans by 1828. The Democratic Republicans became simply Democrats, and most National Republicans became Whigs. The Democrats and their predecessors have consistently claimed to champion the "common man" and were initially the party of the average citizen but gradually shifted to advocate for society's lowest class, today a primary constituency for those who rely on government support for their basic needs, essentially, the welfare advocate party. While Thomas Jefferson sincerely believed that "that governs best which governs the least," and the Democratic Party was the states-rights party for many decades after Jefferson, the modern Democratic Party now strongly favors nationalism, imposing severe limitations on states' rights, and restricting individual freedom.

Originally, the Federalists supported a stronger national government over the loose confederation of states under the Articles of Confederation. Most people were content living under limited government, which was largely democratic with a small *d* in various statehouses. These individuals were not overly concerned with the long-term effects of the United States' weakness on the international scene. Merchants, bankers, and other capitalists suffered most under the near-anarchy prevailing from 1776 to 1787. This group, along with wealthier plantation owners such as George Washington and middle-class professionals like John Adams, managed to persuade people at the state ratifying conventions to support the Constitution despite many citizens' grave misgivings. Voter turnout for delegates to the state ratifying conventions was reportedly low, reflecting a lack of interest even among those few who had the right to vote at that time. For instance, Rhode Island held a popular vote on ratification in March 1788, where the Constitution was defeated, 237 to 2,708, with the state's population at about 68,000.

In the voting population of the United States as a whole, the Federalists were in a minority from the beginning, although this was at a time when greater restrictions on suffrage kept most people from voting, even many adult white males. As more and more states opened the franchise to all or most adult white males in the early nineteenth century, the Federalist Party became more and more a minority party until they disappeared completely. The Federalist reincarnation as Whigs and then Republicans did not erase their minority status, except briefly when slavery became the overwhelming topic of political discussion in the 1850s, and the Democratic Party became synonymous with treason in the 1860s. Although Republicans dominated the presidency from the Civil War until the Great Depression, the Democrats often controlled at least one house of Congress during this period. The popular vote in presidential elections of this period was usually quite close; twice between 1868 and 1900, the Republican candidate won the election while gaining fewer popular votes than his Democrat opponent.

The Democratic Party has been perceived, throughout United States history, as the democratic party, usually favoring wider suffrage, although Thomas Jefferson, the first Democrat, had no use for the urban proletariat. He was a staunch advocate for the yeoman farmer, an independent tiller of the soil. This stance largely informed the anti-slavery and pro-small landowner clauses in his proposed Northwest Ordinance of 1784. Andrew Jackson, the first elected president to call himself a Democrat, was more a critic of the privileged classes, particularly bankers, than a champion of the lower classes. However, as the hero of New Orleans and an avowed Indian fighter, he was embraced wholeheartedly by the poorest sector of the population, tying them more or less permanently to the Democratic Party.

Chapter 5

The Great Presidents

Very few presidents have attained greatness. The opportunity to seize a historic moment and make the most of it does not come to everyone. George Washington had a clean slate to make the presidency, and the nation, into what he thought they should be. Abraham Lincoln faced destruction of the Union and found the means to save it. Ronald Reagan saw an opportunity to end a destructive world situation and took it.

1) George Washington, No Party but in Sympathy with the Federalists

George Washington is correctly identified as the father of his country, but he can also be called the father of the United States government. After presiding at the Constitutional Convention of 1787, he then filled the first two presidential terms from 1789 to 1797. While president, he personally established many of the unwritten protocols of government operation and successfully wielded his extensive powers to secure the existence of the new government, despite its lackluster support among the general population. Most importantly, he resisted the temptation to grasp absolute power, which would have likely been granted to him for life if he wished it, and instead voluntarily retired after two terms in office. Washington disdained political parties but sympathized with the Federalists. The first Congress, inaugurated in 1789, was in sympathy with Washington, but party differences soon emerged, and Washington faced strong Antifederalist or Republican (call it Democratic Republican) opposition for the remainder of his time in office.

Washington was a real estate speculator highly interested in the lands beyond the Appalachian Mountains. He was one of the first to propose improved communications between the settled east and the developing west. With his knowledge of surveying, a substantial part of the eighteenth-century civil engineering curriculum, he is credited with being an original proposer of the Chesapeake and Ohio Canal, intended to link tidewater on the Potomac River in what was to become Washington, DC, with the Ohio River.

Washington faced a sympathetic Congress only in the first two years of his first term. For the remainder of his presidency, one or both houses of Congress were held partially or completely by the Antifederalists for a substantial part of the time.

Regarding the qualities by which the presidents are evaluated, Washington fares as follows:

1) Enhancing American Greatness

    There is hardly any question that the United States today would not exist if it were not for George Washington's courageous leadership in forming and holding together the country after the contentious adoption of the Constitution. Washington organized the new government, managed to clear up the new country's financial affairs with Hamilton's help, improved relations with Great Britain, and began the process of obtaining amicable treaties with the Native Americans. Washington also, by reluctantly accepting a second term as president, prevented the party factionalism of Thomas Jefferson and Alexander Hamilton from destroying the country.

2) Improving Quality of Life

    Washington lobbied for the adoption of the Bill of Rights, the lack of which caused some states to reluctantly approve the Constitution and slowed ratification by North Carolina and Rhode Island. Washington was a highly visible supporter of westward expansion, having been a speculator in western lands from pre-revolutionary times. He was a promoter of the Chesapeake and Ohio Canal, an early transportation improvement.

3) Meeting Crises

Washington, as president, took the bull by the horns by severely crushing the Whiskey Rebellion, an early anti-tax revolt.

4) Overcoming Opposition

Washington initially had no opposition, being unanimously elected in the Electoral College for both his terms as president. He did begin to face some opposition in his second term when he began to side more often with Alexander Hamilton and the Federalists against Thomas Jefferson and the Republicans.

Washington's rating:

CATEGORY	VALUE	RATING
1) Enhancing American Greatness	10	80%
2) Improving Quality of Life	8	60%
3) Meeting Crises	10	80%
4) Overcoming Opposition	8	00%

Total rating: 20.8

2) Abraham Lincoln, Republican

Many people, regardless of their political affiliation, rank Abraham Lincoln as our greatest president, and a good case can be made for him as the greatest. Abraham Lincoln faced the greatest opposition to doing his job of any president, with eleven states choosing to secede from the Union rather than accept his presidency. He was a minority president in his first term, receiving only 45% of the popular vote and being elected because the remainder of the popular vote was distributed among three other major candidates, resulting in Lincoln having a plurality in most of the states that did not secede. Lincoln accomplished a great deal during his presidency; he initiated the construction of the transcontinental railroad to tie the western states to the rest of the country, and he began the eradication of slavery. While Congress was Republican in both the House and Senate throughout Lincoln's presidency, the leaders of Congress strongly opposed Lincoln's conduct of the war and his policy of leniency toward the South.

While Lincoln was not originally in favor of forcing an end to slavery, this was how he was perceived by Southerners, and secession was essentially a ploy to avoid freeing the slaves. The Civil War was initially fought, from the North's point of view, to "preserve the Union." This was not an abstract concept; the secession of the South essentially nullified the Louisiana Purchase. Arkansas, Louisiana, and Texas were on the west side of the Mississippi, and the remainder of the Confederacy was on the east side, ending United States sovereignty at the southern borders of Missouri and Kentucky. Eventually, Lincoln saw that he could not justify continuing the most destructive war yet seen unless it promised the end of slavery and issued his Emancipation Proclamations after two difficult years of war. The final Emancipation Proclamation also put an end to European, and most significantly British, consideration of open support for the Confederacy.

The tragic irony of the Civil War is that it was unnecessary. Lincoln truly was not an abolitionist and would have been content to allow slavery to continue in the then-existing slave states for as long as it was desired there by Southern leaders. Lincoln believed that slavery would eventually die out, as it was not economically viable. The slave-based cultivation of cotton was barely self-sustaining due to the extremely poor efficiency of slave labor. In addition, the slave population in the cotton-producing areas could not sustain itself, and cotton plantation owners relied on procurement of slaves from Maryland and Virginia when they could not get them internationally after the banning of the international slave trade. The eventual mechanization of the harvesting of cotton did away with the need for large amounts of unskilled labor, but this was decades away at the time of the Civil War. Without the need for their labor, there would be no need for plantation owners to support the slave population, and they would have presumably been freed voluntarily. The integration of the former slaves into Southern society would have been an entirely different matter.

Lincoln faced serious opposition to going to war against the South except from the abolitionists, who considered slavery a moral evil that justified using violence to end it. Most Northerners who welcomed the Civil War and supported it with their blood and treasure were primarily concerned with avoiding the spread of slavery into the West, and this was Lincoln's primary reason for running for president. Economically, Lincoln was a Whig and sat in Congress as a Whig from 1847 to 1849. Lincoln understood the value of the Mississippi River in exporting Midwestern crops and other products, having twice floated flatboats laden with commodities produced in the upper Midwest down to New Orleans for export. He may have seen Confederate control of the lower Mississippi River as it passed between the states of Mississippi and Arkansas, and through Louisiana, as justifying going to war. As he said after the Vicksburg campaign, "Now the Father of Waters goes unvexed to the sea."

A case could be made that Abraham Lincoln is the greatest man who became president of the United States. He rose from extremely humble surroundings, faced severe personal difficulties, and appeared to receive very little personal profit from his political activities.

Abraham Lincoln was a lawyer who was fully in tune with the commercial interests of the United States. His most remunerative court cases were in defending the emerging railroads of the country, particularly in the fast-growing Midwest, from restraints attempted by the opponents of the railroads. He was, to some extent, a speculator who expected to profit from his commercial decisions made as president. He owned property in Council Bluffs, Iowa, that was sure to increase in value when he deemed that the east end of the transcontinental railroad would be located there.

Thanks to the secession of the Southern slave states, both houses of Congress were held by the Republicans throughout Lincoln's presidency, though they were not always in harmony.

Regarding the qualities by which presidents are evaluated, Lincoln fares as follows:

1) Enhancing American Greatness

    By winning the Civil War, Lincoln established the Republican Party's control of the nation. The Republicans, while formed as an anti-slavery party, included the Whigs, who favored increased national wealth with government assistance in the form of land grants for railroads and other internal improvements, a national bank to assure stable financing, a protective tariff to promote industry, and a permanent national debt to keep the financial community in harmony with the national government.

2) Improving Quality of Life

    By ending slavery, Lincoln removed a curse from the American landscape that thwarted the aspirations of people in all walks of life.

3) Meeting Crises

    Lincoln successfully met the worst peril that faced the United States—the secession of a key part of the country.

4) Overcoming Opposition

    Lincoln was initially a minority president, having won only a plurality of the electoral vote in his first election. He was considered little more than an amateur by the leaders of his own party and had to fight to achieve and maintain his leadership. He initially faced opposition for the nomination in 1864.

Lincoln's rating:

CATEGORY	VALUE	RATING
1) Enhancing American Greatness	10	80%
2) Improving Quality of Life	8	10%
3) Meeting Crises	10	100%

4) Overcoming Opposition   8   20%
Total rating: 20.4

3)   Ronald Reagan, Republican

Ronald Reagan accomplished what his seven immediate predecessors failed to do: end the Cold War. He also, perhaps coincidentally, began the recovery from the "stagflation" of the 1960s and 1970s that had reached a dangerously high level during the presidency of Jimmy Carter, the man Reagan replaced. Reagan never had a Republican Congress to work with him. The Senate was Republican in the Ninety-Seventh, Ninety-Eighth, and Ninety-Ninth Congresses, but the House of Representatives was held by the Democrats throughout Reagan's presidency. Reagan was able, in spite of ideological differences, to establish a rapport with Congress; perhaps his Irish ancestry allowed him to find common ground with Tip O'Neill, the Irish-American congressman from Massachusetts who was Speaker of the House of Representatives during Reagan's presidency. The special increase of immigration quotas for the Irish may have been a product of this meeting of the minds.

Ronald Reagan began his career as an actor, achieving mid-level stardom in several motion pictures that were fairly well regarded but were not necessarily blockbusters. He rose to political prominence while an actor, becoming active in the liberal-leaning Screen Actors Guild and eventually its president. He switched from Democrat to Republican during the McCarthy era of the late 1940s and early 1950s, when many members of the motion picture profession were found to be Communists or Communist sympathizers. He was one of the few politicians to successfully switch parties, perhaps because he did so before entering electoral politics on a national level. He went on to become a powerful governor of California before running for president.

The House of Representatives was held by the Democrats throughout Reagan's presidency. The Senate was Republican until the One Hundredth Congress when it, too, went Democrat. Reagan was still able to work well with Congress until near the end of his presidency.

Regarding the qualities by which the presidents are evaluated, Reagan fares as follows:

1) Enhancing American Greatness

    Ronald Reagan successfully moved the United States from the malaise following the embarrassments of the Nixon Administration and the incompetence of the Carter Administration, returning the United States to its position as the supreme world power. Reagan successfully negotiated an arms limitation treaty with the Soviet Union. Reagan's adoption of confrontation and dismissal of détente was key to the dissolution of the Soviet Union. Reagan proposed a Strategic Defense Initiative, dubbed "Star Wars," that would employ futuristic weapons in national defense.

2) Improving Quality of Life

    Reagan's domestic policies returned the country to prosperity after several years of stagnation, partly by ending the excessive inflation that had neared 20% annually during the Carter Administration. While ending inflation, Reagan saw millions of new jobs created in the United States economy and also oversaw tax reduction and income tax simplification. Reagan led the reform of Social Security and Medicare, adding more people to the eligibility lists while increasing taxes to pay for the increased benefits, making the fund solvent for the first time in its history. Ronald Reagan appointed Sandra Day O'Connor to be the first woman on the United States Supreme Court.

3) Meeting Crises

    Reagan successfully overcame the rumblings of the death throes of the Soviet Union, avoiding major disruption as the "Evil Empire" staggered toward dissolution. Reagan also spectacularly survived being wounded in an assassination attempt. The United States and its Western Allies withdrew from Lebanon in 1984 after failing to bring an end to hostilities between Israel and its Arab foes. Reagan became involved in the Iran-Contra scandal in 1986 but emerged relatively unscathed in spite of it becoming an embarrassment to the United States government.

4) Overcoming Opposition

Ronald Reagan was not taken seriously as a presidential candidate in spite of his success as governor of California. Opponents credited the successes of his administration to his staff, not to him, and continued to belittle his accomplishments through to the end of his presidency. Successfully, in the face of strenuous opposition, Reagan fired the nation's air traffic controllers after they began an illegal strike. After the United States Senate became controlled by the Democratic Party, Reagan was unable to get his conservative choices for Supreme Court Associate Justice confirmed and had to settle for a moderate, Anthony M. Kennedy, who was confirmed without dispute.

Reagan's rating:

CATEGORY	VALUE	RATING
1) Enhancing American Greatness	10	60%
2) Improving Quality of Life	8	60%
3) Meeting Crises	10	60%
4) Overcoming Opposition	8	20%

Total rating: 18.4

Chapter 6

The Very Good Presidents

Several presidents accomplished great things, but there were also failures in their administrations or activities and events that were detrimental, but not enough to balance out their major achievements.

4)   Thomas Jefferson, Republican[9]

Thomas Jefferson accomplished one significant act that assured his place as one of our greatest presidents: he purchased the Louisiana Territory from France, covering the entire western Mississippi River Basin, from New Orleans to the Rocky Mountains, despite having grave doubts about his legal authority to do so. In this instance, he was the first of many presidents to change his political philosophy in the face of immense potential gain. Jefferson was the first of nine Democrat presidents (although his party was called "Republican" at the time) to have a Congress fully in sympathy with him throughout his presidency.

Jefferson was one of the most liberal of the Founding Fathers and was rather skeptical of the Constitution adopted in 1788. He was very much in sympathy with the French Revolution, as he felt it to be very much an expression of the democratic ideals of the people. Jefferson might be considered one of the original "bleeding heart

---

[9]   Republican, in cases of presidents in office prior to 1856, refers to the party of Thomas Jefferson, not the party of Abraham Lincoln (see chapter 4).

liberals," but within the context of his times, his heart did not bleed that much. Jefferson is often mistakenly credited with originating the expression, "that government is best which governs the least." However, he did evolve from his strict, states-rights, limited federal government position to becoming something of a nationalist after attaining the presidency and facing the job of governing within the constraints of a strict Constitution.

Jefferson was more than a partisan politician. He was more than willing to use extralegal means to destroy or at least confound his enemies. He manipulated the treason trial of Aaron Burr in a desperate attempt to secure a conviction but failed. Jefferson attempted to bring Napoleon and the British Empire to bay during the Napoleonic Wars with his Embargo Act but succeeded only in causing suffering among American farmers and producers of other goods who were unable to export their products except by smuggling, mostly by overland transport, which became rife.

Both houses of Congress were firmly in friendly hands throughout Jefferson's presidency and largely in sympathy with Jefferson's policies, as he was the founder as well as the leader of what would become the Democratic Party.

Regarding the qualities by which the presidents are evaluated, Jefferson fares as follows:

1) Enhancing American Greatness
    Jefferson's Louisiana Purchase, made in spite of his misgivings about the constitutionality of the move, doubled the size of the United States, making it a nation to be reckoned with on the international scene.
2) Improving Quality of Life
    The original purpose of the Louisiana Purchase was to obtain the port of New Orleans for the benefit of farmers in the American West. This was admirably achieved, allowing the West to prosper and giving all Americans an opportunity to "go west," even within the original boundaries of the United States, and achieve their destiny.

3) Meeting Crises

   Jefferson did not fare so well in international relations, becoming something of a tool of Napoleon in his battle with the British. Following his principles, he reduced the size of the United States government, including the army, navy, and diplomatic service, at a time when all were needed in the tempestuous international situation.

4) Overcoming Opposition

   Jefferson had little domestic opposition during his presidency. The Federalist Party was on the wane, and Jefferson's distaste for the antics of Aaron Burr was shared by many of his fellow citizens, of both parties. Jefferson immediately, upon assuming the presidency, freed all political prisoners arrested by the Federalists under the Alien and Sedition Acts.

Jefferson's rating:

CATEGORY	VALUE	RATING
1) Enhancing American Greatness	10	100%
2) Improving Quality of Life	8	40%
3) Meeting Crises	10	20%
4) Overcoming Opposition	8	00%

Total rating: 15.2

5) John Adams, Federalist

John Adams appointed John Marshall to the Supreme Court, setting the judicial branch on its path to becoming an equal and important third branch of the federal government. Adams also was the father of the United States Navy. By creating a permanent Navy and successfully thwarting the aims of France in the XYZ Affair, Adams ensured that the United States received the respect it deserved in the eyes of the rest of the world. The House of Representatives and the Senate were both Federalist throughout Adams's single term as president, marking the last time that party would wield significant power on the national scene.

John Adams, despite being one of the strongest advocates for revolution and independence, became a firm proponent of an alliance with Britain after independence was achieved, a position shared by most of his Federalist colleagues.

The Federalists controlled both houses of Congress throughout the presidency of John Adams. However, Federalist party leadership was in the hands of Alexander Hamilton, who was seldom in complete agreement with Adams.

Regarding the qualities by which the presidents are evaluated, John Adams fares as follows:

1) Enhancing American Greatness

   John Adams made the Navy a permanent part of the United States' defense establishment. Adams successfully ended the XYZ Affair, thwarting France's attempt to control American foreign policy. In preparation for war with France over the affair, Adams called George Washington back to active duty as head of the army. Adams and the Federalists also enacted the Alien and Sedition Acts, severely curtailing the Bill of Rights, in reaction to the war scare. Eventually, Adams sent commissioners to France and ended the threat of war.

2) Improving Quality of Life

   Adams appointed many competent and distinguished men to the United States courts, including appointing John Marshall as Chief Justice of the Supreme Court, helping to ensure that the United States would be a country under the rule of law.

3) Meeting Crises

   As mentioned above, John Adams successfully resolved the XYZ Affair.

4) Overcoming Opposition

   Adams was not a personable politician and had difficulty with personal relationships. He opposed the more extreme followers of fellow Federalist Alexander Hamilton, who largely controlled the Federalist Party. Despite this, Adams was generally successful in all he attempted to do as president.

Adams' rating:

CATEGORY	VALUE	RATING
1) Enhancing American Greatness	10	40%
2) Improving Quality of Life	8	40%
3) Meeting Crises	10	40%
4) Overcoming Opposition	8	40%

Total rating: 14.4

6) James K. Polk, Democrat

James Knox Polk assured the fulfillment of America's "Manifest Destiny" by adding Oregon and the Great Southwest to the territory of the United States. The fact that he did so primarily to add more slave states to the Union is irrelevant, as the territory gained by the Mexican War ended up as free states: California before the Civil War, Nevada before the end of the Civil War; Colorado, Utah, New Mexico, and Arizona after the Civil War. Concurrently with the Mexican War, Polk negotiated a treaty with what is now Colombia to allow the United States to build a railway or canal across the Panamanian isthmus.

James K. Polk was not a popular politician and was only nominated as a presidential candidate after his Democratic Party could not agree on a choice between the more prominent members of the party.

Polk started with a Democrat Congress, but the House turned Whig in the Thirtieth Congress.

Regarding the qualities by which the presidents are evaluated, Polk fares as follows:

1) Enhancing American Greatness

    James K. Polk was the most energetic and enthusiastic of all the expansionist presidents. His primary motive was the expansion of slavery, but none of the territory acquired by the United States during his presidency, except Texas, which was already on the path to statehood before Polk took office, became slave territory, slave states, or part of the Confederacy. With Texas, Oregon, and the Southwest, Polk added more territory to the United States than the Louisiana or Alaska purchases.

2) Improving Quality of Life

    Polk's aggressive capture of California greatly increased the wealth of the United States, especially after the discovery of gold in 1848. This increased the money supply, allowing economic expansion, as well as providing opportunities for hundreds of thousands of people in the new mining frontier.

3) Meeting Crises

    While it could be said that Polk created the crises he successfully overcame, nevertheless many Americans who had emigrated to Texas welcomed the intervention of the United States in their struggle against Mexican government oppression.

4) Overcoming Opposition

    Polk had little domestic opposition to his policies. Some felt he was not as aggressive in his efforts to obtain Oregon as he was in going after Texas and the Southwest, but the only real opposition to his policies was from some of the same Easterners who objected to the Louisiana Purchase on the grounds that it diluted their influence in Washington.

Polk's rating:

CATEGORY	VALUE	RATING
1) Enhancing American Greatness	10	80%
2) Improving Quality of Life	8	20%
3) Meeting Crises	10	40%
4) Overcoming Opposition	8	00%

Total rating: 13.6

7) Theodore Roosevelt, Republican

Theodore Roosevelt was America's first progressive president and ran under the Progressive, "Bull Moose" banner in 1912 after he served the remainder of the assassinated McKinley's second term and his own four-year presidential term, and after one term by his anointed successor, William Howard Taft. Theodore Roosevelt was a Republican throughout his presidency and had a Republican Congress for the whole time he was president.

Theodore Roosevelt was responsible for the construction of the Panama Canal by the United States. While his means of doing this caused some unfavorable feeling among the nations of Latin America, it improved the prestige of the United States in the world at large. It also helped the defense posture of the United States by easing communication between the East, Atlantic Coast, and the West, Pacific Coast of the United States. Improved water transportation between the East and West Coasts also helped reduce the effective monopoly that railroads had in freight transportation in the United States.

Theodore Roosevelt was one of the most popular politicians to hold the office of president and surely could have been reelected to as many terms as he chose to serve if he had not stepped down in 1908. It is fairly certain that he regretted his announcement that he would not run for another term as president in 1908 almost as soon as he made the announcement. He was a very ambitious person who wanted very much to be in charge of things. His "New Nationalism" placed the federal government as supreme over state and individual rights, contrary to the Ninth and Tenth Amendments. This did not bother most people as they saw "TR" as fighting for them against the "Establishment" and the "Robber Barons."

Both houses of Congress were Republican throughout Theodore Roosevelt's presidency, although there was a constant battle for control between the conservative and the progressive members. TR generally sided with the progressives.

Regarding the qualities by which the presidents are evaluated, Theodore Roosevelt fares as follows:

1) Enhancing American Greatness

By initiating the successful construction of the Panama Canal, even though by creating a revolution in Colombia leading to independence for Panama, Theodore Roosevelt placed the United States among the first rank of world powers. His sending of the Great White Fleet on a world tour advertised the fact. His Roosevelt Corollary to the Monroe Doctrine cemented the position of the United States as leader of the Western Hemisphere nations. Theodore Roosevelt's arbitration of the Russo-Japanese War earned him the Nobel Peace Prize.

2) Improving Quality of Life

Theodore Roosevelt successfully brought the biggest of the big businessmen of the United States to understand that they were answerable to the government and people of the United States for their actions. He intervened in the 1902 strike of the anthracite coal miners, on the side of the miners, forcing the coal mine owners to enter into arbitration to end the strike. Roosevelt pressured Congress to pass the Hepburn Act, strengthening regulation of the railroads of the United States, in 1906.

3) Meeting Crises

Theodore Roosevelt was not as aggressive a trust-buster as he was sometimes portrayed. By maintaining a relationship with J. P. Morgan and other financiers of the era, Roosevelt kept the Panic of 1907 from being a serious drag on the economy.

4) Overcoming Opposition

Theodore Roosevelt was an extremely popular president, with his only serious opposition coming from the leaders of the great trusts that he was endeavoring to keep under control. This opposition manifested itself in the refusal of the Republican Party to nominate him for president in 1912, even though it was apparent that the incumbent, Taft, would likely come in third if Roosevelt ran as an independent or third-party candidate in that election and the Democrats nominated a progressive candidate.

Theodore Roosevelt's rating:

CATEGORY	VALUE	RATING
1) Enhancing American Greatness	10	60%
2) Improving Quality of Life	8	60%
3) Meeting Crises	10	20%
4) Overcoming Opposition	8	00%

Total rating: 12.8

Chapter 7

The Better-than-Average Presidents

Many presidents served out their terms while making modest improvements in the state of the union and not doing anything seriously detrimental; others, such as Richard Nixon, combined great accomplishments with disasters.

8) Dwight Eisenhower, Republican

Eisenhower was perhaps the epitome of the middle-of-the-road presidents; he was also, perhaps, the closest to a nonpartisan statesman of any president since Washington. As a retired general, Eisenhower was pursued by both major political parties to be their candidate in the 1952 presidential election. Eisenhower chose the Republicans as he felt their party philosophy to be more in tune with that of Middle America, and may have felt he could do better than Roosevelt and Truman internationally. Eisenhower had a Republican Eighty-Third Congress but thereafter both the House and Senate were controlled by the Democrats.

Dwight Eisenhower was responsible for initiating the construction of the Interstate Highway system in the United States, making it much easier for Americans to travel within the country. His interest in highways dated from his early army experience in participating in a cross-country convoy of army vehicles shortly after World War I. He may have also gotten a bit of an anti-railroad attitude from his father, a blue-collar railroad employee, and may have been interested in loosening the railroads' grip on the long-distance freight business. The Interstate Highways also improved the distribution of consumer goods throughout the United States.

Eisenhower rose swiftly from relative obscurity to be the leader of the World War II allied forces fighting Nazi Germany. He was considered a Far Eastern expert prior to World War II but had little to do with the defeat of totalitarian Japan. He continued to demonstrate his administrative and diplomatic abilities after the war as president of Columbia University and as the head of the North Atlantic Treaty Organization. He appeared to be of a somewhat liberal turn politically, but when both major parties in the United States asked him to be their presidential candidate in 1952, he chose the Republicans.

Both houses of Congress were under Republican control when Eisenhower took the oath of office as president. They soon changed hands and remained Democrat throughout Eisenhower's presidency.

Regarding the qualities by which the presidents are evaluated, Eisenhower fares as follows:

1) Enhancing American Greatness

As president, Eisenhower demonstrated leadership on the international scene responding to crises in Southeast Asia and the Middle East. He attended a summit meeting with the leaders of Great Britain, France, and Russia, although it accomplished little. He addressed the United Nations where he called for planning for the peaceful use of atomic energy, leading to the formation of the International Atomic Energy Agency. Eisenhower condemned the United Kingdom and France for their heavy-handed handling of the Suez Crisis. Continuing past United States policy, he failed to assist the Hungarians in their uprising against the Russian-backed Hungarian communists. After receiving congressional approval, he promulgated what was to be called the "Eisenhower Doctrine," offering help to countries requesting assistance against armed aggression by international communism. This led to military intervention in Lebanon and Taiwan. But Cuba was lost to communism under Eisenhower's watch.

2) Improving Quality of Life

Eisenhower's stewardship in promoting the Interstate Highway system gave Americans greater ease of travel and more expeditious delivery of consumer goods. Eisenhower expanded Social Security, increased the minimum wage—to $1 per hour!—and began the desegregation of schools in the United States, using federal troops to help integration in the South. In his farewell address, Eisenhower warned the people of America to beware of undue influence by the military-industrial complex.

3) Meeting Crises

Eisenhower managed to dodge a bullet when a U-2 spy plane pilot was downed inside the Soviet Union. This event did cause the cancellation of a summit conference between Eisenhower and Soviet Premier Nikita Khrushchev.

4) Overcoming Opposition

Eisenhower had little opposition during his two presidential terms, although some pundits felt that he was a figurehead and that others were actually running the government.

Eisenhower's rating:

CATEGORY	VALUE	RATING
1) Enhancing American Greatness	10	40%
2) Improving Quality of Life	8	60%
3) Meeting Crises	10	20%
4) Overcoming Opposition	8	00%

Total rating: 10.8

9) Richard M. Nixon, Republican

In a popularity contest (see chapter 12), Richard Nixon would have, at the end of his presidency, come in close to dead last. His reputation improved somewhat as time went on, but he is still viewed unfavorably by most people. Not so in 1968, when, even a year before the election, polls showed Nixon to be more popular than Lyndon Johnson, or at least less unpopular. Both the House and Senate were held by the Democrats throughout Nixon's presidency. In the 1968 presidential election, Nixon had the advantage of George Wallace running as a third-party candidate. Wallace's far-right position took some ultraconservative votes but made Nixon seem to be a middle-of-the-roader when compared to the ultraliberal, for the time, Hubert Humphrey, the Democrat candidate. Richard Nixon probably had more to do with the improvement in the quality of life within the United States than any other president, by encouraging the creation of the Environmental Protection Agency under his watch. The EPA has had a profound effect on the quality of air and water within the United States.

In international relations, Nixon's visit to Communist China while president had a major effect on the international balance of power, greatly improving the status of the United States internationally. It also pushed the Soviet Union into a more defensive stance, leading eventually to its dissolution.

Richard Nixon would probably have been impeached and removed from office in the wake of the Watergate scandal if he had not resigned. His arrogant disregard for political realities in the 1972 election campaign caused him the loss of support of many within his own party as well as people and political operatives in general. His many beneficial acts were completely ignored once it became apparent to most people that he had had a personal hand in the Watergate break-in or its cover-up. With both houses of Congress firmly in the hands of the opposition party, Nixon's impeachment and removal from office were highly likely, although an escape as per Andrew Johnson was not impossible; Nixon's resignation made it moot.

Both houses of Congress were Democrat throughout Nixon's presidency.

Regarding the qualities by which the presidents are evaluated, Nixon fares as follows:

1) Enhancing American Greatness

    Richard Nixon effectively broke the close bonds between the Union of Soviet Socialist Republics and the People's Republic of China, putting the United States in sole first place among the world's powers. Nixon's administration had the good fortune to be in place during the culmination of the United States space program when Neil Armstrong and Edwin Aldrin landed on the Moon in July of 1969.

2) Improving Quality of Life

    The creation of the Environmental Protection Agency under Nixon's watch brought about an immediate improvement in the air and water that people of the United States had to breathe and drink. Nixon also pursued improvements in urban life elsewhere that had been initiated previously.

3) Meeting Crises

    Nixon held his own during several international incidents, but his handling of the Watergate scandal completely negated the public perception of his performance in other arenas. The United States Supreme Court entered an era of controversy when Lyndon Johnson attempted to place Abe Fortas as Chief Justice. Fortas's confirmation process became drawn out, and he had to withdraw his name when irregularities in his past surfaced. Nixon ended up nominating Warren Burger as Chief Justice, and Burger was quickly confirmed. Eventually, Nixon named two associate justices to the Supreme Court, resulting in the first conservative Supreme Court majority since the early Franklin Roosevelt Administration.

4) Overcoming Opposition

    Nixon narrowly lost the presidential election of 1960. In spite of likely voter fraud in Illinois and Texas, whereby John F. Kennedy narrowly won the general election, Nixon chose not to pursue a recount, even though there was evidence of systemic corruption in the Kennedy campaign, going back to the Democratic Party nomination process. Nixon's sending of United States troops into Cambodia, expanding the Vietnam War, caused his popularity to plummet. The killing of protesters and bystanders by National Guard troops at Kent State University in Ohio quickly turned public opinion in the United States against the war. Nixon's Cambodian venture resulted in Congress passing a war powers act over Nixon's veto, limiting the president's ability to engage in military activity without Congressional approval. Accomplishing what he did during his presidency in spite of being almost completely hamstrung during his second administration is testimony to Richard Nixon's ability to overcome opposition.

Nixon's rating:

CATEGORY	VALUE	RATING
1) Enhancing American Greatness	10	40%
2) Improving Quality of Life	8	60%
3) Meeting Crises	10	00%
4) Overcoming Opposition	8	20%

Total rating: 10.4

10) Donald J Trump, Republican

It is difficult to objectively evaluate Donald Trump as of March 2024, even three years after he left office, due to the effect the coronavirus scare had on his presidency and the fact that his presidential career has not yet concluded. He faced strenuous opposition throughout his term, including two impeachments followed by acquittals in the Senate, but he completed four years in office. As of April 2024, he is the leading Republican candidate for the 2024 presidential election. The Senate was Republican throughout Trump's presidency, but the House of Representatives turned Democrat in the 116th Congress.

Regarding the qualities by which presidents are evaluated, Trump's performance is considered as follows, noting that criticism of his presidency continues as he attempts to gain a second, nonconsecutive term in 2024:

1) Enhancing American Greatness

    Trump succeeded in reducing the loss of high-paying skilled manufacturing jobs overseas and renegotiated trade agreements with Mexico, Canada, and China to benefit American exports. He rebuilt the American military structure after years of neglect by his predecessor. He opposed the trend toward globalism, prevalent in the United States and Western Europe for decades, which would diminish the United States' international status and potentially lead to a loss of sovereignty in several areas.

2) Improving Quality of Life

    The economy began recovering the day after the 2016 election results were announced, continuing through the first half of Trump's first term. This recovery contrasted with the modest recovery during the previous eight years, which was largely attributed to significant federal government stimulus spending. Trump made inroads into the federal bureaucracy, which has been perceived as reducing Americans' freedoms in many areas.

3) Meeting Crises

    The number of illegal aliens crossing the southern border between the United States and Mexico decreased significantly during Trump's presidency. The effectiveness of his response to the coronavirus crisis remains a subject of debate as of August 2024.

4) Overcoming Opposition

    The Democratic Party took immediate steps to destroy the Trump presidency even before his inauguration in January 2017. Despite two impeachment attempts failing to remove him from office, he was defeated in his 2020 reelection campaign.

Trump's rating:

CATEGORY	VALUE	RATING
1) Enhancing American Greatness	10	80%
2) Improving Quality of Life	8	50%
3) Meeting Crises	10	00%
4) Overcoming Opposition	8	-40%

Total rating: 8.8

11) Chester A. Arthur, Republican

Chester A. Arthur, known as a political hack until he became president, was transformed by the assassination of James A. Garfield by a self-proclaimed political spoils seeker into an advocate of political reform in Washington. Specifically, Arthur promoted reform in the civil service, signing the Pendleton Act, which removed much of the civil service from the political sphere in the federal government. Throughout Arthur's presidency, either the Senate or the House of Representatives was under Democrat opposition control.

In spite of his surprisingly competent performance as president, Arthur was denied the opportunity by his party to run for a full term of his own.

The House of Representatives was Republican at the beginning of Garfield's (and Arthur's) term but changed to Democrat in 1883. The Senate became Republican at the beginning of Arthur's term and remained so.

Regarding the qualities by which presidents are evaluated, Arthur fares as follows:

1) Enhancing American Greatness

Arthur continued the advancement of the United States into prominence in world affairs. He attempted to prevent Congress from enacting an extremely high protective tariff. Arthur proposed an agreement among Western Hemisphere countries to prevent war and, more than one hundred years before its time, to unite in a common currency to improve trade.

2) Improving Quality of Life

Arthur took steps to rein in the spoils system, which dated from the Jackson Administration, that hampered good government in Washington by turning most government employees out onto the street whenever the administration changed. Arthur was instrumental in adopting Standard Time in the United States. He attempted to get the United States Senate to approve a treaty with Nicaragua to construct an Atlantic-Pacific canal. Arthur proposed federal aid to education, a radical idea at the time, and proposed clarifying the rules on presidential succession.

3) Meeting Crises

Little of moment occurred during Arthur's administration except for the assassination of Garfield, which resulted in his presidency. He vetoed some pork-barrel measures but was overruled by Congress.

4) Overcoming Opposition

Arthur overcame disdain on the part of others in government, due to his previous reputation as a party hack, to take a leadership role in reforming the government in Washington.

Arthur's rating:

CATEGORY	VALUE	RATING
1) Enhancing American Greatness	10	40%
2) Improving Quality of Life	8	10%
3) Meeting Crises	10	00%
4) Overcoming Opposition	8	40%

Total rating: 8.0

The Crime of the Democrats

12) William McKinley, Republican

William McKinley allowed the United States to become an imperial nation by fighting the Spanish-American War and annexing Hawaii. The Spanish-American War faced domestic opposition within the United States and elsewhere, and among the people in the territories involved. Cuba became a free country, as did the Philippines, while the people of Puerto Rico chose to remain a territory under the protection of the United States. Congress was controlled by the Republicans throughout McKinley's presidency. Although party leadership was centered elsewhere than in the Executive Mansion during McKinley's presidency, he received credit for most of the positive results of efforts in Washington during his presidency, primarily because of his success in working with Congress. McKinley was regarded by some as a figurehead, with Mark Hanna, a prominent Republican industrialist, considered to be his handler.

The House of Representatives and the Senate were Republican throughout McKinley's presidency.

Regarding the qualities by which presidents are evaluated, McKinley fares as follows:

1) Enhancing American Greatness

    McKinley presided over the annexation of Hawaii and the victory over Spain in the Spanish-American War. He thus placed the United States squarely in the world-power camp and thwarted, at least temporarily, the isolationists of the US. McKinley had United States troops participate in putting down the Boxer Rebellion in China but did so in such a way as to gain the appreciation of the Chinese people.

2) Improving Quality of Life

    Under McKinley's watch, industrialization in the United States took a major step forward, thanks to increased protective tariffs and a return to the gold standard, providing increased prosperity for most Americans. McKinley's substantial victory over William Jennings Bryan in the election of 1896, and his repeat victory in 1900 by a larger margin, effectively ended the cheap money campaign of the populists and kept the United States on a prosperous road. The overall wealth of the United States and its citizens reached, by the end of the McKinley Administration, perhaps its greatest level, relatively speaking, of any time in the history of the Republic.

3) Meeting Crises

The gold crisis, with William Jennings Bryan campaigning for president, was an extremely volatile issue in the 1890s. McKinley and the Republicans successfully thwarted Bryan and his followers.

4) Overcoming Opposition

McKinley had little trouble overcoming opposition from the Left during his administration.

McKinley's rating:

CATEGORY	VALUE	RATING
1) Enhancing American Greatness	10	40%
2) Improving Quality of Life	8	30%
3) Meeting Crises	10	10%
4) Overcoming Opposition	8	00%

Total rating: 7.4

13) William Howard Taft, Republican

William Howard Taft, a lawyer before entering public service, served in various roles, notably under Theodore Roosevelt, who endorsed Taft as his successor in 1908. The Republican Party controlled Congress during Taft's first two years in office, but as the Democrats began to align with the Progressive movement, the House and then the Senate became Democrat in the Sixty-Second Congress.

Like a later president, George H. W. Bush, Taft had a diverse public service career. He was pleased to be appointed Chief Justice of the United States Supreme Court by Warren Harding.

Regarding the qualities by which presidents are evaluated, Taft fares as follows:

1) Enhancing American Greatness
   William Howard Taft continued the beneficial progressive reforms initiated by Theodore Roosevelt, without stifling American business.
2) Improving Quality of Life
   Taft was a committed progressive. He drafted the constitutional amendments providing for the direct election of senators and the income tax. He continued and expanded the trust-control activities of his predecessor, Theodore Roosevelt. Taft, while president, proposed banking and currency reforms that later led to the Federal Reserve System.
3) Meeting Crises
   Taft faced few crises during his administration.
4) Overcoming Opposition
   Although a progressive, Taft was criticized for not being aggressive enough in pursuing progressive policies. In his reelection attempt in 1912, as the Republican candidate, he finished a distant third behind Woodrow Wilson and Theodore Roosevelt.

Taft's rating:

CATEGORY	VALUE	RATING
1) Enhancing American Greatness	10	50%
2) Improving Quality of Life	8	40%
3) Meeting Crises	10	00%
4) Overcoming Opposition	8	-20%

Total rating: 6.6

14) Herbert Hoover, Republican
Herbert Clark Hoover was perhaps the greatest humanitarian to have served as president. Having made a fortune as a mining engi-

neer and businessman, Hoover devoted his later life to public service. He managed the distribution of food and other necessities to refugees in Belgium and other parts of Europe during and after World War I. Unfortunately for him, he was president of the United States when the stock market crashed in October of 1929. Although he initiated many important programs to combat the Depression, many felt he did not offer sufficient sympathy to those suffering from its ravages, and Congress ignored him after 1930.

Hoover was inaugurated with a Republican Congress, but the House turned Democrat in the Seventy-Second Congress in 1931, while the Senate remained Republican until 1933.

Regarding the qualities by which presidents are evaluated, Hoover fares as follows:

1) Enhancing American Greatness
    Hoover played a leading role in international efforts to mitigate the effects of the Depression that began in 1929.
2) Improving Quality of Life
    Hoover initiated most of the key federal government programs put into effect to ease the hardships suffered by the American people during the Great Depression. He called for, and received from Congress, an income tax cut and initiated several public works programs.
3) Meeting Crises
    Internationally famous for leading relief efforts for the Belgian people during and after World War I, Hoover did not perform similar duties for the American people as the Depression deepened in the 1930s but did initiate federal programs to provide funding for useful work for the unemployed.
4) Overcoming Opposition
    Despite a complete lack of cooperation from Congress, Hoover managed to initiate some programs to ease the effects of the Great Depression.

Hoover's rating:

CATEGORY	VALUE	RATING
1) Enhancing American Greatness	10	00%
2) Improving Quality of Life	8	-30%
3) Meeting Crises	10	50%
4) Overcoming Opposition	8	40%

Total rating: 5.8

15) Calvin Coolidge, Republican

Calvin Coolidge was one of the most disparaged presidents, perhaps because of his taciturn ways and seeming lack of humor. This was a misapprehension, as those who knew of his response to the woman who bet she could get him to say more than three words ("You lose") are well aware. Coolidge also famously posed, while president, in an Indian chief's headdress while on vacation in South Dakota. The House of Representatives and the Senate were Republican throughout Coolidge's presidency. Coolidge was the first vice president to regularly sit in on cabinet meetings, perhaps because of Harding's lack of confidence in his own leadership qualities. He was firmly in the capitalist camp while "Red Scares" were causing concern around the country. He famously said, "The chief business of America is business."[10]

The House and Senate were firmly Republican throughout Coolidge's presidency.

Regarding the qualities by which the presidents are evaluated, Coolidge fares as follows:

1) Enhancing American Greatness

Coolidge restored the respect of the United States worldwide after the scandals of the Harding Administration came to light. Coolidge famously refused to ease off on demanding that the Allies of World War I repay their war

---

[10] In an address to Society of American Newspaper Editors on January 17, 1925.

debts to the United States: "They hired the money, didn't they?" Coolidge's secretary of state, Frank Kellogg, won the 1929 Nobel Peace Prize for negotiating the Kellogg-Briand Pact, outlawing war.

2) Improving Quality of Life

Coolidge did what he could to stabilize the economy during the heady days of the Roaring Twenties. He reduced the national debt and vetoed spending bills, some of which were passed by Congress over his veto.

3) Meeting Crises

Coolidge successfully weathered the exposure of the Teapot Dome and Elk Hills scandals, but he chose to retire rather than deal with the dangerous financial situation that was looming and led to the Great Depression.

4) Overcoming Opposition

Coolidge had no significant national political opposition as president. He easily won the election of 1924, even though there was a Progressive Party candidate (Robert M. La Follette) in the field who won some electoral votes. Presumably, Coolidge could have easily obtained the Republican nomination in 1928 if he had chosen to run. In Washington, Coolidge faced formidable opposition consisting of Democrats and Republican progressives.

Coolidge's rating:

CATEGORY	VALUE	RATING
1) Enhancing American Greatness	10	40%
2) Improving Quality of Life	8	40%
3) Meeting Crises	10	00%
4) Overcoming Opposition	8	-20%

Total rating: 5.6

16) Gerald R. Ford, Republican

Gerald Ford faced the daunting task of addressing the aftermath of Richard Nixon's resignation in 1974. Handicapped by being the only president never elected to the presidency or vice presidency, Ford and his family nevertheless became quite popular residents of the White House. However, his popularity could not surmount several public gaffes and the controversial pardoning of Richard Nixon, leading to his narrow defeat in the 1976 presidential election to Jimmy Carter, 240 to 297 in the Electoral College (39,148,940 to 40,828,929; by 2.1% in the popular vote).

Ford inherited a Congress controlled by the Democrats.

Regarding the qualities by which the presidents are evaluated, Ford fares as follows:

1) Enhancing American Greatness

Gerald Ford maintained the United States' international status after the Watergate scandal, leveraging his reputation as a competent foreign affairs member of the House of Representatives. In 1975, he met in Helsinki, Finland, with leaders of the Soviet Union and over thirty other countries to sign an agreement that guaranteed the boundaries of European countries and secured human rights for the residents of all signing countries.

2) Improving Quality of Life

Ford's pardon of Richard Nixon and provisional amnesty to Vietnam War protesters resolved internal tormenting issues, though he faced criticism from all sides for these actions. Economic challenges were widespread throughout the 1970s and 1980s, largely due to the Arab oil embargo and resulting high energy prices, leading to chronic inflation, recession, and high unemployment. Ford's economic policies and efforts to reduce dependence on foreign oil moderated inflation but contributed to the recession that deepened before the end of his presidency.

3) Meeting Crises

Ford's responses to the North Vietnamese violation of the truce were disregarded by Congress, resulting in the fall of governments in South Vietnam, Laos, and Cambodia to Communism. His efforts to negotiate further arms reduction treaties were hindered by dwindling popularity, casting doubt on his election prospects in 1976.

4) Overcoming Opposition

Initially supported by nearly everyone in the general population and Washington to rescue the presidency, Ford found himself increasingly isolated or shunned by the end of his term, further weakening the presidential office.

Ford's rating:

CATEGORY	VALUE	RATING
1) Enhancing American Greatness	10	30%
2) Improving Quality of Life	8	30%
3) Meeting Crises	10	10%
4) Overcoming Opposition	8	-20%

Total rating: 4.8

17) James Monroe, Republican[11]

James Monroe's presidency coincided with the "Era of Good Feeling," a period not so much characterized by universal goodwill as by the United States functioning as a single-party state. Following the disappearance of the Federalist Party, serious politicians rallied under the "Republican" Party banner, the contemporary iteration of the Antifederalist Party, which would later evolve into the Democratic Party. Despite presiding over the recession of 1819, the country's first significant economic downturn, Monroe remained an exceedingly popular president.

---

[11] Republican, in cases of presidents in office prior to 1856, refers to the party of Thomas Jefferson, not the party of Abraham Lincoln (see chapter 4).

Throughout Monroe's presidency, Congress was controlled by the Republicans (initially former Antifederalists, who would later be known as Democratic Republicans and then simply Democrats).

Regarding the qualities by which presidents are evaluated, Monroe fares as follows:

1) Enhancing American Greatness

    While much of the work was executed by his secretary of state, John Quincy Adams, the Monroe Administration is famous for its clarification of issues in the Western Hemisphere. Monroe facilitated treaties that defined the boundary between the United States and British territories in North America, later known as the Dominion of Canada. In 1819, the United States acquired Florida from Spain. The Monroe Doctrine, asserting that the New World was off-limits for further European colonization, remains recognized as a principle of international law respecting the sovereignty of Latin American countries.

2) Improving Quality of Life

    Monroe's presidency is generally regarded as a time of peace, prosperity, and growth. During Monroe's administration, an agreement was made with Great Britain to eliminate fortifications along the United States–Canada border, a notable achievement.

3) Meeting Crises

    The Monroe Administration experienced minimal turmoil, with no significant crises necessitating resolution.

4) Overcoming Opposition

    The period known as "The Era of Good Feeling" truly was a time of widespread popularity for the president, although this acclaim did not persist long after his departure from office.

Monroe's rating:

CATEGORY	VALUE	RATING
1) Enhancing American Greatness	10	20%
2) Improving Quality of Life	8	30%
3) Meeting Crises	10	00%
4) Overcoming Opposition	8	00%

Total rating: 4.4

18) George H. W. Bush, Republican

George Herbert Walker Bush's presidency is primarily remembered for its continuation of Ronald Reagan's policies, leading to the dissolution of the Union of Soviet Socialist Republics in December 1991. The end of the Soviet Union diminished ideological tensions in Europe and elsewhere, enhancing the quality of life globally.

George Herbert Walker Bush, a utilitarian president, had served in various government roles before his election to the nation's highest office in 1988. Starting as a congressman, Bush held several executive positions, including head of the Central Intelligence Agency and Ambassador to the United Nations, before eventually becoming vice president.

Throughout his presidency, Bush faced a Congress controlled by the Democrats.

Bush eventually lost the support of conservatives by raising taxes, a move seen as a breach of his pledge of "no new taxes." His apparent lack of empathy for the less fortunate cost him the support of liberals. Notably, not long before the 1992 election, an unfavorable incident in Japan received extensive media coverage.

Regarding the qualities by which presidents are evaluated, George H. W. Bush fares as follows:

1) Enhancing American Greatness
   As president, George H. W. Bush maintained pressure on the Soviet Union, contributing to its dissolution. He

led an international coalition to expel Iraq from Kuwait, earning a 90% approval rating from the American public.
2) Improving Quality of Life

George H. W. Bush oversaw continued prosperity for the American people and supported free trade in North America between Canada, Mexico, and the United States, preparing the United States for increased economic globalization. While buying foreign goods lowered costs for US consumers, foreign competition led many domestic manufacturers, especially in consumer goods, to go out of business or relocate overseas, resulting in job losses in the US.
3) Meeting Crises

Bush maintained a friendly stance toward Chinese leaders despite increased oppression by the Chinese government against their people. He removed Manuel Noriega from the presidency of Panama after Noriega refused to step down following a fraudulent election.
4) Overcoming Opposition

Despite dealing with an increasingly Democrat-controlled Congress, Bush faced little opposition during the early part of his term but lost the confidence of the majority of the American people by the end of his term, becoming one of the few American presidents elected to office and then losing his bid for a second term.

George Herbert Walker Bush's rating:

CATEGORY	VALUE	RATING
1) Enhancing American Greatness	10	10%
2) Improving Quality of Life	8	10%
3) Meeting Crises	10	20%
4) Overcoming Opposition	8	-10%

Total rating: 3.0

19) John Quincy Adams, "Republican,"[12] later National Republican

John Quincy Adams was likely the unhappiest of all presidents. His career in government, both before and after his presidency as Monroe's secretary of state and as a congressman, was much more fruitful and appreciated. Adams won the presidency in the House of Representatives over Andrew Jackson, who had received the most popular and electoral votes in the 1824 election. Jackson did not secure a majority of the electoral vote, leading to the election being decided in the House, for the second and, as of March 2024, the last time. Jackson's supporters, much like the followers of the loser in every disputed election since, loudly and persistently cried fraud, making Adams's life miserable throughout his term. Jackson's followers controlled the Senate and House of Representatives during all of Adams's single term, ensuring that none of Adams' proposed programs passed through Congress. Initially, John Quincy Adams identified as a "Republican" or Democratic Republican. However, the "Republican" Party soon split due to the intense disagreements between Adams' followers and Jackson's, leading Adams to become a National Republican while Congress remained "Republican," though most members considered themselves Jacksonians. These Jacksonians eventually named their party the Democratic Party.

John Quincy Adams was forced to deal with a Democratic Republican or overtly hostile Jacksonian Congress throughout his presidency.

Regarding the qualities by which presidents are evaluated, John Quincy Adams fares as follows:

1) Enhancing American Greatness

    Adams continued the strong foreign policies he advocated as Secretary of State under James Monroe but had little opportunity to accomplish anything concrete during his presidency.

---

[12] Republican, in cases of presidents in office prior to 1856, refers to the party of Thomas Jefferson, not the party of Abraham Lincoln (see chapter 4).

2) Improving Quality of Life

John Quincy Adams was the first president to strongly advocate for internal improvements, aiming to increase the country's wealth. He lifted the first shovel of earth in the construction of the Chesapeake and Ohio Canal. Although canals proved to be not as effective in improving transportation facilities as the railroads that were first coming into use during Adams' term, his promotion of internal improvements, despite the lack of funding from a Democratic Congress, benefited the young country.

3) Meeting Crises

Apart from political opposition to his policies, John Quincy Adams faced no real crises during his administration.

4) Overcoming Opposition

Adams encountered significant political opposition, as noted. He was unsuccessful in overcoming it. His accomplishments were the result of his executive powers, not his political leadership.

John Quincy Adams' rating:

CATEGORY	VALUE	RATING
1) Enhancing American Greatness	10	00%
2) Improving Quality of Life	8	30%
3) Meeting Crises	10	00%
4) Overcoming Opposition	8	00%

Total rating: 2.4

20) Zachary Taylor, Whig

Zachary Taylor was a hero of the Mexican War who did not receive a majority of the popular vote in the Election of 1848 but had a comfortable plurality over Lewis Cass, the Democrat candidate, and Martin Van Buren, the Free-Soil Party candidate. Presumably, Van Buren assured Taylor's election by splitting the New York vote, as his votes (he was a former Democrat) supposedly would have gone to Cass, giving Cass New York's electoral votes and the election. Not much was expected of Taylor as president, as most of the major issues of the day seemed insoluble, and he had no record in politics. However, Taylor boldly stated his solutions to slavery extension and other issues. He stepped on many toes and died before implementing his proposed program. His death remains a mystery today, although some still believe he was poisoned, murdered by opponents of the restriction of slavery. Despite being a Southerner and a slaveholder, Taylor favored the Whig program of a protective tariff to encourage domestic manufactures. He also proposed setting up an Agriculture Bureau to aid farmers and was a zealous advocate of a transcontinental railroad; both measures were enacted during the Lincoln Administration after the southern states seceded and the Democrats lost control of Congress.

The Democrats controlled both houses of Congress throughout Taylor's short presidency.

Regarding the qualities by which the presidents are evaluated, Taylor fares as follows:

1) Enhancing American Greatness

    Taylor was instrumental in winning the Mexican War with his overwhelming victories. His Whig politics earned him the enmity of President James K. Polk, who used his position as commander in chief to keep Taylor out of as much of the final victory in the war as possible. Taylor worked strongly to make California the thirty-first state, despite the slavocracy's unwillingness to admit another free state. California, as a free state, was admitted to the Union as the thirty-first state on September 9, 1850, just two months after Taylor's death. The entry of California permanently ended the parity between slave and free states in the Senate, likely making secession and the Civil War inevitable as the South saw itself becoming a minority member of the Union and no longer in control of the government.

2) Improving Quality of Life

Taylor opposed the Compromise of 1850, believing it to be too proslavery. His death in office allowed the Compromise to be enacted. Had Taylor not died, the Civil War might have been fought ten years earlier, potentially resulting in a quicker Union victory with fewer casualties and less destruction. This could have meant a better reconstruction settlement with less long-term rancor and a possibility of better future racial harmony. Unfortunately, due to events, this is only speculation.

3) Meeting Crises

The slaveholding South was on its way to permanently controlling the Federal Government when Taylor was elected. Taylor faced a Democrat Congress that was favorable to the extension of slavery as a means of avoiding civil war.

4) Overcoming Opposition

Taylor brooked no opposition to his policies, clearly stating that he was prepared to use the army to end treason when Southerners were preparing to take over New Mexico and install slavery there by force. His death ended his efforts as Fillmore, his vice president, took a more moderate position upon moving into the Oval Office.

Taylor's rating:

CATEGORY	VALUE	RATING
1) Enhancing American Greatness	10	20%
2) Improving Quality of Life	8	20%
3) Meeting Crises	10	00%
4) Overcoming Opposition	8	-20%

Total rating: 2.0

21) Rutherford B Hayes, Republican

Rutherford B. Hayes limited himself in the presidency by immediately announcing he would serve only one term. Single-term presidencies had been the norm for a period before the Civil War, but with the reduction in presidential power following Abraham Lincoln's assassination, Congress was able to overpower a president with limited patronage capabilities. Hayes thought this was beneficial, proposing a single six-year term for the president, which would ensure permanent lame-duck status. Hayes was a proponent of civil service reform, although it did not occur until after his presidency.

The Democrats controlled the House of Representatives throughout Hayes's term. He had a Republican Senate upon inauguration, but it switched to Democrat in the Forty-Sixth Congress.

Regarding the qualities by which presidents are evaluated, Hayes fares as follows:

1) Enhancing American Greatness

Hayes attempted, with limited success, to ameliorate the plight of Native Americans in the American West, reduce corruption in federal employment, and protect the enfranchisement of freed Blacks in the South after Reconstruction. His efforts conveyed the aspiration for America to become a better place.

2) Improving Quality of Life

Hayes removed federal troops from the states of the former Confederacy, effectively ending Reconstruction. This decision removed a significant source of tension in American society, although it led to decades of second-class citizenship for former slaves and their descendants.

3) Meeting Crises

The primary crisis of Hayes's administration was his acceptance of the presidency. It was widely believed that his opponent, Samuel Tilden, deserved victory, but the resolution of disputed electoral votes ensured Hayes's victory. Hayes attempted to mitigate conflicts between Native Americans and settlers in the West, albeit one-sidedly,

through an executive order prohibiting the sale of firearms to Native Americans.
4) Overcoming Opposition

Hayes was derisively referred to as "His Fraudulency" among other terms. He was unpopular with both Republicans and Democrats, and it was fortunate he accomplished what he did during his single term, as he would not be nominated for a second term.

Hayes' rating:

CATEGORY	VALUE	RATING
1) Enhancing American Greatness	10	00%
2) Improving Quality of Life	8	00%
3) Meeting Crises	10	00%
4) Overcoming Opposition	8	20%

Total rating: 1.6

Chapter 8

The "Average" Presidents

The presidents in this group can be said to have not accomplished great things, but neither did their actions lead to disasters, great or small. Some have been ridiculed as "do nothing" presidents, but there have been periods in US history when Congress took the initiative in Washington and was unwilling to give it up without a fight. Two of these presidents have been largely ignored by historians as their terms of office were extremely short.

22) Benjamin Harrison, Republican

Benjamin Harrison's four-year presidency is often seen as the epitome of the "nominal" or "average" presidency, as lacking in accomplishments in the history books as that of his grandfather, William Henry Harrison. Benjamin Harrison held the belief that Congress was the true voice of the people and that the president's role, especially in domestic matters, should be limited to following Congress's will.

Regarding the qualities by which presidents are evaluated, Benjamin Harrison's tenure is assessed as follows:

1) Enhancing American Greatness
   Harrison, alongside Secretary of State James G. Blaine, hosted the first Pan-American Congress in Washington in

1889. He expanded the United States Navy but engaged in international arbitration to resolve disputes, anticipating Theodore Roosevelt's policy of "speak softly and carry a big stick."

2) Improving Quality of Life

Benjamin Harrison supported the high protective tariffs enacted by Congress, which protected American industry and provided more and better-paying jobs to working-class Americans, albeit at the cost of higher prices. He cautioned that the prosperity of the American worker would be jeopardized by the lower tariffs proposed by the Democrats, who gained control of the House of Representatives in the 1892 elections.

3) Meeting Crises

The Sherman Anti-Trust Act was passed during Benjamin Harrison's administration, providing the mechanism for control of the emerging huge trusts that would dominate American heavy industry, but successful prosecutions would not occur until later. Harrison also strongly advocated for the enactment of an anti-lynching law by Congress, enabling him to use federal force to combat racial lawlessness in the South.

4) Overcoming Opposition

The Republicans controlled both the House and Senate at the beginning of Benjamin Harrison's presidency. However, the House switched to Democrat control in the Fifty-Second Congress, and Harrison lost his reelection bid in 1892 in a three-way race.

Benjamin Harrison's rating:

CATEGORY	VALUE	RATING
1) Enhancing American Greatness	10	00%
2) Improving Quality of Life	8	10%
3) Meeting Crises	10	00%

4) Overcoming Opposition 8 -10%
Total rating: 0.0

23) James A Garfield, Republican

James A. Garfield had almost no opportunity to impact the American people positively as president due to his assassination shortly after taking office. This situation, of course, also minimized the potential damage he might have caused, had he been inclined to do so. One of his goals as president was civil service reform; unfortunately, he was assassinated by a disappointed office seeker.

James A. Garfield was inaugurated with a Republican House of Representatives. The Senate, during the Forty-Seventh Congress, was volatile but ultimately controlled by Republicans by the time of his assassination.

Regarding the qualities by which presidents are evaluated, Garfield's tenure is assessed as follows:

1) Enhancing American Greatness

As Garfield entered the White House, individuals like John D. Rockefeller and Andrew Carnegie were developing their companies, positioning the United States on its path to becoming a world power.

2) Improving Quality of Life

Upon Garfield assuming the presidency, the United States was emerging from the depression and labor strife of the 1870s. Garfield did nothing to hinder that recovery.

3) Meeting Crises

Garfield had no opportunity to address any crises that might have emerged during his brief seven-month presidency.

4) Overcoming Opposition

Garfield was a beneficiary of the "payoffs" if they could be called that from the Credit Mobilier scandal. This allowed some opposition to him to arise before and during his presidency.

Garfield's rating:

CATEGORY	VALUE	RATING
1) Enhancing American Greatness	10	00%
2) Improving Quality of Life	8	00%
3) Meeting Crises	10	00%
4) Overcoming Opposition	8	00%

Total rating: 0.0

24) William Henry Harrison, Whig

William Henry Harrison was the first member of the Whig Party, also known as the Anti-Andrew Jackson Party, to win the presidency. His victory occurred after the negative consequences of Jackson's fiscal policies affected Jackson's successor, Martin Van Buren. Harrison secured over 53% of the popular vote in the 1840 election, partly due to the Whig Party's innovative campaign tactics, which included parades, banners, songs, and slogans.

William Henry Harrison was incapacitated from his inauguration until his death thirty-one days later, leaving him with no presidential record to evaluate. His inaugural address, however, revealed his Whig inclinations; he advocated for a single presidential term and strongly denounced "executive interference in the legislation of Congress," arguing that the president's constitutional duty to inform Congress and recommend measures did not equate to the right to originate legislation. This stance aimed to reduce the power of an imperialist like Andrew Jackson and became a continuing philosophy of the Whig and, later, Republican Party, albeit with many exceptions.

The House of Representatives was under Whig control when William Henry Harrison took office, and the Senate shifted to the Whigs shortly thereafter.

Regarding the qualities by which presidents are evaluated, William Henry Harrison's contributions are mostly from before his presidency:

1) Enhancing American Greatness

   William Henry Harrison played a pivotal role in opening the Old Northwest—now the states of Ohio, Indiana, Illinois, Michigan, and Wisconsin—for settlement, despite infringing on the rights of Native Americans, which was not widely condemned at the time.

2) Improving Quality of Life

   As the governor of the Indiana Territory, Harrison fostered conditions beneficial to the welfare of pioneer settlers, contributing to Indiana's statehood in 1816.

3) Meeting Crises

   Harrison successfully led the Battle of Tippecanoe in 1811 near present-day Lafayette, Indiana, neutralizing the threat posed by Tecumseh and the Shawnees to Midwestern pioneers.

4) Overcoming Opposition

   Despite being mocked by Democrats as a frontier bumpkin, Harrison triumphed in the 1840 presidential election against incumbent Martin Van Buren. His election as the first Whig president, while the vast majority of voters in the United States considered themselves Democrats, was Harrison's only presidential achievement.

William Henry Harrison's rating:

CATEGORY	VALUE	RATING
1) Enhancing American Greatness	10	00%
2) Improving Quality of Life	8	00%
3) Meeting Crises	10	00%
4) Overcoming Opposition	8	00%

Total rating: 0.0

25) Grover Cleveland (1st Term), Democrat

Grover Cleveland capitalized on the Republican Party's nomination of James G. Blaine, who was tainted by corruption allegations, in the 1884 presidential election. Cleveland narrowly won, securing only 50.3% of the popular vote. The defection or abstention of many liberal Republicans, who detested Blaine, likely tipped the election in Cleveland's favor.

During Cleveland's first term, the House of Representatives was Democrat-controlled, while the Senate was held by Republicans.

In evaluating Grover Cleveland's first term, the following aspects are considered:

1) Enhancing American Greatness
    Cleveland epitomized honest governance and played a significant role in dispelling the aura of corruption that lingered from the Reconstruction era.
2) Improving Quality of Life
    Cleveland opposed high tariffs, contributing to a lower cost of living for Americans.
3) Meeting Crises
    Cleveland's first administration witnessed a peak in industrial conflict, marked by events such as the Haymarket Riot in Chicago. He facilitated the creation of the Department of Labor to help resolve management-labor disputes, though it did not achieve cabinet status until much later. Additionally, the Interstate Commerce Commission, the first federal regulatory agency, was established during his term, though its initial efforts to check railroad abuses were largely ineffectual.
4) Overcoming Opposition
    Cleveland faced criticism from Republicans for his stance against pensions for Grand Army of the Republic veterans and from Democrats for his opposition to the free coinage of silver.

Cleveland (1)'s rating:

CATEGORY	VALUE	RATING
1) Enhancing American Greatness	10	-20%
2) Improving Quality of Life	8	20%
3) Meeting Crises	10	20%
4) Overcoming Opposition	8	-20%

Total rating: 0.0

Chapter 9

The Below-Average Presidents

Twenty-one presidents were found to be above average, four presidents to be "average," with ratings of 0.0, and twenty-one presidents to be below average. Twelve presidents, those discussed in this chapter, are only slightly below average. Four presidents are rated "poor" and five are rated "bad" to complete the total of below-average presidents to be twenty-one. While the midpoint rating number of 0.0, representing a neutral 00% score on all rating factors, is considered average, in reality, the average of all forty-six presidents' ratings is -1.03. Twenty-seven presidents had ratings above that number, and nineteen had ratings below it.

Based on a different quantitative rating system developed by C-Span, as used in their 2021 rankings discussed in chapter 14, on a scale of zero to 100 for ten different categories for a total potential score of 1000, with only 44 presidential ratings—Trump was not rated and Cleveland was rated only once, combining his two separate terms into one—27 presidents achieved a score of more than 500, or 50%. The median scores were 568, achieved by Andrew Jackson, and 543, achieved by William Howard Taft, with 20 presidents having higher ratings and 20 presidents having lower ratings. The C-Span rating system is in fairly good agreement with the other rankings as identified by Wikipedia (see chapter 14), suggesting that the presidential ranking system developed in this book is more rigorous than the mainstream. On the other hand, a libertarian ranking as promulgated by Ivan Eland in *Recarving Rushmore*, not included in the mainstream ranking composite, ranks four presidents as average, only ten as above average ("good" and "excellent"), and twenty-seven as below average ("poor" and "bad"). Only one president, Dwight Eisenhower, receives a similar ranking by all three methodologies.

26) Grover Cleveland (2nd Term), Democrat

Grover Cleveland is the only president of the United States to have served nonconsecutive terms. He was defeated for reelection by Benjamin Harrison in 1888 but then defeated Harrison in his bid for reelection in 1892. As conditions and Cleveland's public standing were somewhat different in his two terms, he is listed twice here and is officially considered the twenty-second and twenty-fourth president by the United States government. Most presidential ratings and rankings evaluate Cleveland once, combining his two terms into one. As can be seen, there is not a great deal of difference between his two terms. Cleveland in his first term rated a neutral 0.0. In his second term, he rates slightly above the average rating of all the presidents, with a rating of -0.8 as opposed to the average rating of all 46 presidents of -1.03.

Both the House of Representatives and Senate were Democrat at the beginning of Cleveland's second term, while changing to Republican before he left office.

Regarding the qualities by which the presidents are evaluated, Grover Cleveland in his second term fares as follows:

1) Enhancing American Greatness
    Cleveland resisted the annexation of Hawaii, which was not achieved until the McKinley Administration.
2) Improving Quality of Life
    Cleveland, with the help of the Republicans, was able to repeal the Sherman Silver Purchase Act, which was rapidly draining gold from the United States Treasury.

3) Meeting Crises
Labor unrest and other factors caused a drag on the United States economy that led to a depression that was not ended by the time of the 1896 election.
4) Overcoming Opposition
Cleveland was again under attack from Democrats for his conservative policies, particularly his support of the gold standard and his opposition to the Pullman Strike and Coxey's Army of unemployed. He was replaced as the Democratic Party nominee in the 1896 presidential election by William Jennings Bryan, an outspoken populist.

Cleveland (2)'s rating:

CATEGORY	VALUE	RATING
1) Enhancing American Greatness	10	-20%
2) Improving Quality of Life	8	-30%
3) Meeting Crises	10	20%
4) Overcoming Opposition	8	20%

Total rating: -0.8

27) U S Grant, Republican

Ulysses Simpson Grant was the great hero of the American Civil War. His leadership placed the Union armies on the path to victory and led to a successful conclusion of the military phase of the southern rebellion. Earlier, Grant participated in the Mexican War as a junior officer and came away with a negative feeling about the war, believing it to be an unjustified conflict—a sentiment shared by many people then and now. He and two other presidents rate slightly below the nominal 0.0 rating of all the presidents, with ratings of -0.8, -1.0, and -2.0, as compared to the average rating of all 46 presidents of -1.03. Congress was totally Republican-controlled when Grant assumed the office of President, but the House went Democrat in the 44th Congress before the end of Grant's second term.

Regarding the qualities by which the presidents are evaluated, Grant fares as follows:

1) Enhancing American Greatness
   Grant achieved a measure of success in foreign relations with his appointment of Hamilton Fish as secretary of state.
2) Improving Quality of Life
   Grant supported Congress in its harsh Reconstruction policy against the South. He proposed the annexation of Santo Domingo as a haven for the freed slaves, but Congress rejected this plan.
3) Meeting Crises
   Corruption among some of Grant's appointees in the federal government led to several scandals, such as the Whiskey Ring—particularly ironic since he tended to display the symptoms of alcoholism whenever he was forced by his duties, particularly in the Army, to be apart from his wife, Julia, for protracted periods. The scandals of his administration were resolved with no indication of personal involvement by Grant.
4) Overcoming Opposition
   Opposition to what was perceived as Grant's weakness as president led to significant opposition to his reelection, but he easily defeated the Democratic candidate and Horace Greeley, running as a Liberal Republican, in the presidential election of 1872. Grant was seriously considered for a third term, disconnected from his first two, in the election of 1880, but various factors, including his health and the opposition of the liberals in the Republican camp, prevented it from happening.

Grant's rating:

CATEGORY	VALUE	RATING
1) Enhancing American Greatness	10	00%
2) Improving Quality of Life	8	00%
3) Meeting Crises	10	-10%
4) Overcoming Opposition	8	00%

Total rating: -1.0

28) George W. Bush, Republican

George Walker Bush was one of the half-dozen or so presidents whose election was so close and contentious that it affected his performance in his first term of office. At the end of the 2000 presidential election day, the outcome in several states was in doubt. The news media first declared a victory for the Democrat Party candidate, Al Gore, then reversed itself to declare Bush the victor, then backed off on that. Eventually, Bush was named the victor after the United States Supreme Court got involved, particularly regarding the counting of votes in Florida, one of the undecided states. As with John Quincy Adams after the 1824 election, Rutherford B. Hayes after the 1876 election, and Donald Trump more recently, George W. Bush was not initially accepted as president by a large segment of the population of the country. Fortunately for Bush, he won reelection with a clear majority of the popular and electoral vote in 2004, and the complaints died down. Like Benjamin Harrison, coincidentally another victor in a contentious presidential election, George W. Bush can be considered a "nominal" or "average" president, as he had no great blunders and no great successes during his presidency. He received a 00% rating in three of four categories as described in chapter 4. He rates slightly below the average rating of all the presidents, with a rating of -2.0, as opposed to the average rating of all forty-six presidents of -1.03.

In the 101st Congress, the House was Republican when George W. Bush was first inaugurated, while the Senate was Democrat-controlled. The Senate soon turned Republican, but both houses were in Democrat hands by the time "W" left office.

Regarding the qualities by which the presidents are evaluated, George W. Bush fares as follows:

1) Enhancing American Greatness

George W. Bush made an immediate and powerful response to the horrific events of September 11, 2001. He led the United States in a strenuous effort to halt international terrorism, particularly to bring the perpetrators of the September 11, 2001, attacks on the World Trade Center, the Pentagon, and elsewhere to justice. He was instrumental in the creation of the cabinet-level Department of Homeland Security to help protect against terrorist attacks within the United States. In foreign policy, Bush tipped the United States toward Russia, China, India, Pakistan, and Japan while distancing from other traditional allies, upsetting world diplomacy.

2) Improving Quality of Life

George W. Bush took preemptive steps to avoid a recession that appeared to be looming at the end of the Clinton Administration. He began an education initiative to try to end substandard public school education in the United States. His "No Child Left Behind" initiative reversed the traditional Republican Party lack of support for education direction at the national level.

3) Meeting Crises

George W. Bush led an international coalition that went on the offense against the perpetrators of the September 11 and other terrorist acts, driving Osama bin Laden and his Al Qaeda group into hiding. He made a strong effort to convert Iraq from a dictatorship to democracy. Unfortunately, his removal of Saddam Hussein from power in Iraq resulted in further destabilization in the Middle East. The intelligence that was used to justify the invasion of Iraq was later shown to be faulty. The Bush

Administration led a successful international campaign to combat AIDS, improving treatment and substantially reducing the HIV infection rate. Under Bush, the federal government was forced to react to a major financial crisis when many large financial institutions in the United States and elsewhere began to fail in September 2008.

4) Overcoming Opposition

George W. Bush successfully overcame partisan opposition to his election in 2000 but lost the House of Representatives and the Senate to the Democrats in the 110th Congress.

George Walker Bush's rating:

CATEGORY	VALUE	RATING
1) Enhancing American Greatness	10	00%
2) Improving Quality of Life	8	00%
3) Meeting Crises	10	-20%
4) Overcoming Opposition	8	00%

Total rating: -2.0

29) Warren Harding, Republican

Warren Gamaliel Harding won the presidential election of 1920 with the highest percentage of the popular vote ever recorded in a presidential election, 63.8%. This outcome was largely due to the public's strong aversion to the aftermath of World War I and the final months of the Wilson Administration. It was more a vote *against* Wilson and the Democrats than a vote *for* Harding. Harding took his presidential responsibilities seriously, vetoing a generous veterans' bonus bill that did not provide for obtaining the funds to pay the bonus.

Both the House of Representatives and the Senate were Republican throughout Harding's presidency.

Regarding the qualities by which the presidents are evaluated, Harding fares as follows:

1) Enhancing American Greatness

   Despite a personal lack of presidential timbre, Harding created a highly respected cabinet that took a leading role in world politics after World War I, despite the refusal of the United States to join the League of Nations. Harding hosted the Washington Conference for the Limitation of Armaments, which slowed down the growth of armaments. Unfortunately, his cabinet also included a few less-than-honest cronies who left a permanent severe stain on the Harding administration.

2) Improving Quality of Life

   Harding initiated the idea of a national budget, thereby putting some order in federal spending and helping control the growth of the federal government. Harding's pressure on the big steel companies eventually resulted in a shorter working day for steelworkers.

3) Meeting Crises

   The major crisis of the Harding Administration came after his death when the Teapot Dome and other scandals came to light, none of which involved any actual wrongdoing by Harding but exemplified his failure to control his colleagues and poor judgment in the selection of some of his subordinates.

4) Overcoming Opposition

   Harding really had no opposition during his presidency. Congress remained solidly Republican throughout his tenure in the White House.

Harding's rating:

CATEGORY	VALUE	RATING
1) Enhancing American Greatness	10	20%

2) Improving Quality of Life	8	20%
3) Meeting Crises	10	-60%
4) Overcoming Opposition	8	00%

Total rating: -2.4

30) Millard Fillmore, Whig

Millard Fillmore, the second "president by accident," accomplished little to further Zachary Taylor's agenda; people still had little use for an unelected president. He did fulfill one Whig aim by providing the first land grants for railroad construction. Fillmore later ran for president under the American Party (otherwise known as "Know-Nothings"), an anti-Catholic, anti-immigrant group, but lost, coming in third behind the Democrat and Republican candidates in 1856. He was one of the first third-party candidates to "throw" an election, as he probably took more votes away from John C. Fremont, the Republican candidate in 1856, than from James Buchanan, the Democrat candidate, giving Buchanan the victory. Fremont and Fillmore, who were substantially in agreement on most issues, combined for approximately 54% of the popular vote in 1856. By 1856, the Republican Party had been sufficiently established so that if the Republican candidate for president, John C. Fremont, had won, secession might have been avoided as the government in Washington would have been firmly in the hands of its friends, and the southern slave power would not have had the advantages it had in 1860–61, advantages that some believe were due to treasonous activities on the part of the president, James Buchanan.

Congress was Democrat throughout Fillmore's presidency.

Regarding the qualities by which the presidents are evaluated, Fillmore fares as follows:

1) Enhancing American Greatness

    Fillmore approved the Compromise of 1850, which did little to improve the prestige of the United States abroad.

2) Improving Quality of Life

The Compromise of 1850 was actually a concession to the slaveholding south, doing little to improve the living conditions of Americans elsewhere, and included the Fugitive Slave Act, which made life more unpleasant for African Americans, whether slave or free. It did ease the tensions between North and South, somewhat.

3) Meeting Crises

Fillmore's approval of the Compromise of 1850 made the slave vs. free conflict worse, as the slaveholders felt it was not enough to satisfy them, and Free-Soilers and abolitionists considered it an abject surrender to slavery.

4) Overcoming Opposition

Fillmore was quite unpopular by the end of his presidency and was not given the nomination as the Whig candidate for president in 1852.

Fillmore's rating:

CATEGORY	VALUE	RATING
1) Enhancing American Greatness	10	-10%
2) Improving Quality of Life	8	00%
3) Meeting Crises	10	-10%
4) Overcoming Opposition	8	-20%

Total rating: -3.6

31) Andrew Johnson, Democrat

There is no question that Andrew Johnson had the worst time of any president, having been elected in 1864 to be Abraham Lincoln's vice president, as a Democrat, solely to form a "fusion" party (called the Union ticket) in the summer of 1864 when things were not going well for the country. He failed miserably in meeting the situation following Lincoln's assassination, but the fact that he survived impeachment against overwhelming odds when just being a Democrat was tantamount to treason in some people's eyes says something.

Andrew Johnson faced an extremely hostile Republican Congress throughout his presidency.

Regarding the qualities by which the presidents are evaluated, Andrew Johnson fares as follows:

1) Enhancing American Greatness

    Andrew Johnson attempted, without success, to implement Abraham Lincoln's method of returning the former Confederate states to the Union.

2) Improving Quality of Life

    Andrew Johnson attempted, without success, to find a practical means to provide employment in the South for the freed slaves. Johnson failed to implement a program, favored by some Radical Reconstructionists, of redistributing confiscated or abandoned former plantation land to freed slaves.

3) Meeting Crises

    Upon the assassination of Abraham Lincoln, the first overt assassination of an American president, Andrew Johnson took over the Executive Branch of the federal government but was unable to control many of his subordinates, including a few cabinet members, and was forced to accept the Tenure of Office Act, passed over his veto.

4) Overcoming Opposition

    Andrew Johnson successfully survived impeachment by the radical majority in Congress.

Andrew Johnson's rating:

CATEGORY	VALUE	RATING
1) Enhancing American Greatness	10	00%
2) Improving Quality of Life	8	00%
3) Meeting Crises	10	-80%
4) Overcoming Opposition	8	50%

Total rating: -4.0

32) John Tyler, Whig to Democrat

John Tyler, once a Democrat but a foe of Andrew Jackson, ran as the vice presidential candidate with William Henry Harrison's Whig Party presidential candidacy. His true leanings were suspect by the Whig Party faithful, and as soon as he became president, he showed his true colors by reverting to Democratic Party politics. Not trusted by either the Whigs or Democrats, he accomplished little in office, becoming a man without a party. After William Henry Harrison's death, there was some doubt as to whether Tyler, the first vice president to succeed to the office of president upon the death of a president, could be considered more than an acting president; an attempt was made to make him the first president to be impeached, but it failed. Tyler was the first president to have a veto overridden by Congress. He advocated the admission of Texas as a slave state, to help provide a slavocracy majority in the Senate, although Texas was not admitted until Tyler's term was over. Thanks to Daniel Webster, his secretary of state, Tyler's administration saw the resolution of the Maine-Canada boundary and a trade treaty with China.

The House of Representatives was Democrat, and the Senate was Whig throughout Tyler's presidency.

Regarding the qualities by which the presidents are evaluated, Tyler fares as follows:

1) Enhancing American Greatness

    Tyler was a champion of expansion, particularly in the southwest, where he thought that slavery had a chance of success. Some international success occurred in the State Department while it was held by Daniel Webster, selected by William Henry Harrison. Webster resigned, however, after the work he had started under William Henry Harrison was completed. This included the Webster-Ashburton Treaty, settling a United States–Canada border dispute, and the trade treaty with China.

2) Improving Quality of Life

    Tyler continued the Democratic Party policy of opposition to public improvements.

3) Meeting Crises
    Tyler strongly favored the annexation of Texas, which led to the Mexican War under his successor, James K. Polk.
4) Overcoming Opposition
    Tyler was the first president in history to have a veto overridden, on his last day in office, March 3, 1845.

Tyler's rating:

CATEGORY	VALUE	RATING
1) Enhancing American Greatness	10	-20%
2) Improving Quality of Life	8	-10%
3) Meeting Crises	10	-20%
4) Overcoming Opposition	8	-20%

Total rating: -6.4

33) Martin Van Buren, Democrat

Even Democrats and liberal journalists regard Martin Van Buren as a poor president, but the outcome of his presidency wasn't entirely his fault. Van Buren had the unfortunate luck to become president just as Andrew Jackson's financial policies resulted in the worst economic depression the country had yet seen, perhaps second only to the Great Depression of the 1930s.[13] This was, to some extent, karma, as Van Buren, the "Wizard of Kinderhook," was in some ways the brains behind the Jackson presidency, and his New York cronies had a hand in the fiscal machinations that led to the almost complete collapse of the economy when Jackson won his bank war. As Jackson's vice president, Van Buren could have become president earlier if the 1835 assassination attempt on Jackson had succeeded.

During Van Buren's presidency, a US Navy expedition discovered the continent of Antarctica, and US warships interfered with

---

[13] David Saville Muzzey, *A History of Our Country: A Textbook for High School Students* (Boston, 1936), 304.

American ships active in the African slave trade. Van Buren was personally anti-slavery and ran as the Free-Soil candidate in the 1848 presidential election but probably did not affect the outcome.

Congress was Democrat throughout Van Buren's presidency.

Regarding the qualities by which the presidents are evaluated, Van Buren fares as follows:

1) Enhancing American Greatness

    In attempting to correct the errors of the Jackson Administration, mostly orchestrated by Van Buren and his cronies, Van Buren proposed an independent treasury system to remove the revenues of the United States government from private banks. Internationally, Van Buren sent a naval expedition around the world but accepted arbitration in most disputes between the United States and other countries.

2) Improving Quality of Life

    Van Buren declared it was not the province of the federal government to alleviate the sufferings of its citizens when financial panic turned into a depression shortly after he was inaugurated.

3) Meeting Crises

    Van Buren managed to avoid full-scale war when boundary disputes with Britain over the Canadian-Maine border erupted.

4) Overcoming Opposition

    Van Buren faced little opposition until the end of his term. Then, as the Whigs chanted, "Van, Van, is a used-up man," Van Buren lost the 1840 election in a landslide.

Van Buren's rating:

CATEGORY	VALUE	RATING
1) Enhancing American Greatness	10	-20%
2) Improving Quality of Life	8	-30%

3) Meeting Crises   10   -20%
4) Overcoming Opposition   8   -20%
Total rating: -8.0

34) Jimmy Carter, Democrat

Carter ran for president on a policy of economy in government based on the "zero" budgeting techniques he used as governor of Georgia. He also stressed his Naval experience with nuclear reactors as qualifying him on energy issues while the United States was still suffering from the Arab oil embargo. Carter accomplished little in Washington as his outsider status provided him little leverage in his battles with Washington professionals.

Although serving with a Democrat Congress throughout his presidential term, Carter received little encouragement or support from his party fellows in Congress.

Regarding the qualities by which the presidents are evaluated, Carter fares as follows:

1) Enhancing American Greatness

Jimmy Carter hosted a summit conference between Menachem Begin of Israel and Anwar Sadat of Egypt, which was hoped to be a prelude to the end of hostilities in the Middle East. These hopes were eventually dashed as other Arab nations viewed Sadat, who was eventually assassinated by members of the Egyptian Islamic Jihad, as a traitor to the Arab cause. Carter first cut defense spending and then increased it, contributing to the uncertainty with which foreign governments viewed the United States. Fidel Castro in 1980 duped Carter into accepting approximately 125,000 Cuban "refugees," who were actually undesirables, including criminals, whom Castro was happy to be rid of, in what was called the Mariel Boatlift. In 1977, Carter signed a treaty turning over the Panama Canal and the Canal Zone to Panama in 1999. Carter negotiated a new Strategic Arms Limitation Treaty (SALT II) with the Soviet

Union but had to forego ratification as the Soviets invaded Afghanistan in December 1979, shortly after agreeing on the treaty. Carter took several punitive steps against the Soviets in retaliation, including a grain embargo and a boycott of the 1980 Moscow Summer Olympics. Carter won the Nobel Peace Prize in 2002.

2) Improving Quality of Life

Domestically, Carter's presidency can be summed up by a phrase uttered publicly by his victorious opponent in the 1980 presidential election, Ronald Reagan: "Are you better off than you were four years ago?" The answer was a resounding "NO." Carter's popularity suffered in 1980 due to a severe recession that peaked that year. Carter gave full amnesty to all Vietnam era draft resisters. Inflation grew to unprecedented heights while Carter was president, negating the intended beneficial economic effects of tax cuts enacted during his administration. The federal Department of Energy and Department of Education were created during Carter's presidency.

3) Meeting Crises

In spite of strenuous efforts, Carter was unable to resolve the Iran Hostage Crisis, which arose after Carter allowed the Shah, who had been in exile, to come to the United States for medical treatment.

4) Overcoming Opposition

It was a foregone conclusion that Carter could not win the 1980 election, but he insisted on holding on to his delegates at the Democratic National Convention. He lost the general election with barely 41% of the popular vote to Ronald Reagan, the Republican nominee, 35,481,435 to Reagan's 43,899,248 while liberal Republican John Anderson received 5,719,437. Carter won 49 electoral votes to Reagan's 489. Carter was one of the few presidents to have his vetoes overridden when Congress was controlled by his own party.

Carter's rating:

CATEGORY	VALUE	RATING
1) Enhancing American Greatness	10	-20%
2) Improving Quality of Life	8	-30%
3) Meeting Crises	10	-30%
4) Overcoming Opposition	8	-10%

Total rating: -8.2

35) Franklin D. Roosevelt, Democrat

Franklin Delano Roosevelt, throughout his presidency, was one of the most popular presidents, although his winning margins in the Electoral College and the popular vote eventually declined significantly. Unfortunately, he failed at his main missions. His policies did not end the Great Depression in the United States and are considered by some to have prolonged it. He also failed to end totalitarianism in Europe or Asia. The Soviet Union, with no real opposition from the United States, took over from Nazi Germany as the oppressor of Eastern Europe, and Communist China, with Russian assistance, replaced Japan as the dominant force in East Asia.

Franklin Delano Roosevelt is credited with inspiring the people of the United States with confidence in the United States government and faith in democracy at a time when many, including Charles Lindbergh and Joseph P. Kennedy, seemed to think that fascism was the wave of the future. The first of Roosevelt's famous "fireside chats" explained why he closed the nation's banks. While he may have helped reduce the popularity of communism among the lower classes in the United States, his and Congress's liberal programs resulted in a large infusion of communists and communist sympathizers into the federal government who remained undetected for decades. When the Supreme Court began declaring Roosevelt's radical New Deal programs unconstitutional, Roosevelt tried to pack the court by adding more justices of his choice and political persuasion. This resulted in a fierce backlash against Roosevelt, and he backed off before his popularity dropped too much. Many aged, conservative Supreme

Court justices began retiring shortly thereafter, eventually allowing Roosevelt to reshape the Court as he intended.

Franklin Delano Roosevelt's exemplary political skills propelled him to the peak of presidential power after his initial success in 1932 was practically guaranteed as the vast majority of the people of the United States were desperate for a change in administration in Washington as the economic depression deepened under the presidency of Herbert Hoover, the last Republican in a nearly unbroken series going back to Abraham Lincoln's victory in 1860. Roosevelt's innovative use of radio as a means of communicating directly with the public contrasts sharply with his secret machinations (see below) to maintain the Democratic Party in power in Washington. After Roosevelt's economic policies failed to end the depression, Roosevelt lost interest in domestic politics as the international situation darkened. He was unable to interest the country in an active international anti-fascist role but was extremely active, up to the limit of his executive powers, in supporting the United Kingdom in its war against Nazi Germany. Unfortunately, Roosevelt failed disastrously in several areas prior to and during World War II.

Even before the United States entered the war, German submarines were successfully destroying shipping in the North Atlantic. Supposedly to prevent panic among the American populace, but more likely to avoid culpability and loss of confidence in his administration, Roosevelt ordered the sinking of merchant shipping off the east coast of the United States to be kept secret and failed to take any measures to reduce the damage. This led to much greater losses that could have been avoided.

The failure of the United States military forces to protect the US Navy fleet at Pearl Harbor is considered a major failing, and several high-level officers were court-martialed over it. The truth is that United States and British intelligence forces had broken the Japanese codes and were aware of what was taking place but failed to provide adequate warning to the forces in Hawaii.

In Europe, Roosevelt gave in to British demands for retribution against the Germans for their attacks on English cities, particularly London. Thousands of bombers and crews were lost in so-called "strategic" bombing that killed hundreds of thousands of German, French, and other civilians as well as many members of bomber crews while doing little to slow the German war effort. If these air attacks had been directed to tactical use against the German Army, it is likely that the war in Europe could have been significantly shortened. It would also have resulted in much less devastation and distress across Europe during and after the war, and recovery could have occurred sooner. It might also have resulted in the "Iron Curtain" having been erected hundreds of miles further east, easing Cold War pressures.

Franklin Roosevelt served his entire 12-year presidential career with the full support of Congress, which remained with Democrat majorities in both houses from 1933 to 1945.

Regarding the qualities by which presidents are evaluated, Franklin Delano Roosevelt fares as follows:

1) Enhancing American Greatness

Franklin Roosevelt attempted to do as much as possible to thwart the fascist totalitarian governments of Germany, Italy, and Japan from expanding but was largely hindered by the isolationism of the United States Congress. He achieved some revision of neutrality rules out of Congress and provided aid to Great Britain and its allies. He prepared, with Winston Churchill, the Atlantic Charter in August 1941, outlining war aims against Germany and Japan. Upon the United States entering World War II, Roosevelt immediately mobilized the nation's full strength to defeat Hitler and Japan. However, his errors in Hawaii and Europe prolonged the war and increased its devastation. Unfortunately, he allowed Joseph Stalin, dictator of the Soviet Union, to completely overrun Eastern Europe, resulting in the enslavement of those very Eastern European people whom the United States, France, and Great Britain went to war in Europe to protect. Roosevelt's diplomatic recognition of the Soviet Union encouraged Stalin in his repressive and expansionist activities. The liberation of France did little to improve the international status of the

United States, as France later, under the very Charles De Gaulle whom Roosevelt helped put in power in France, took an independent, almost anti–United States stance in post–World War II politics. Franklin Roosevelt's strategic failures against Japan necessitated the dropping of atomic bombs to force Japan into surrender. In Asia, it was the Chinese who emerged as the greater threat after the Japanese were defeated.

2) Improving Quality of Life

Franklin Roosevelt was elected in 1932 in opposition to what was considered Herbert Hoover's lackluster efforts to end the depression that began in 1929. In spite of massive increases in government expenditure and gross increases in federal government controls over society, by such measures as the Agricultural Adjustment Act, the National Industrial Recovery Act, the Tennessee Valley Authority, the Federal Communications Commission, the Federal Housing Administration, the National Resources Board, the Rural Electrification Administration, and the Home Owners Loan Corporation, the depression was not ended; government intervention may have thwarted a recovery that had begun in 1937, leading to a recession in 1938. Roosevelt by executive order took the country off the gold standard, a move constitutionally reserved for Congress. The depression did not end until the country entered a full war economy in 1942. These activities increased the power of the national government over the states, undermining federalism with programs like the Federal Emergency Relief Administration, Social Security, and the Civilian Conservation Corps, relieving the state and local governments of the expense of providing direct relief to the destitute: young, old, and working-class.

When the United States entered World War II, Roosevelt obtained rigid price and wage controls, hundreds of billions of dollars in appropriations, censorship, a ban on strikes and lockouts, and secret development of the atomic bomb.

3) Meeting Crises

The first crisis faced by Franklin Delano Roosevelt was the Great Depression. While it did not have the deleterious effect on the United States as did the depression of 1837, it did have a severe negative impact on a great many Americans. Roosevelt's major accomplishment in combating the Great Depression was acting as a cheerleader to convince the American people that good times would return. His attempt to increase the number of Supreme Court Justices was seen as "packing" the court and was defeated. Over his twelve years as president, Roosevelt appointed nine Supreme Court justices, nearly filling the entire bench (see Appendix F). When choosing a running mate for the 1944 presidential election, in the midst of World War II, Roosevelt, in spite of his poor and worsening health (many think he should have never run, in 1944 or 1940), picked Harry Truman, a relatively unknown, unsophisticated United States Senator from Missouri as his running mate, and then ignored him and left him out of policy discussions and important briefings. This resulted in a completely unqualified, unprepared person holding the most important job in the world at the most critical time in human history.

4) Overcoming Opposition

Franklin Delano Roosevelt won 59.1% of the popular vote in 1932, 62.5% in 1936, 55% in 1940, and 53.8% in 1944. After his 1936 reelection, his popularity dwindled as many felt he had served long enough. The Twenty-second Amendment, placing a term limit on the presidency, is part of his legacy.

Franklin Delano Roosevelt's rating:

CATEGORY	VALUE	RATING
1) Enhancing American Greatness	10	-40%
2) Improving Quality of Life	8	-40%
3) Meeting Crises	10	-10%
4) Overcoming Opposition	8	-10%

Total rating: -9.0

36) Harry Truman, Democrat

Harry S. Truman inherited the presidency from Franklin Delano Roosevelt, but despite Roosevelt's extremely poor health, no effort was made to prepare Truman for the job. Truman had to end both the war in Europe and the war in Asia and had to keep both the real "victors" of the war, Russia and China, at bay. He did not do well at either task but might have performed better if given proper training prior to taking his job. Truman largely continued the policies and programs of Franklin Roosevelt, with many of the same staff and cabinet members as those who served under Roosevelt.

Truman inherited Franklin Delano Roosevelt's Democrat majorities in both houses of Congress but lost both to the Republicans in 1946. He regained them in the following election but they were lost by the Democrats again in the elections of 1952 when Truman chose not to be a candidate.

Regarding the qualities by which presidents are evaluated, Truman fares as follows:

1) Enhancing American Greatness

Truman ordered the dropping of atomic bombs on Japan, essentially ending World War II, a decision that remains controversial to this day. Truman was slow to recognize the expansionist aims of Joseph Stalin, head of the Soviet Union, after the end of World War II in Europe. Truman ended up bogged down in a land war in Korea after the Russians and Communist Chinese urged the

The Crime of the Democrats

North Koreans to invade the South in 1950. Truman fired General Douglas MacArthur, head of US and other United Nations troops in Korea, rather than accede to his requests to fight all out against the Communists, blaming the firing on "insubordination." Truman enunciated the "Truman Doctrine" as a counter to Communism, specifically to prevent outside forces, particularly Soviet Russia, from interfering in the domestic policies of sovereign nations. Truman applied his doctrine only to Greece, where the communist threat was relatively weak and largely domestic, in a successful endeavor, while allowing Czechoslovakia, Romania, Bulgaria, Hungary, Poland, and East Germany to become Russian Soviet satellites without any effort or offers of aid above the Marshall Plan, the aid of which each of these countries refused on orders from Moscow. Truman's administration propounded the "Containment" policy, intended to restrict the expansion of Communism, with poor results. Truman signed the treaty forming the North Atlantic Treaty Organization in 1949, in response to Communist encroachments including the blockading of Berlin, Germany. Truman immediately recognized the state of Israel on its creation in 1948, at once winning the enmity of the entire Arab world.

2) Improving Quality of Life

Truman enacted strong controls on the economy after World War II ended, in a futile attempt to control inflation. He seized United States steel mills in an effort to prevent strikes but was overruled by the Supreme Court.

3) Meeting Crises

Truman failed to prevent the takeover of the Chinese mainland by Mao Zedong's communists.

4) Overcoming Opposition

Truman was unable to enact most of his proposals as president due to opposition by a combination of Republicans and Southern Democrats. He chose not to run for reelection in 1952, although he was constitutionally allowed to do so.

Truman's rating:

CATEGORY	VALUE	RATING
1) Enhancing American Greatness	10	-20%
2) Improving Quality of Life	8	-50%
3) Meeting Crises	10	-30%
4) Overcoming Opposition	8	-10%

Total rating: -9.8

37) William J. Clinton, Democrat

Clinton entered the presidency with a Democrat Congress and a strong agenda for social programs, including additional child welfare programs and expanded Medicare. When the cost and scope of these proposed programs were fully explained to the public, Clinton's entire liberal program was rejected out of hand, as both the House of Representatives and the Senate turned Republican in the 104th Congress elected in 1994 and remained so throughout Clinton's presidency. Clinton accepted the defeat of his Democrat Congress and went so far as to accept the leadership of Newt Gingrich, Republican Speaker of the House, who provided a balanced budget and no annual federal deficit by the end of Clinton's administration, the first time the federal budget had balanced since 1969.

Several scandals erupted during Clinton's presidency, some relating to his career as governor in Arkansas, such as the Whitewater land deal affair and the Rose law firm, and others of a personal nature, including activities involving a White House intern and the suicide of Vincent Foster, an aide to President Clinton. In a case that went to the United States Supreme Court, a former employee of the State of Arkansas, Paula Jones, accused Clinton of sexual harassment.

President Clinton entered office with Democrat majorities in both houses of Congress but lost them both to the Republicans in the next election. The House of Representatives and the Senate remained Republican until after Clinton left office.

Regarding the qualities by which presidents are evaluated, Clinton fares as follows:

1) Enhancing American Greatness

　　After the end of the Soviet Union, engineered by the previous administration, Clinton squandered the "peace dividend" and allowed the armed forces of the United States to deteriorate. An attempt at using United States combat troops to provide humanitarian aid in Somalia failed disastrously. Clinton was able to broker a deal between Yasser Arafat and Israeli Prime Minister Benjamin Netanyahu, but it did not lead to long-term gains. Clinton ordered the American military to attack targets in Iraq after reports surfaced of hidden weapons of mass destruction.

2) Improving Quality of Life

　　Clinton's pressure on banks to increase their lending to people at the lower end of the economic ladder eventually, in combination with other Administration actions, resulted in massive foreclosures and aggravated the crisis in the banking industry in the United States. Clinton attempted but failed to get health care reform legislation enacted. Clinton signed agreements enacting expanded North American and worldwide trade as a culmination of globalization efforts begun under his predecessor, George Herbert Walker Bush.

3) Meeting Crises

　　Clinton's handling of a Bureau of Alcohol, Tobacco, and Firearms (ATF) incident in Waco, Texas, resulted in the deaths of eighty or more people, including seventeen children.

4) Overcoming Opposition

　　Clinton successfully overcame impeachment by the House of Representatives, even though thirty-one members of his own Democratic Party in the House of

Representatives voted with the Republican majority for impeachment. Two votes were held during his trials in the Senate. He won the first, fifty-five to only forty-four for removal from office, and won the second by a fifty-fifty tie vote. A two-thirds majority, sixty-seven votes, was required for conviction. Before the end of his second term, Clinton had largely abrogated his leadership position and turned the initiative in Washington over to the Republican-controlled Congress. This resulted in the enactment of balanced-budget legislation, tax cuts, and limiting increases in Medicare.

Clinton's Rating:

CATEGORY	VALUE	RATING
1) Enhancing American Greatness	10	-40%
2) Improving Quality of Life	8	-40%
3) Meeting Crises	10	-50%
4) Overcoming Opposition	8	00%

Total rating: -12.2

Chapter 10

The Poor Presidents

Several presidents entered office with high hopes and public support but were not up to the challenge, perhaps facing greater, more difficult tasks than they expected. As Harry Truman said about his presidential desk, "The buck stops here."

38) John F. Kennedy, Democrat

John F. Kennedy, considered a political lightweight by many, including the Russians, owed his election to the presidency more to his father's millions than to any innate leadership, diplomatic, or political qualities he might have possessed. There is considerable suspicion that Joseph P. Kennedy, John F.'s father, financed some dirty tricks in West Virginia and perhaps elsewhere to secure his son the Democratic Party presidential nomination over the leading contender, Hubert Humphrey of Minnesota. Additionally, the Kennedys may have assisted Richard J. Daley, the Irish-American mayor of Chicago, in manufacturing votes in Illinois to secure Kennedy's win in the 1960 presidential election over Richard Nixon of California. Kennedy seemed to toughen up after taking some particularly hard knocks early in his presidency but was assassinated before he could benefit from his experiences.

Kennedy was perhaps the first real "public relations" president, with considerable effort expended before, during, and after his presidency to keep his image polished. Congress was solidly in the hands of the Democrats throughout Kennedy's presidential term.

Regarding the qualities by which presidents are evaluated, Kennedy fares as follows:

1) Enhancing American Greatness

After the Bay of Pigs invasion failure, the Soviets deemed Kennedy a weak president, prompting several Soviet advances. One was in Berlin, where a wall was built surrounding West Berlin, greatly reducing the number of people escaping from East Germany to West Berlin. Several other Soviet moves prompted the Kennedy Administration to make a forceful move against the advance of communism. Kennedy's decision to mount a military campaign in Vietnam to assist the South Vietnamese in repelling communist infiltration eventually failed, costing the United States prestige abroad. No one knows how many state secrets may have been revealed to the opposition through Kennedy's supposed liaisons with women of questionable virtue. Kennedy was instrumental in forming the Peace Corps, which, despite its intentions, often served more as a postcollege overseas vacation for upper-middle-class American children than a tool for improving United States foreign relations. After a halt in nuclear weapons testing during the Eisenhower Administration, the Russians resumed detonating nuclear bombs shortly after Kennedy's administration began in 1961. A Nuclear Test Ban treaty was eventually signed in 1963. The United States space program was actively accelerated during the Kennedy Administration, leading to the first moon landing in 1969.

2) Improving Quality of Life

Kennedy was unable to get congressional approval for his many proposed domestic programs for a wide variety of purposes. He was instrumental, while as a senator, in defeating a proposed Constitutional Amendment that would have allocated each state's electoral vote according to the percentage of the popular vote—a proposal favored at that time by conservatives, but later by liberals, as an approach to having the popular vote decide the winner of presidential elections. The minimum wage was raised to $1.25 per hour for most positions during his administration. Kennedy actively promoted improved civil rights for Black Americans, particularly in Alabama and Mississippi.

3) Meeting Crises

Kennedy faced numerous crises during his short tenure, with suboptimal responses. He largely ignored the Bay of Pigs invasion, leading to severe animosity from the participants and supporters of the exercise, which was sponsored by the United States government. His response to the Russian installation of offensive missiles in Cuba was more vigorous, but he allowed the Russians a "win" by trading the removal of preexisting NATO missiles from Turkey for the withdrawal of Russian missiles from Cuba. Kennedy's response to the Berlin Wall's erection—a significant Russian affront against the US—was to begin a massive buildup of United States troops in Vietnam, a major error.

4) Overcoming Opposition

Despite his popularity, Kennedy struggled to secure significant liberal social legislation from Congress and faced reduced prestige abroad as the Soviets continued to achieve victories in many areas, despite increased US defense spending.

Kennedy's rating:

CATEGORY	VALUE	RATING
1) Enhancing American Greatness	10	-40%
2) Improving Quality of Life	8	-20%
3) Meeting Crises	10	-80%
4) Overcoming Opposition	8	-30%

Total rating: -16.0

39) James Madison, "Republican"[14]

James Madison was one of the leading figures in the development and adoption of the United States Constitution but became an advocate for states' rights after its adoption, shifting away from the centralizing policies of Alexander Hamilton, Washington's Secretary of the Treasury. Madison played a crucial role in the formation of the "Republican" (later Democrat) party, emphasizing Antifederalism, which marked the beginning of the southern "states' rights" strategy. Madison, and several other Virginians such as John Randolph and Patrick Henry, expected Virginia to be the leading member of the new unified nation under the proposed Constitution but lost their enthusiasm when the smaller states demanded equal rights with the larger. Virginia was one of the last of the thirteen colonies to ratify the Constitution, and Randolph actually campaigned against it. Madison, as noted earlier, worked with Thomas Jefferson after the new government went into effect to undermine the Constitution's authority.

James Madison inherited a Republican Congress, in the Jeffersonian sense (i.e., Democrat in the modern sense) from Thomas Jefferson. He maintained this political landscape throughout his presidency, passing it to James Monroe in 1817.

Regarding the qualities by which presidents are evaluated, Madison fares as follows:

1) Enhancing American Greatness

Madison was goaded into declaring war on Great Britain, resulting in the War of 1812. The conflict ended with a peace treaty that returned things to their antebellum status.

2) Improving Quality of Life

The British victories during the War of 1812 emboldened Native American campaigns against American fron-

---

[14] Republican, in cases of presidents in office prior to 1856, refers to the party of Thomas Jefferson, not the party of Abraham Lincoln (see chapter 4).

tiers, which were not quelled until notable defeats by Andrew Jackson and William Henry Harrison.
3) Meeting Crises
Madison was forced to abandon Washington when the British attacked and set fire to the Capitol, the White House, and other buildings.
4) Overcoming Opposition
Madison, akin to Bill Clinton nearly two centuries later, adopted a pragmatic approach after his popularity waned, embracing previously opposed measures such as the establishment of a national bank and higher tariffs, policies favored by Federalists. However, just before leaving office, he vetoed the Bonus Bill proposed by John C. Calhoun, which aimed to use federal funds for extensive infrastructure development, maintaining his stance against extensive federal involvement in such projects.

Madison's rating:

CATEGORY	VALUE	RATING
1) Enhancing American Greatness	10	-50%
2) Improving Quality of Life	8	-20%
3) Meeting Crises	10	-80%
4) Overcoming Opposition	8	-20%

Total rating: -16.2

40) Woodrow Wilson, Democrat

Woodrow Wilson's brief political career before becoming president, including a single term as Governor of New Jersey, was seen as an advantage since he lacked the political baggage of his rivals for the Democratic Party nomination in 1912. Wilson's progressivism, particularly appealing to disaffected Republican progressives, was a key factor in his political appeal, despite his policies largely reflecting a Southern perspective on progressivism. While Wilson is credited with progressive achievements such as the income tax and the direct election of senators, these initiatives were actually initiated by his Republican predecessor, William Howard Taft. Wilson's significant legislative achievement was his role in the enactment of the Federal Reserve Act, although it had been conceived under Republican auspices and had several contentious pieces of legislation that underwent numerous revisions before its passage, with Wilson playing a crucial role in securing agreement on the final bipartisan bill.

Wilson enjoyed a Democrat-controlled Congress until 1918, when Democrats lost control of both houses. Wilson's presidency is evaluated based on several key aspects:

1) Enhancing American Greatness

    Woodrow Wilson pushed the United States into World War I, preventing a victory by Germany, after early attempts to avoid entry into the conflict. His efforts at the peace conference gave away the conditions of the peace to Great Britain and France, in return for their agreeing to foundation of a League of Nations, Wilson's pet project that the United States eventually refused to join. The harsh peace terms forced onto the Central Powers, Germany and Austria, by the Allies after Wilson gave them a free hand led directly to the Great Depression of the 1930s and World War II. An argument can also be made that the policies of Wilson, Britain, and France allowed the success of the communist revolution in Russia, the effects of which lasted for seventy years, if, in fact, they are concluded now. Wilson's heavy-handed expansion of United States interventionism in Latin America resulted in resentment of the United States by the people of those countries that lasted for decades.

2) Improving Quality of Life

    Wilson orchestrated the passing of highly restrictive laws that practically turned the United States into a police state, in supposed advancement of prosecution of the Great War (World War I). Wilson's progressive economic policies were frankly socialist in regard to the nation's railroads, caving to the demands of labor unions for government control of the railroads, which amounted to confiscation with inadequate compensation, and left them a shambles after government control ended.

Wilson obtained reduction in tariffs after he was elected president, but the advent of World War I shortly after meant that fewer foreign goods were available for import into the United States. Wilson and the Democrat-controlled Congress did accomplish considerable consumer-friendly legislation, including creating the Federal Trade Commission, the Clayton anti-trust act, and child labor legislation. Wilson also pushed adoption of the Adamson Act, benefitting railroad employees.

3) Meeting Crises

Wilson continually ignored serious challenges to the sovereignty of the United States by agents of the central powers and torpedoing of American vessels by German submarines. Wilson did not see fit to ask for a declaration of war until Congress passed the Adamson Act, a pro-labor measure that also gave the president vigorous powers to act on the domestic economy of the United States. After obtaining Democrat control of Congress with his anti-war rhetoric, Wilson proceeded to demand, and receive, a declaration of war from Congress and obtained what was tantamount to dictatorial powers throughout American participation in the conflict. As noted above, his obsession with the League of Nations squandered his leadership position as the de facto head of the Allied Powers at the time of the Armistice, resulting in devastation and chaos in Europe that lasted, essentially, until the 1950s.

4) Overcoming Opposition

After Wilson was unable to get approval of the United States Senate for the Versailles Treaty, including the League of Nations, he went on a nationwide speaking tour trying to build public support for the treaty. He failed to move public opinion and succumbed to a stroke and had to return to Washington, completely debilitated. In spite of his condition, he refused to give up executive power but acted through his wife. This led to the complete abandonment of Wilson and Wilsonianism by the public and the politicians.

Wilson's rating:

CATEGORY	VALUE	RATING
1) Enhancing American Greatness	10	-50%
2) Improving Quality of Life	8	-50%
3) Meeting Crises	10	-20%
4) Overcoming Opposition	8	-70%

Total rating: -16.6

41) Barrack Obama, Democrat

After a brief career in elected politics, Barack Obama captured the enthusiasm of liberals nationwide and defeated Hillary Clinton for the Democrat nomination for president of the United States in 2008. Like Bill Clinton before him, Obama entered the Oval Office with a perceived mandate for liberal change and initially had a Democrat Congress to support him. However, like Clinton, Obama soon discovered that the public was not as supportive of his liberal agenda as he had thought. The House of Representatives turned Republican in the 112th Congress and remained so for the duration of Obama's presidency. The Senate also turned Republican in the 114th Congress in 2014 and stayed that way through the end of Obama's term.

Regarding the qualities by which presidents are evaluated, Obama fared as follows:

1) Enhancing American Greatness

    Obama's major foreign affairs accomplishment was the execution of Osama bin Laden, long after he had become a hunted fugitive irrelevant in international affairs. This was a political assassination, contrary to the rule of law, and in stark contrast to the arrest, trial, and execution of Saddam Hussein in Iraq during George W. Bush's administration.

2) Improving Quality of Life

    Obama failed to make any serious efforts to curtail domestic terrorism in the United States, allowing suspected terrorists to operate freely. His anti-business bias, exemplified by the Affordable Care Act, or Obamacare, stifled free enterprise and held back a true recovery from recession for the entire length of the Obama Administration, until the results of the 2016 presidential and congressional elections were announced and it became apparent that the pro-business (and pro-employee) philosophy of the new Trump Administration would be in place soon.

3) Meeting Crises

    Several terrorist attacks on American facilities abroad left the United States government with only unanswered questions. Obama's friendly attitude and actions toward Iran could be considered treason. Despite federal government expenditures in the trillions of dollars via various "recovery" programs, the United States economy remained flat throughout the Obama presidency.

4) Overcoming Opposition

    Obama easily overcame opposition within the Democratic Party by appointing Hillary Clinton as his secretary of state. The Republicans nominated candidates for the 2008 and 2012 elections who failed to gain the support of the party's more conservative members, contributing to Obama's electoral victories.

Obama's rating:

CATEGORY	VALUE	RATING
1) Enhancing American Greatness	10	-80%
2) Improving Quality of Life	8	-60%
3) Meeting Crises	10	-40%
4) Overcoming Opposition	8	-20%

Total rating: -18.4

Chapter 11

The Bad Presidents

A very few presidents have had such a negative effect on the welfare of the country that they can be called bad. The worst, of course, are James Buchanan and Franklin Pierce, whose actions led directly to the Civil War. Every poll of historians or other experts lists these two near or at the bottom in presidential rankings.

42) Joseph Biden, Democrat

Joseph Biden, originally from Pennsylvania, served multiple terms as a United States senator representing Delaware. He was vice president during the eight years of Barack Obama's presidency. His political career was unremarkable until he won the 2020 Democrat presidential primary, largely due to support from Black Democrats in the South Carolina Democrat Presidential Primary. He went on to win the presidency in 2020 over the Republican incumbent, Donald Trump, in a highly contentious race. Following Biden's victory, the economy deteriorated, inflation reached levels not seen in nearly fifty years, the southern border saw a massive influx of prospective immigrants, and the federal debt soared as Democrats, controlling both Congress and the presidency, launched spending programs in attempts to address these and other issues.

The House of Representatives was Democrat-controlled when Biden took office, but the Republicans gained control in the 2022 midterm election. The Democrats maintained control of the Senate by a slim majority, relying on non-Democrat senators and the vice president.

Regarding the qualities by which presidents are evaluated, Biden fared as follows:

1) Enhancing American Greatness
   Biden's evacuation of US personnel from Afghanistan was criticized for lacking proper military support and preparation, leading to unnecessary loss of life and billions of dollars' worth of equipment falling into Taliban hands.
2) Improving Quality of Life
   Under Biden, the COVID-19 pandemic continued until public disinterest set in. Inflation reached levels not seen since the Carter Administration.
3) Meeting Crises
   The Biden administration faced several terrorist attacks on American facilities abroad without clear responses. His handling of illegal immigration at the southern border has been highly criticized.
4) Overcoming Opposition
   Biden overcame opposition within the Democratic Party when endorsed by a leading Black Democrat congressman.

Biden's rating:

CATEGORY	VALUE	RATING
1) Enhancing American Greatness	10	-80%
2) Improving Quality of Life	8	-50%
3) Meeting Crises	10	-50%
4) Overcoming Opposition	8	-40%

Total rating: -20.2

The Crime of the Democrats

43) Lyndon Johnson, Democrat

Lyndon Johnson was a typical Southern politician but with stronger ties to Franklin Roosevelt's New Deal than most Southerners. As Senate Majority Leader in the 1950s, he remained a Southern Democrat. Post–World War II, Johnson recognized that the Democratic Party needed to find new voters to maintain its dominance in American politics, given the increasing wealth of the average American and their growing inclination towards the Republicans. He identified the largely disenfranchised Black population as a potential source of new Democrat voters and began to court them. After becoming president in 1963 following John F. Kennedy's assassination, Johnson initiated a massive program of enhanced welfare benefits, primarily targeting African Americans. Combined with the cost of the Vietnam War escalation after the Tonkin Gulf Resolution, these actions necessitated large tax increases while still enlarging the federal deficit, initiating an inflation spiral. These actions, along with the anti-Goldwater rhetoric of Johnson's 1964 presidential campaign, marked the beginning of the increased ideological split between the two major political parties in the United States and saw the switch of Southern Democrats to the Republican Party.

The United States Congress, in both houses, was under Democratic control throughout Lyndon Johnson's presidency.

Regarding the qualities by which presidents are evaluated, Lyndon Johnson fares as follows:

1) Enhancing American Greatness

   Johnson escalated American involvement in Vietnam following the alleged attack by North Vietnamese torpedo boats in the Gulf of Tonkin, resulting in over fifty thousand American deaths without achieving victory, while the prestige and respect for the United States plummeted worldwide. Johnson was accused of imperialism for sending US troops to the Dominican Republic to quell a revolt.

2) Improving Quality of Life

   Johnson's promises to Black people dubbed the "War on Poverty" were slow to be fulfilled, resulting in massive race riots and the destruction of large portions of several major, and smaller, cities. Federal troops were deployed to Detroit in 1967 and Washington, DC, in 1968 to restore order. Johnson's administration saw the creation of federal aid to education, medical care for senior citizens, the Department of Housing and Urban Development, and the Department of Transportation.

3) Meeting Crises

Growing protests against Johnson's Vietnam policy, combined with race riots, necessitated the deployment of federal troops in Washington, DC.

4) Overcoming Opposition

Johnson was unable to surmount increasing opposition to his policies, especially regarding the Vietnam War, leading him to decline nomination as the Democratic Party candidate for president in 1968.

Lyndon Johnson's rating:

CATEGORY	VALUE	RATING
1) Enhancing American Greatness	10	-60%
2) Improving Quality of Life	8	-40%
3) Meeting Crises	10	-80%
4) Overcoming Opposition	8	-40%

Total rating: -20.4

44) Andrew Jackson, Democrat

Andrew Jackson, the last Revolutionary War veteran to become president and the only one to have been a prisoner of war, was highly opinionated, quick to take offense, and deeply prejudiced. He demonstrated no friendship toward either the Indigenous peoples or African Americans, as his actions and policies clearly indicated. He was strongly patriotic, having "won" the War of 1812 almost single-handedly with the Battle of New Orleans—although that battle was irrelevant, actually fought after the war was officially over and a peace treaty had been signed. Jackson took the side of Union over states' rights during the Nullification Crisis of 1832, predicting that the states' rights issue would rise again around slavery.

Jackson, perhaps the most racist president, aggressively pursued the removal of Native Americans from lands desired by Whites, with his orchestration of the Cherokee removal to west of the Mississippi—known as the "Trail of Tears"—being particularly genocidal.

National political parties were in the final stages of their realigning. The Republicans evolved into the Democratic Republicans, then the Jacksonians, and finally the Democrats, controlling both houses of Congress throughout his presidency. The Whigs emerged as the anti-Jackson party but failed to secure a majority in the federal government at the time.

Jackson was highly opinionated and very dictatorial, but he was easily led by cronies and crafty persons such as members of his "Kitchen Cabinet," behind-the-scenes type of politicians who had their own interests in mind. These people used Jackson's anti-bank bias to get the center of banking and financial institutions away from Nicholas Biddle and the Philadelphia community and into the hands of their friends on Wall Street in New York City.

Regarding the qualities by which presidents are evaluated, Jackson fares as follows:

1) Enhancing American Greatness
   Andrew Jackson appointed his henchman, Roger B. Taney, as Chief Justice led to the Dred Scott Decision, inflaming national tensions and making the Civil War inevitable.
2) Improving Quality of Life
   Jackson decided to put the Bank of the United States out of business, as a means of ruining his political enemy, Nicholas Biddle. The Bank of the United States was the only financial institution providing stability to the currency system in the United States. When Jackson issued his Specie Circular, requiring only gold to be used in payments to the United States Treasury, the economy took a

downturn. Without the financial stability provided by the Bank of the United States, a severe depression soon came, although it did not make its heaviest mark until the following Van Buren administration. Jackson was an energetic supporter of westward expansion at the expense of the natives. He failed to honor Indian treaties, even those he negotiated.

3) Meeting Crises

In the case of *Cherokee Nation v. Georgia*, Jackson refused to enforce a decision by John Marshall's Supreme Court stating that the Indians were "domestic dependent nations" and had a right to their property until they voluntarily ceded it. Jackson reportedly said, "John Marshall has made his decision. Now let him enforce it." The court's decision was never enforced, and the Cherokees were eventually forced to leave their land. During the nullification crisis, Jackson bullied the leader of the nullification party, John C. Calhoun, into backing down. While this was a positive result, Jackson was, in fact, a personal enemy of Calhoun's and welcomed the opportunity to humiliate him. Considering Jackson's career, he may not have been a true opponent of nullification to the extent that the incident with Calhoun suggests. At the risk of war, Jackson pressured France to make payments for damages done to American shipping during the Napoleonic wars, resolving the issue and resulting in resumption of good relations with France. Jackson recognized Texas independence on his last day in office, leaving to his successors the resolution of the issue of annexation of Texas.

4) Overcoming Opposition

Jackson had many powerful enemies and single-handedly caused the Whig Party to be created more as an anti-Jackson party than for any other political purpose (the Whigs originated in England as the party opposing the power of the king and favoring Parliament). The Whigs tended to be primarily a party of the financially and socially elite, while Jackson's followers coalesced into what they began to call the Democratic Party, representing, in Jackson's words regarding the bank war, "the humble members of society, the farmers, mechanics, and laborers." Jackson was victorious for a time, but his handpicked successor went down to crashing defeat in his bid for reelection after the results of Jackson's policies became apparent.

Jackson's rating:

CATEGORY	VALUE	RATING
1) Enhancing American Greatness	10	-40%
2) Improving Quality of Life	8	-70%
3) Meeting Crises	10	-60%
4) Overcoming Opposition	8	-60%

Total rating: -20.4

45) James Buchanan, Democrat

James Buchanan was a seasoned Pennsylvania politician known for his early involvement in railroad development, notably with the Harrisburg, Portsmouth, Mount Joy, and Lancaster Rail Road in the 1830s, a line that eventually formed a key part of the Pennsylvania Railroad system. At sixty-five, Buchanan brought extensive experience from various executive and legislative roles to the presidency.

Universally regarded as one of the United States' worst presidents, Buchanan's attempts to appease the slave states prior to the Civil War and his facilitation of Federal arms transfers to the South as secession loomed are seen by many as acts of treason. His presidency began with a Democrat-controlled Congress, but by its end, both the House of Representatives and the Senate had shifted to Republican control.

Evaluating Buchanan's presidency:

1) Enhancing American Greatness

    Buchanan's unsuccessful endeavors to purchase Alaska and Cuba did little to elevate America's international standing. His support for Chief Justice Taney's Dred Scott Decision exacerbated tensions between the North and South, diminishing American prestige.

2) Improving Quality of Life

    Buchanan attempted to force admission of Kansas as a slave state to minimize the majority held in the Senate by the free states since the admission of California in 1850, followed by Minnesota and Oregon, all free states, so that the Senate consisted of thirty-six members from free states and thirty from slave states by 1860, with other potential free states and no potential slave states in the wings. His efforts failed but resulted in "Bloody Kansas."

3) Meeting Crises

    Buchanan's denial of responsibility for secession contrasted sharply with his administration's provision of weapons to the South, actions some believe could have warranted impeachment for treason. While claiming powerlessness against secession, he did not hesitate to deploy federal troops against Mormon rebels in Utah Territory.

4) Overcoming Opposition

    Announcing he would not seek a second term early in his presidency, Buchanan quickly became a lame duck, with Democratic Party leadership shifting to Stephen A. Douglas. Buchanan's post-presidency was largely spent defending his legacy against accusations of aiding the South and contributing to the Civil War's onset.

Buchanan's rating:

CATEGORY	VALUE	RATING
1) Enhancing American Greatness	10	-50%
2) Improving Quality of Life	8	-90%
3) Meeting Crises	10	-60%
4) Overcoming Opposition	8	-60%

Total rating: -23.0

46) Franklin Pierce, Democrat

Franklin Pierce, a New Englander from New Hampshire, exhibited pro-South and proslavery tendencies throughout his presidency. Aligning with Democrat policy, his primary objective was to appease the South and maintain an even representation in the Senate between slave and free states. Efforts to purchase Mexico and Cuba to create more slave states, coupled with his rejection of Hawaii's annexation due to its likely free state status, underscored his alignment. His endorsement of the Kansas-Nebraska Act, which negated the Missouri Compromise and opened western territories to slavery, directly contributed to the Civil War's inevitability. On a positive note, Pierce's term saw the negotiation of a trade treaty with Japan and promoted the Atlantic cable and land grants for railroads.

Widely regarded as one of the United States' worst presidents, Pierce's willingness to expand slavery across the nation to satisfy southern slaveholders and his disregard for the slave population and the future of the free labor force in a slave-dominated society have led to his categorization as the worst US president by some.

During Pierce's presidency, the Senate remained under Democratic control, while the House transitioned from Democratic to American Party control in the Thirty-Fourth Congress.

Evaluating Pierce's presidency:

1) Enhancing American Greatness
   Pierce's staunch support for the proslavery Compromise of 1850, including the Fugitive Slave Act,

severely limited African Americans' rights, reflecting his alignment with proslavery policies.
2) Improving Quality of Life
The Kansas-Nebraska Act's signing, which effectively nullified the Missouri Compromise and opened new territories to slavery, ignited northern opposition, leading directly to the Civil War and resulting in over half a million American casualties.
3) Meeting Crises
In order to cool the increasing furor of the slave states over Northern opposition, Pierce attempted to purchase Cuba from Spain to prevent the freeing of its slaves and thereby avert a slave rebellion in the United States, as well as to form another slave state. He also refused admission to Hawaii, which would have been a free state. His Cuba efforts failed.
4) Overcoming Opposition
Despite his desire for a second term, Pierce was not renominated for the 1856 presidential election due to opposition from northern Democrats. Although he had some support for the 1860 Democrat candidacy, Pierce ultimately retired from electoral politics.

Pierce's rating:

CATEGORY	VALUE	RATING
1) Enhancing American Greatness	10	-60%
2) Improving Quality of Life	8	-80%
3) Meeting Crises	10	-80%
4) Overcoming Opposition	8	-70%

Total rating: -26.0

There are many factors involved in evaluating a US president, whether for ranking purposes or for a simple assessment of their presidency. One factor that can be determined for each president, independent of his peers, is presidential strength. Some presidents thrive on adversity, meeting challenges with the necessary effort to overcome them. Other presidents may fail to overcome obstacles or may lead the country in a direction that was unwisely chosen. Still, others may use their overwhelming popularity to justify actions that, perhaps in retrospect, were unwise. Furthermore, some presidents, due to being very unpopular, had difficulty achieving worthy goals, or may have failed at them.

While there is considerable material available in this volume to justify the rankings in the table below (Table 11-1), the strength ranking of the presidents is admittedly much more subjective. Presidential strength can change within a term, as popularity or other factors can change radically. While a general grouping of strong, weak, and moderate presidents can be fairly easily obtained, ranking all forty-six presidents can be difficult. The difference in ranking of the presidents by multiple evaluators under this criterion would possibly show even more variation than the differences seen in the twenty-one different mainstream presidential rankings illustrated in Appendix E (see chapter 14). However, "strong" vs. "weak" transcends party affiliation, at least to some extent, so political bias would be a lesser factor in a strength ranking.

The following table lists the presidents in (1) chronological order, (2) with their ranking (highest to lowest), and (3) in decreasing order of strength (strongest to weakest), with party affiliation:

	PRESIDENT CHRONOLOGICALLY		PRESIDENT THIS RANKING		PRESIDENTIAL STRENGTH	PARTY[15]
1	WASHINGTON	1	WASHINGTON	1	JACKSON	DEM
2	J ADAMS	2	LINCOLN	2	WILSON	DEM
3	JEFFERSON	3	REAGAN	3	REAGAN	REP
4	MADISON	4	JEFFERSON	4	T ROOSEVELT	REP
5	MONROE	5	J ADAMS	5	JEFFERSON	DEM
6	J Q ADAMS	6	POLK	6	F D ROOSEVELT	DEM
7	JACKSON	7	T ROOSEVELT	7	TRUMAN	DEM

---

[15] Modern equivalent.

8	VAN BUREN	8	EISENHOWER	8	EISENHOWER	REP
9	W H HARRISON	9	NIXON	9	LINCOLN	REP
10	TYLER	10	G H W BUSH	10	POLK	DEM
11	POLK	11	ARTHUR	11	WASHINGTON	REP
12	TAYLOR	12	MCKINLEY	12	NIXON	REP
13	FILLMORE	13	TAFT	13	L JOHNSON	DEM
14	PIERCE	14	HOOVER	14	J ADAMS	REP
15	BUCHANAN	15	COOLIDGE	15	TRUMP	REP
16	LINCOLN	16	FORD	16	MONROE	DEM
17	A JOHNSON	17	MONROE	17	OBAMA	DEM
18	GRANT	18	J Q ADAMS	18	HAYES	REP
19	HAYES	19	TAYLOR	19	TAYLOR	REP
20	GARFIELD	20	HAYES	20	TYLER	DEM
21	ARTHUR	21	B HARRISON	21	CLEVELAND (1)	DEM
22	CLEVELAND (1)	22	GARFIELD	22	PIERCE	DEM
23	B HARRISON	23	TRUMP	23	ARTHUR	REP
24	CLEVELAND (2)	24	W H HARRISON	24	CLEVELAND (2)	DEM
25	MCKINLEY	25	CLEVELAND (1)	25	G W BUSH	REP
26	T ROOSEVELT	26	CLEVELAND (2)	26	TAFT	REP
27	TAFT	27	G W BUSH	27	COOLIDGE	REP
28	WILSON	28	GRANT	28	HOOVER	REP
29	HARDING	29	HARDING	29	J Q ADAMS	REP
30	COOLIDGE	30	FILLMORE	30	A JOHNSON	DEM
31	HOOVER	31	A JOHNSON	31	MCKINLEY	REP
32	F D ROOSEVELT	32	TYLER	32	GRANT	REP
33	TRUMAN	33	VAN BUREN	33	KENNEDY	DEM
34	EISENHOWER	34	CARTER	34	CLINTON	DEM
35	KENNEDY	35	F D ROOSEVELT	35	FILLMORE	REP
36	L JOHNSON	36	TRUMAN	36	HARDING	REP
37	NIXON	37	CLINTON	37	G H W BUSH	REP
38	FORD	38	KENNEDY	38	BUCHANAN	DEM
39	CARTER	39	MADISON	39	B HARRISON	REP
40	REAGAN	40	WILSON	40	VAN BUREN	DEM
41	G H W BUSH	41	OBAMA	41	GARFIELD	REP
42	CLINTON	42	BIDEN	42	FORD	REP
43	G W BUSH	43	L JOHNSON	43	CARTER	DEM
44	OBAMA	44	JACKSON	44	MADISON	DEM

| 45 | TRUMP | 45 | BUCHANAN | 45 | W H HARRISON | REP |
| 46 | BIDEN | 46 | PIERCE | 46 | BIDEN | DEM |

Table 11-1   Presidents, Ranking, Strength

Chapter 12

The Popularity Contest

The public perception of a political candidate largely revolves around the presentation of that candidate by the media, who are influenced to a great degree by the evaluations of scholars and political scientists. Politicians, particularly when campaigning for office, frequently try to mask their actual political philosophy and party affiliation to attract votes from those considering themselves independents or even actual members of the other party, under the assumption that party loyalists will vote for them anyway and it can't hurt to attract a few other voters. This can be especially true at the presidential level, while also applying to a greater or lesser extent in other contests. A party's success at the polls can be more dependent on its treatment by the media and "experts" than its position on the issues.

Some good presidents were also popular, but dying in office generally does more for a president's popularity than good performance. The popular vote is also not a good leading indicator for either popularity or good performance. Some of the presidents with the highest percentage of the popular vote ended up least popular, and some performed poorly. In general, presidents perform better in popularity than Congress or the press, but there have been exceptions. Regardless of who or what is responsible for good times or bad, the President usually gets the credit or the blame. People generally remember the good times and forget the bad times, so many presidents have a higher degree of popularity than they perhaps should hold.

Some of the presidents most popular throughout their terms were Democrats: John Kennedy, Franklin Delano Roosevelt, Bill Clinton, and Barack Obama possibly all could have been elected for life; Kennedy and FDR were. In all these cases, their key virtue was expressed sympathy for the plight of the common man or the poor, regardless of whether they accomplished anything material to improve the lives of such persons. Such a persona is truly a valuable asset for a politician running for office in a democracy. The "I feel your pain" mantra of Bill Clinton assured him eternal high popularity numbers in spite of his lackluster, even scandalous, presidency. In fact, all the most popular presidents representing the Democratic Party after 1900 were progressives, whose main vote-getting mechanism was the promise of redistribution of wealth, as opposed to increasing prosperity for all.

The popular vote is not necessarily a reflection of the popularity of a president, as the popular vote can be, and often is, a vote against someone or something. Warren Harding's high popular vote total in 1920 was more a vote against Woodrow Wilson, or Woodrow Wilson's policies, and a statement of dissatisfaction with the aftermath of World War I, than a positive statement about Warren Harding. Richard Nixon's popular vote in 1972 was as much or more against George McGovern and his expressed liberal political philosophy than a positive endorsement of Richard Nixon.

The most unpopular presidents were John Quincy Adams, Andrew Johnson, and Herbert Hoover. Their unpopularity was mostly due to political opposition that was assisted by a hostile press. Hoover became the mirror image of William Clinton, being perceived as completely unsympathetic to the plight of the poor in spite of his initiation of many assistance programs at the start of the Great Depression of the 1930s.

Several presidents started out with high popularity but lost it by the time their terms were over. These include Warren Harding, Richard Nixon, and Jimmy Carter.

Some of the most unpopular presidents were those who were elected president without gaining a majority or even a plurality of the popular vote. Two early presidents were elected without obtaining a majority of the electoral vote; they were chosen by the House of Representatives. Thomas Jefferson, in 1800, tied with Aaron Burr in the Electoral College. As Jefferson was the intended president and Burr was the intended vice president, there was little opposition to Jefferson's selection as president by the House. It was recognized almost immediately that Burr's numerical electoral tie with Jefferson was due to a constitutional flaw; this was soon remedied by the Twelfth Amendment. Burr's failure to willingly cede the presidency to Jefferson caused him severe public censure, and Burr eventually became a renegade. On the other hand, in 1824, when Andrew Jackson, John Quincy Adams, Henry Clay, and William Crawford split the electoral vote, and the president was chosen by the House of Representatives from the three candidates with the highest vote totals, Jackson, Adams, and Crawford, the Jackson people complained long and bitterly when the House chose Adams over Jackson in spite of Jackson having a plurality of the electoral vote. Adams was hounded throughout his presidency and received no cooperation from Congress for his proposals and received a crushing defeat at the hands of Jackson in the ensuing presidential election of 1828.

A few other presidents were elected with a majority of the electoral vote while not receiving a majority of the popular vote. Four of these presidents—Rutherford B. Hayes, Benjamin Harrison, George W. Bush, and Donald Trump—were clearly the winners based on the rules set out in the Constitution. However, the supporters of the losing candidates (Democrats in every case), who received more popular votes than the winners, never ceased complaining. Proposals have been made to change the method of electing the president to more closely follow the popular vote, but the extra two electoral votes for each state, insisted upon by the smaller states at the time of adoption of the Constitution, remain and are likely to continue, in spite of the United States today being more of a nation than the confederacy it was when the Constitution was adopted. After all, from July 2, 1776, when independence was voted, until June 21, 1788, when the ninth state ratified the Constitution and it took effect, all decisions on a national level were taken on a "one state, one vote" basis. Popular vote applied only in state elections.

The smaller states were, as a rule, quick to ratify the Constitution, with Delaware, New Jersey, and Georgia ratifying unanimously at their conventions. Meanwhile, two of the largest states at the time, Virginia and New York, hesitated until the ninth ratification (by New Hampshire) put it into effect, and then joined the new Union. The smaller states in 1787 (except for cantankerous Rhode Island) were happy to join the Union, primarily because of the equal representation in the Senate and corresponding extra weight in the selection of the president. The same would undoubtedly hold true today if an attempt were made to eliminate this feature of the Constitution. The larger states definitely have the advantage in the House of Representatives, as was the case at the time of the ratification of the Constitution. This issue and slavery were the two main points of contention at that time. In 1788, representation in the House of Representatives was allocated as follows (Table 12-1):

Virginia	10 Representatives
Massachusetts	8 Representatives
Pennsylvania	8 Representatives
New York	6 Representatives
Maryland	6 Representatives
Connecticut	5 Representatives
North Carolina	5 Representatives
South Carolina	5 Representatives
New Jersey	4 Representatives
New Hampshire	3 Representatives
Georgia	3 Representatives
Rhode Island and Providence Plantations	1 Representative
Delaware	1 Representative

Table 12-1   Original House of Representatives (1788)

In spite of having a minority in the House of Representatives, the Virginians and their Southern cohorts were able to control the federal government, and the presidency, almost continuously up until the Civil War.

Looking at all the presidential elections in which the winner did not receive a majority of the popular vote, the number of changes in the person of the elected president that would have occurred if the popular vote were decisive might not overly favor one party (see table 12-2). See pages 161–164 for more detail on these elections. Five Democrats and seven Republicans were minority-popular-vote presidential winners, and the thirteenth, John Quincy Adams, ran under the same party banner, "Republican,"[16] as all the other major candidates in that election. In some cases, as with Taylor, Cleveland, Truman, Nixon, and Trump, a third candidate's votes probably would have gone to the winner if the third-party candidate had not run, giving the winner a majority of the popular vote. On the other hand, John Quincy Adams, James Buchanan, Abraham Lincoln, Rutherford B. Hayes, Benjamin Harrison, Woodrow Wilson, William Clinton, and George W. Bush were clearly not the choice of the majority of voters.

Election Year	Winner (major candidates)	Percent of Popular Vote	House	Senate
1824	John Quincy Adams, R	31.4%	D	D
1848	Zachary Taylor, R	47.3%	D	D
1856	James Buchanan, D	45.3%	D	D
1860	Abraham Lincoln, R	45.0%	R	R
1876	Rutherford B Hayes, R	48.5%	D	R
1888	Benjamin Harrison, R	49.6%	R	R
1892	Grover Cleveland, D	47.2%	D	D, R
1912	Woodrow Wilson, D	45.3%	D	D
1948	Harry Truman, D	49.9%	D	D
1968	Richard Nixon, R	43.6%	D	D

---

[16] Republican, in cases of presidents in office prior to 1856, refers to the party of Thomas Jefferson, not the party of Abraham Lincoln (see chapter 4).

1992	William Clinton, D	43.3%	D	D
2000	George W. Bush, R	48.4%	R	D
2016	Donald Trump, R	49.5%	R	R

R = Federalist, National Republican, Whig, or modern Republican

D = Antifederalist, Jeffersonian Republican, Democratic Republican, or Democrat

Table 12-2   Presidential Winners with Minority of Popular Vote

Therefore, three Democrats, four Republicans, and one pre-1856 "Republican" were chosen by a minority of the voters. Two of these, Hayes and Benjamin Harrison, defeated candidates who received a majority of the popular vote. On only two occasions did the minority vote presidential winner come from the party that was the loser in both houses of Congress.

There has frequently been agitation for term limits for elected politicians, and after Franklin Delano Roosevelt's presidency, a Constitutional Amendment, the twenty-second, to limit presidents to no more than two full terms, plus two years of a preceding president's term, was adopted. There is still occasionally a call for a single presidential term of six years. If this were in effect, it would not change the length of the average president's term much, as it is, as of 2020, a little over five years. Unfortunately, it would deprive the country of the full services of that rare president who could fill a much longer term to the satisfaction of an overwhelming majority of the people. It also would produce instant lame-duck status, reducing the President's stature in the governmental triumvirate and probably fatally crippling his political effectiveness. If there were no limitation on presidential terms, a few presidents could have been reelected for life, or until they decided to retire for medical or other physical reasons; some perhaps should have been.

Several presidents were elected for life, albeit inadvertently: William Henry Harrison, Zachary Taylor, Abraham Lincoln, James A. Garfield, William McKinley, Warren G. Harding, Franklin Delano Roosevelt, and John Fitzgerald Kennedy all died in office. Lincoln, Garfield, McKinley, and Kennedy were assassinated, while the others—Harrison, Taylor (presumably), Harding (presumably), and

Roosevelt—died of natural causes. Several other presidents died shortly after leaving office, so that if they had been reelected, they would not have lasted long. There are a few presidents who most likely could have been reelected as long as they wanted to serve, or until they died in office: George Washington, Andrew Jackson, Abraham Lincoln, U. S. Grant, William McKinley, Franklin Delano Roosevelt, Dwight Eisenhower, John F. Kennedy, and Ronald Reagan. Republicans Eisenhower, McKinley, Grant, Lincoln, and Reagan all increased their popular vote on reelection over their initial winning vote. Democrat Andrew Jackson had lower popular vote totals for reelection than for his initial election; Franklin Delano Roosevelt increased his popular vote percentage for his first reelection in 1936, but his vote percentage dwindled thereafter; Kennedy's reputation eventually suffered, so his future vote total probably would have declined as well.

Vote-getting power is not a sure means of determining the best president according to experts' standards. Some of the presidents with the highest winning percentage of the popular vote left office in disgrace, such as Warren Harding, Lyndon Johnson, and Richard Nixon; or lost their reelection bid: Martin Van Buren.

Of the forty-six presidents to date, only twenty have been elected as sitting presidents: Washington, Jefferson, Madison, Monroe, Jackson, Lincoln, Grant, McKinley, Theodore Roosevelt (only elected once), Wilson, Coolidge (only elected once), Franklin Roosevelt (reelected three times), Truman (only elected once), Eisenhower, Lyndon Johnson (only elected once), Nixon, Reagan, Clinton, George W. Bush, and Obama. Ten Republicans and ten Democrats, an even split. Only twelve served a full two terms (or more, in the case of FDR), and one of these, Wilson, was an incapacitated invalid for the last year and a half of his presidency. Of the nine perpetually popular presidents listed above, five are listed in the top third of this ranking, and three are in the bottom third; in a comparison of the four rankings cited in chapter 14, by C-Span (2021), CBS News (Siena 2022), Newsweek (APSA 2018), and the Wall Street Journal (2000), seven, five, six, and seven are placed in the top third, and two, four, three, and one are placed in the middle third, respectively, with one in the bottom third in one poll.

Chapter 13

The Popular Vote

The vote in a presidential election in the United States is essentially a popularity contest. The individual with the most favorable publicity and the most appealing persona almost always secures victory. Champions of unpopular programs, such as tax increases, or those blamed for any sort of disaster, typically find themselves at a disadvantage.

The winners of the popular vote, their percentages, and their outcomes are listed below in descending order. Winners prior to 1824, when the popular vote was not tabulated, are excluded, even though the results of those elections were, in some instances, noteworthy: George Washington received 100% of the electoral vote in both of his elections, facing no opposition; James Monroe received 99.6% once (he would have achieved 100% but for a single elector voting against his state's decision) and 92% on another occasion.

Warren G Harding (R), 1920, 63.8%

Harding died in office, possibly of food poisoning, perhaps a heart attack and pneumonia; some say suicide, others suggest murder, after the malfeasance of some of his cabinet members began to become known, at least to him. The 1920 presidential vote may have been a protest against the Wilson Administration. The House of Representatives and the Senate shifted from Democrat to Republican before Harding's election and remained Republican until the depression of the 1930s.

Franklin Delano Roosevelt (D), 1936, 62.5%

FDR had convinced people, during his first term, that he had their best interests at heart in fighting the Great Depression of the 1930s. The worst of the Depression was, in fact, over by the election of 1936. Roosevelt went on to win a third and a fourth term, although with lesser percentages of the popular vote. The House of Representatives and the Senate shifted from Republican to Democrat by the time Roosevelt was inaugurated in 1933 and remained so beyond his presidency.

Richard Nixon (R), 1972, 61.8%

This was largely a protest against the perceived socialist policies of Nixon's opponent, George McGovern. Not unlike the 1964 election (see below), the public's perception of the losing candidate was largely the result of the negative campaign tactics of the winner. Nixon may have also benefited from the "dirty tricks" of the Committee to Reelect the President, which included the notorious Watergate break-in. The House and Senate remained Democrat throughout Nixon's presidency.

Lyndon Johnson (D), 1964, 61.3%

Johnson had an opponent in 1964, Barry Goldwater, who seemed to many to be promising a nuclear holocaust if elected. The Johnson campaign seized on this with a lurid advertising campaign, portraying Goldwater as a warmonger, and won the election handily. Johnson went on to massively escalate the Vietnam War, resulting in tens of thousands of deaths of American soldiers, but with no clear sign of victory, and declined to run for an additional term as his popularity declined to near zero in 1968. Despite Johnson's eventual unpopularity, the House of Representatives and the Senate remained under Democrat control throughout his presidency.

Theodore Roosevelt (R), 1904, 60.6%

After succeeding the assassinated William McKinley in 1901, Teddy Roosevelt achieved tremendous popularity as a "trustbuster" and as the very popular, jingoistic builder of the Panama Canal. He declined to run again in 1908, stating that he had already served the traditional maximum of two terms (including almost all of McKinley's second term). He changed his mind in 1912 but could not secure the Republican nomination due to his reputation as a more-than-moderate progressive. He ran in 1912 as a third-party progressive "Bull Moose" candidate, throwing the election to the Democrat, Woodrow Wilson. Roosevelt reversed himself on progressivism before he died in 1919. The House and Senate were Republican throughout Roosevelt's presidency.

Ronald Reagan (R), 1984, 59.2%

After being ridiculed as an actor-politician in his first term, Reagan proved himself a strong president with numerous ideas on how to improve the lot of the American people, cruising to an easy victory in 1984 with 97.6% of the electoral vote. His popularity continued in spite of some scandals in his second term, and he likely could have been elected for life. Reagan began his presidency with a Republican Senate but lost it to the Democrats by the end of his second term. The House was Democrat throughout Reagan's presidency.

Franklin Delano Roosevelt (D), 1932, 59.1%

Herbert Hoover was widely blamed for (1) not avoiding the Great Depression, which began in Hoover's first year in office, and (2) not doing enough to combat the Great Depression after its effects were felt. An easy victory in 1932 required little effort on Roosevelt's part. The House of Representatives and the Senate remained Democrat throughout Roosevelt's presidency.

Herbert Hoover (R), 1928, 58.8%

The nation was prosperous, World War I was largely forgotten, and people felt the best way to keep things as they were was to vote for Herbert Hoover in 1928, the candidate of the party that had been in control of the government for the last seven years. The House of Representatives and Senate were both securely Republican at the start of Hoover's presidency, but the House was lost to the Democrats in the 1930 election.

Martin Van Buren (D), 1836, 58.2%

Van Buren was the anointed successor to the people's hero, Andrew Jackson. It was fairly well known that Van Buren was the "brains" behind the Jackson presidency. His main competitor in 1836 was Henry Clay. If the votes of minor candidates are included, when his opponents, the Whigs, strategized that different Whig candidates should run in different parts of the country where they were most popular, Van Buren's percentage of the vote is only 50.9%. In spite of Clay's scheming, the House of Representatives and the Senate were solidly Democrat throughout Van Buren's term of office.

Dwight Eisenhower (R), 1956, 56.0%

Eisenhower was an extremely popular president. His experience as Commander of Allied Forces in Europe during World War II and as head of NATO, the North Atlantic Treaty Organization, gave people confidence in his abilities; his performance in his first term gave little reason to doubt those abilities, and he was easily reelected. Eisenhower's popularity did not help the Republicans in Congress. He had Democrat majorities in both houses of Congress throughout his second term.

Andrew Jackson (D), 1828, 56.0%

Jackson had been campaigning hard for four years since his loss to John Quincy Adams in the House of Representatives in 1824–1825. His consistent, constant, loud complaint that he was the choice of the people, by virtue of his plurality of the 1824 popular vote, paid off. Jackson had Democrat or "Jacksonian" majorities in both houses of Congress throughout his presidency.

Ulysses S. Grant (R), 1872, 55.9%

Grant was a war hero, considered the savior of the Union, second only to the martyred Lincoln. In spite of, or perhaps because of, liberal Republican and Democrat bashing of Grant, he increased his popular vote from his 1868 victory total.

Dwight Eisenhower (R), 1952, 55.4%

Eisenhower was a popular war hero and career military man with a very clean record; the previous administration had been tainted with scandal, and there was public unrest arising from a variety of sources. Eisenhower was perceived to be a statesman unsullied by political dealings. He started his presidency with a Republican House and Senate, but both soon turned Democrat and stayed that way.

Abraham Lincoln (R), 1864, 55.1%

After a shaky first three years, Lincoln's presidency was doing well, and it was clear that the Union armies were on their way to victory. The House and Senate were firmly in Republican hands in the 39th Congress.

Andrew Jackson (D), 1832, 55.0%

Jackson's vote percentage dropped slightly from 1828. His vote total increased slightly, by about 6%, while the country's population increased about 13%. Jackson had Democrat or "Jacksonian" majorities in both houses of Congress throughout his presidency.

On the other end of the scale, several presidents won the Electoral College while obtaining less than 50% of the popular vote. Some of these elections had three or more major candidates, so that the winner may have had a plurality of the popular vote (see page 151).

John Quincy Adams (NR), 1824, 31.8%

This was a four-man race, with Andrew Jackson, Henry Clay, and William Crawford also participating. All were prominent public figures. The three highest electoral vote-getters went on to a race, per the Constitution, in the House of Representatives, where the vote was by state, with each state delegation getting one vote. In what was called a "corrupt bargain" by the supporters of Andrew Jackson, Henry Clay threw his support to Adams, who then won the vote in the House and subsequently appointed Henry Clay as secretary of state. There was nothing illegal or immoral about this, but Adams was hounded by Jackson supporters throughout his presidency and was not able to get any of his programs through Congress.

William Clinton (D), 1992, 43.3%

This was a three-man race, with Clinton obtaining a plurality of the popular vote and a clear majority of the electoral vote.

Richard Nixon 1968 (R), 43.6%

This was a three-man race, with Nixon obtaining a plurality of the popular vote and a clear majority of the electoral vote. The third-party candidate's votes probably would have largely gone to Nixon if it had been only a two-man race, or those voters would have stayed home, so Nixon would have had a majority of the popular vote as well as the electoral vote. However, the third-party candidate made Nixon appear less conservative, perhaps helping him with independent voters (see page 71).

Abraham Lincoln (R), 1860, 45.0%

This was a four-man race, with Lincoln obtaining a plurality of the popular vote and a clear majority of the electoral vote. It is quite possible that, had the Southern Democrat candidate stayed out of the election, the Northern Democrat, Stephen A. Douglas, would have won most of his votes, but Lincoln still would have won the electoral vote.

Woodrow Wilson (D), 1912, 45.3%

This was a three-man race, with Wilson obtaining a plurality of the popular vote and a clear majority of the electoral vote. The Republican candidate, William Howard Taft, and the Bull Moose

(Progressive) Party candidate, Theodore Roosevelt, split the conservative vote. If only Taft or Roosevelt had been running, he most likely would have won the election, and Wilson would have been defeated.

James Buchanan (D), 1856, 45.3%

This was a three-man race, with Buchanan obtaining a plurality of the popular vote and a clear majority of the electoral vote. Together, John C. Fremont of the new Republican Party and Millard Fillmore, a former Whig running under the American Party banner, garnered a large majority of the popular vote. It is probable that if Fillmore had not run, Fremont would have taken most of his votes and won the election easily.

Grover Cleveland (D), 1892, 47.2%

This was a three-man race, with Cleveland obtaining a plurality of the popular vote and a clear majority of the electoral vote. The votes of the third party's candidate, James Weaver of the Populist or People's Party, would likely have gone to Cleveland, or those voters would have stayed home, so Cleveland's percentage of the popular vote would have been higher if it had been a two-man race.

Zachary Taylor (W), 1848, 47.3%

This was a three-man race, with Taylor obtaining a plurality of the popular vote and a clear majority of the electoral vote. The third-party candidate, Martin Van Buren, ran under the Free-Soil Party banner. As Van Buren was a former Democrat, it is difficult to say whether he took votes away from Taylor or from Lewis Cass, the Democrat candidate. If all of Van Buren's votes had gone to Cass instead, which is unlikely, Cass would have had a clear majority of the popular vote and may have won the election.

George W. Bush (R), 2000, 48.4%

This was a very closely contested race, with Bush winning by a Supreme Court decision giving him the electoral votes of Florida in the infamous "chads" case.

Rutherford B. Hayes (R), 1876, 48.5%

This was a close election, with the electoral votes of two states in dispute. Hayes had to obtain all the disputed electoral votes to win, which he did. Most analysts conclude that Hayes' opponent was unfairly denied all or some of those electoral votes, so that Hayes should have lost the election.

Donald Trump (R), 2016, 49.5%

There were several candidates in this race who won substantial numbers of popular votes without winning any electoral votes. The plurality of popular votes was won by Hillary Clinton, the liberal or Democrat candidate, by about 60.4 million to 60 million, or 50.2% when counting only hers and Donald Trump's votes. A substantial majority of the popular vote was won by conservative candidates over liberal candidates, approximately 64.6 million to 61.6 million, so that Clinton's share of the total presidential vote in 2016 was only 47.8%. Trump won 305 electoral votes, 56.7%, to 233 for Clinton.

Benjamin Harrison (R), 1888, 49.6%

Harrison, the Republican, defeated the Democrat candidate, the incumbent Grover Cleveland, despite losing the popular vote. Cleveland was an unpopular conservative Democrat who opposed the free coinage of silver, a concept popular among many of the Democratic Party faithful, some of whom may have stayed away from the polls during the 1888 election.

Harry Truman (D), 1948, 49.9%

This was a four-man race, with Truman obtaining a plurality of the popular vote and a clear majority of the electoral vote. It was widely predicted that the unpopular incumbent, Truman, would lose the election, and many called the election for his Republican opponent, Thomas Dewey, before late returns gave the election to Truman. Bracketing Truman's election to the presidency in 1948 were the only two Congresses controlled by the Republicans between 1931 and 1981: the eightieth and the eighty-third.

Several presidents were elected with just over 50% of the popular vote, but less than 52.5%, so they could hardly be said to have a mandate. These include: U. S. Grant's first term, William McKinley's first term, Barack Obama's second term, Woodrow Wilson's second term, Ronald Reagan's first term, George W. Bush's second term, Jimmy Carter, Grover Cleveland's first and second terms, John F. Kennedy, and James A. Garfield. Interestingly, however, Grant, McKinley, Reagan, and Bush, all Republicans, in their second election improved their vote margins over their first election, while Obama and Cleveland, both Democrats, had a lower percentage of the popular vote in their second election as compared to their first. Wilson's second election was in a close two-man race as opposed to his first in a three-man race, so his vote percentage was bound to go up, win or lose.

The other side of the popularity coin is in the reelection contest. Sitting presidents usually have a tremendous advantage when they run for reelection, as they already have name recognition and some sort of record to run on. Nevertheless, several sitting presidents have lost in their attempts at reelection. These include John Adams, John Quincy Adams, Grover Cleveland, Benjamin Harrison, William Howard Taft, Herbert Hoover, Gerald Ford, Jimmy Carter, George H. W. Bush, and Trump, all but two of whom were Republicans. Gerald Ford was the only totally unelected president, having replaced Spiro Agnew without facing an election as vice president after Agnew resigned, and then having been advanced from vice president when Richard M. Nixon resigned the presidency. Other vice presidents who attained the office of president upon the death of their predecessor, such as Chester Arthur, would have liked to run for president on their own but were denied the nomination by their party. A few ex-presidents, such as Millard Fillmore, who became president when Zachary Taylor died in office, and also Martin Van Buren and Theodore Roosevelt, ran, after their presidencies, as third-party candidates but were defeated.

Chapter 14

The Polls and Presidential Ranking

The Typical Polls

Officially, Grover Cleveland is both the twenty-second and twenty-fourth president. Most polls have combined his two terms to produce one ranking. This ranking includes Cleveland twice, even though both ratings for Cleveland are similar, placing Grover Cleveland at no. 24 and no. 25 in the presidential ranking, with ratings of 0.0 and -0.8, respectively.

There can be considered to be three schools of presidential rankings. The presidential ratings and resultant rankings developed in this book can be considered from a conservative point of view. Most published rankings are more aligned with a liberal philosophy of government, valuing the properties and accomplishments of the presidents differently. Strict libertarians hold presidents to a much more rigid standard of constitutionality, and their presidential ratings bear little resemblance to the others. The following table compares mainstream rankings as displayed in Wikipedia and elsewhere, the rankings developed herein, and a libertarian ranking as compiled by Ivan Eland (see table 14-1).

Only two presidents were ranked similarly in all three systems: Washington at 3, 1, and 7, in the aggregate mainstream, this ranking, and libertarian, respectively, and Eisenhower at 8, 8, and 9, respectively. Two other presidents, Monroe and George W. Bush, had ranking ranges of ten or less. All these presidents share a public perception as disinterested public servants or even as statesmen. Only two presidents, Washington and Eisenhower, were ranked in the top ten by all three systems. On the other end of the scale, Pierce, Buchanan, and George W. Bush were ranked twenty-third or worse by all three systems. A few presidents had uniformly mediocre rankings, such as Ford with 29, 16, and 16, respectively; Taft with 24, 13, and 20, respectively; John Quincy Adams at 23, 19, and 12, respectively; and Monroe, 16, 17, and 25, respectively. For comparison of all rankings of all presidents, corrections must be made for William Henry Harrison and Garfield, and all presidents after Franklin Delano Roosevelt. The mainstream rankings are a composite of several separate rankings, and not all include the more recent presidents, making for a serious disturbance in comparison of the ranking numbers.

In table 14-2, C-Span ranked Cleveland only once, while this ranking included him once for each of his two nonconsecutive terms. In adjusting this comparison, C-Span and this ranking, using the same numerology, have identical rankings for one president, Grover Cleveland. This ranking and C-Span did come within 5 points of each other on the rankings of an additional fourteen presidents, which is remarkable considering the apparent difference in criteria, as discussed below.

President	Mainstream Ranking[17]	This Ranking	Libertarian Ranking
Washington	3	1	7
Adams	15	5	22
Jefferson	5	4	26
Madison	14	39	28
Monroe	16	17	25
John Quincy Adams	23	19	12
Jackson	9	44	27
Van Buren	26	33	3
William Henry Harrison	41 (13 votes)	24	no ranking
Tyler	39	32	1

[17] Twenty-one ranking votes but not all evaluated all forty-six presidents.

Terry L. Koglin

Polk	12	6	38
Taylor	37	20	13
Fillmore	40	30	14
Pierce	42	46	24
Buchanan	45	45	23
Lincoln	1	2	29
Andrew Johnson	43	31	17
Grant	35	27	19
Hayes	27	21	4
Garfield	32 (13 votes)	23	no ranking
Arthur	30	11	5
Cleveland (1st Term)	21	25	2
Benjamin Harrison	33	22	15
Cleveland (2nd Term)	21	26	2
McKinley	18	12	39
Theodore Roosevelt	4	7	21
Taft	24	13	20
Wilson	7	40	41
Harding	44	29	6
Coolidge	31	15	10
Hoover	34	14	18
Franklin Roosevelt	2	35	31
Truman	6 (20 votes)	36	40
Eisenhower	8 "	8	9
Kennedy	11 (19 votes)	38	36
Lyndon Johnson	13 "	43	32
Nixon	38 "	9	30
Ford	29 "	16	16
Carter	28 "	34	8
Reagan	17 (17 votes)	3	35
George H. W. Bush	25 (16 votes)	18	33
Clinton	19 (15 votes)	37	11
George W. Bush	36 (10 votes)	28	37

Obama	10 (6 votes)	41	34
Trump	46 (3 votes)	10	no ranking
Biden	20 (1 vote)	42	no ranking

Table 14-1 Comparison of Presidential Ranking Systems

C-Span		This Ranking, adjusted
#1	Abraham Lincoln	2
#2	George Washington	1
#3	Franklin D. Roosevelt	34
#4	Theodore Roosevelt	7
#5	Dwight D. Eisenhower	8
#6	Harry Truman	35
#7	Thomas Jefferson	4
#8	John F. Kennedy	37
#9	Ronald Reagan	3
#10	Barrack Obama	40
#11	Lyndon Johnson	41
#12	James Monroe	17
#13	Woodrow Wilson	39
#14	William McKinley	12
#15	John Adams	5
#16	James Madison	38
#17	John Quincy Adams	19
#18	James K. Polk	6
#19	Bill Clinton	36
#20	Ulysses S. Grant	26
#21	George H. W. Bush	18
#22	Andrew Jackson	42
#23	William Howard Taft	13
#24	Calvin Coolidge	15

#25	Grover Cleveland (once only)	25 (rated twice)
#26	Jimmy Carter	33
#27	James A. Garfield	23
#28	Gerald Ford	16
#29	George W. Bush	27
#30	Chester A. Arthur	11
#31	Richard Nixon	9
#32	Benjamin Harrison	22
#33	Rutherford B. Hayes	21
#34	Martin Van Buren	32
#35	Zachary Taylor	20
#36	Herbert Hoover	14
#37	Warren G. Harding	28
#38	Millard Fillmore	29
#39	John Tyler	31
#40	William Henry Harrison	24
#41	Donald Trump	10
#42	Franklin Pierce	44
#43	Andrew Johnson	30
#44	James Buchanan	43
None	Joseph Biden	—

Table 14-2   Comparison of Latest C-Span (2021) to This Ranking

C-Span and this ranking differed by 20 points or more on only ten presidents. Not surprisingly, eight of the ten are Democrats, all rated much higher by C-Span. The greatest difference, 31 points, was with Franklin D. Roosevelt, who had international diplomacy problems in his inability to thwart Joseph Stalin's gain of hegemony in Eastern Europe, and domestically, with his failure to end the Great Depression. This president was an aggressive advocate for the poor, at the expense of the middle class, with a great rapport with the mass media, and his Democratic Party remains in that position today. Donald Trump has the equal difference in ratings, for opposite reasons. Trump is rated thirty-one points higher in this ranking than by C-Span. Trump is widely perceived as an advocate for the middle class as opposed to the poor.

The C-Span 2021 survey of presidential historians determined their rankings of the presidents. The advisors for C-Span rated each president on a scale of one to ten on ten different qualities of presidential leadership, with each quality given the same weight: Public Persuasion, Crisis Leadership, Economic Management, Moral Authority, International Relations, Administrative Skills, Relations with Congress, Vision/Setting an Agenda, Pursued Equal Justice for All, and Performance Within Context of Times (see www.cspan.org/presidentsurvey2021/). It is debatable whether each of these categories is equally important, but opinion would most likely be divided as to which categories are more important than others, so probably by consensus of the historians no differentiation was made. Pursued Equal Justice for All, Public Persuasion, Moral Authority, and Vision/Setting Agenda could be factors at least partially associated with popularity. C-SPAN's Historians Survey on Presidential Leadership rankings, with points scored for each president, is shown in table 14-3.

Of the ten C-Span criteria, two are not considered by this ranking: Administrative Skills and Performance Within Context of Times. Economic Management could be considered a part of Improving Quality of Life, and International Relations is a part of Enhancing American Greatness. Overcoming Opposition could consist of Public Persuasion, Moral Authority, Relations with Congress, and Vision/Setting Agenda. Just one evaluation category is rated similarly by both C-Span and this ranking and can be directly compared: Crisis Leadership or Meeting Crises. The relative bias of these two systems of rating can be determined by comparing the value obtained in this category for each president by each system (see table 14-4).

As can be readily seen, this ranking is more critical on crisis management, as, of the forty-four presidents compared, twenty-five presidents have higher C-Span crisis management ratings than this rating assessment, while eighteen presidents have lower ratings by C-Span than this ranking, and one, William Howard Taft, has the same rating for both: 50 and 50.0. There could be some political bias in these ratings, as C-Span ranks 15 Democrats higher than does this ranking but only three are ranked lower (counting Cleveland only once and not counting Tyler), while with Republicans, C-Span ranks ten Republican presidents higher than does this ranking while rating twelve Republican presidents lower than does this ranking.

C-Span Ranking (2021)	President	Overall Score
#1	Abraham Lincoln	897
#2	George Washington	851
#3	Franklin D. Roosevelt	841
#4	Theodore Roosevelt	785
#5	Dwight D. Eisenhower	734
#6	Harry S. Truman	713
#7	Thomas Jefferson	704
#8	John F. Kennedy	699
#9	Ronald Reagan	681
#10	Barrack Obama	664
#11	Lyndon B. Johnson	654
#12	James Monroe	643
#13	Woodrow Wilson	617
#14	William McKinley	612
#15	John Adams	609
#16	James Madison	604
#17	John Quincy Adams	603
#18	James K. Polk	599
#19	William J. Clinton	594
#20	Ulysses S. Grant	590
#21	George H. W. Bush	585
#22	Andrew Jackson	568

#23	William Howard Taft	543
#24	Calvin Coolidge	535
#25	Grover Cleveland	523
#26	Jimmy Carter	506
#27	James A. Garfield	506
#28	Gerald R. Ford	498
#29	George W. Bush	495
#30	Chester A. Arthur	472
#31	Richard M. Nixon	464
#32	Benjamin Harrison	462
#33	Rutherford B. Hayes	456
#34	Martin Van Buren	455
#35	Zachary Taylor	449
#36	Herbert Hoover	396
#37	Warren G. Harding	388
#38	Millard Fillmore	378
#39	John Tyler	354
#40	William Henry Harrison	354
#41	Donald Trump	312
#42	Franklin Pierce	312
#43	Andrew Johnson	230
#44	James Buchanan	227
#45	Biden	NO RATING

Table 14-3   C-Span 2021 Ranking and Numerical Ratings

However, the C-Span ratings agree with these ranking ratings to within twenty points for thirty-one presidents: Washington, Lincoln, Reagan, Jefferson, John Adams, Polk, Eisenhower, Nixon, Arthur, McKinley, Taft, Coolidge, Ford, Monroe, G. H. W. Bush, John Quincy Adams, Taylor, Hayes, Benjamin Harrison, Garfield, William Henry Harrison, Cleveland, Grant, G. W. Bush, Fillmore, Andrew

Johnson, Tyler, Van Buren, Carter, Buchanan, and Pierce, while disagreeing by more than 50% on only two presidents: Madison and Kennedy. The greatest discrepancy is with John F. Kennedy, where C-Span gave a rating of 73.9 while this ranking accorded Kennedy only a 10. Kennedy not only began the quagmire in Vietnam by placing ground troops there but also gave the Soviets the excuse to build the Berlin Wall (and allowed them to do so), and his handling of the Cuban Missile Crisis had only one final result: NATO removing its missiles from Turkey. Kennedy was extremely popular with the people at large, before, during, and after his presidency, due to a successfully projected persona as a "man of the people" and "super great guy," helped by a very accommodating news media as well as his extremely charming wife.

This further suggests that the more commonly published presidential ratings are based more on popularity contest criteria than on accomplished facts. There appears to be an additional fault in the C-Span methodology; this can be noted by comparing their relative rankings of William Henry Harrison and Franklin Pierce. Leading strongly in the wrong direction, as exemplified by Franklin Pierce, produces a low rating, but providing no leadership, as in the case of William Henry Harrison, also produces a low rating. The methodology of this ranking, which provides a 0 rating for zero crisis management, as in the case of William Henry Harrison, and a negative 80 rating for such poor leaders as Franklin Pierce, is more consistent. Both systems provide a rating of 100 for the most positive crisis management; Abraham Lincoln has the highest rating from both, 100 from this ranking and 96.4 by C-Span.

Siena College included all presidents in their September 13, 2022, ranking (see table 14-5), the latest survey available for comparison. The Siena ranking compares similarly to C-Span with this ranking. Two presidents have the same ranking with Siena and this ranking (adjusted): Abraham Lincoln at number 2 and James Buchanan at number 44.

The American Political Science Association in February 2018 ranked the United States presidents on a scale of zero to 100 in a poll of current and recent members, rating each president on a scale of 0 to 100 for: great = 100, average = 50, failure = zero (see table 14-6). All these rankings are included in Appendix E.

Only one president, James Buchanan, received the same ranking by Newsweek/APSA as by this ranking. Like C-Span and Siena, APSA combined both of Cleveland's two nonconsecutive terms to provide one ranking for him. For fourteen presidents, the APSA ranking was within five marks of this ranking.

President	Rating by This Ranking	Converted	Rating by C-Span 2021
Washington	80	90	91.9
Adams	40	70	62.2
Jefferson	20	60	70.2
Madison	-80	10	60.4
Monroe	0	50	64.9
John Quincy Adams	0	50	54.0
Jackson	-60	20	66.5
Van Buren	-20	40	41.1
William Henry Harrison	0	50	31.9
Tyler	-20	40	38.6
Polk	40	70	66.7
Taylor	0	50	47.4
Fillmore	-10	45	37.9
Pierce	-80	10	25.0
Buchanan	-60	20	16.1
Lincoln	100	100	96.4
Andrew Johnson	-80	10	19.8
Grant	-10	45	63.2
Hayes	0	50	43.0
Garfield	0	50	46.4
Arthur	0	50	45.1

Cleveland	20	60	51.8
Benjamin Harrison	0	50	43.4
Cleveland	20	60	51.8
McKinley	10	55	63.4
Theodore Roosevelt	20	60	80.8
Taft	0	50	50.0
Wilson	-20	40	67.1
Harding	-60	20	43.4
Coolidge	0	50	52.9
Hoover	50	75	35.0
Franklin Roosevelt	-10	45	91.6
Truman	-30	35	80.1
Eisenhower	20	60	77.3
Kennedy	-80	10	73.9
Lyndon Johnson	-80	10	57.5
Nixon	0	50	48.3
Ford	10	55	50.1
Carter	-30	35	39.5
Reagan	60	80	89.1
George H. W. Bush	20	60	50.1
Clinton	-50	25	73.4
George W. Bush	-20	40	51.1
Obama	-40	30	62.8
Trump	0	50	26.5
Biden	-50	25	no rating

Table 14-4   Comparison of C-Span and This Ranking on Crisis Management

Thirteen presidents had APSA rankings that differed by twenty or more points from this ranking. Nine of these were Democrats, and four were Republicans. Like with C-Span and Siena, the major differences among the Democrats' rankings were with very popular presidents, and again, performance seemed to take a back seat to public image or presentation in the development of the ratings by APSA. APSA rated Barack Obama highly, despite the lack of significant accomplishments in his presidency. His rating by APSA, as with the ratings for Franklin Roosevelt and Lyndon Johnson, appears to owe more to his perceived efforts for poor people than to what he accomplished, or failed to accomplish, for them or for the nation as a whole. Disregarding their last-place rating for Donald Trump, made only one year into his presidency, their worst rating was for James Buchanan, universally regarded as one of the worst Presidents the United States ever had. Both this ranking and APSA placed Buchanan second to last.

Only three of the APSA rankings vary by more than five places from the 2017 C-Span rankings: Polk (20th vs. 14th, respectively), Van Buren (27th vs. 34th, respectively), and Kennedy (16th vs. 8th, respectively). James K. Polk and John F. Kennedy received higher rankings from C-Span, while Martin Van Buren received a higher ranking from APSA. The C-Span ranking for Polk is closer to this ranking, the APSA ranking for Kennedy is closer to this ranking, while the C-Span ranking for Van Buren is almost identical to this ranking (34 vs. 33). The 2021 ranking by C-Span deviates somewhat more from the APSA 2018 ranking. Seven C-Span 2021 rankings deviate by more than five points from the APSA 2018 ranking: Monroe (6 pts), John Quincy Adams (7 pts), Andrew Jackson (7 pts), Martin Van Buren (7 pts), James A. Garfield (7 pts), John F. Kennedy (8 pts), and William Clinton (6 pts).

Other Rankings, not discussed above (data from Wikipedia: historical rankings of the presidents of the United States [note: Professor Julian E. Zelizer of Princeton University says that traditional ratings are "weak mechanisms for evaluating"]):

- Arthur Schlesinger Sr. 1948, 1962
- Arthur Schlesinger Jr. 1996
- Murray-Blessing 1982

- Complete Book of US Presidents 1982 survey by Chicago Tribune

"Rating the Presidents: A Ranking of US Leaders from the Great and Honorable to the Dishonest and Incompetent" by William J. Ridings Jr. and Stuart B. McIver

Wall Street Journal 2000: For the forty presidents rated, twenty-one presidents were ranked lower than this ranking by WSJ, and fifteen were ranked higher. Only four presidents, George Washington, Abraham Lincoln, Thomas Jefferson, and Theodore Roosevelt, had the same ranking from both surveys. For Democrats, WSJ ranked fifteen higher than this ranking did.

Siena (2022)		This Ranking, Adjusted
#1	Franklin D. Roosevelt	34
#2	Abraham Lincoln	2
#3	George Washington	1
#4	Theodore Roosevelt	7
#5	Thomas Jefferson	4
#6	Dwight D. Eisenhower	8
#7	Harry Truman	35
#8	Lyndon B. Johnson	42
#9	John F. Kennedy	37
#10	James Madison	38
#11	Barrack Obama	40
#12	James Monroe	17
#13	Woodrow Wilson	39
#14	William Clinton	36
#15	James K. Polk	6
#16	John Adams	5
#17	John Quincy Adams	19
#18	Ronald Reagan	3

#19	Joseph Biden	41
#20	George H. W. Bush	18
#21	Ulysses S. Grant	26
#22	Willam McKinley	12
#23	Andrew Jackson	43
#24	James Earl Carter	33
#25	William Howard Taft	13
#26	Grover Cleveland (combined terms)	25
#27	James A. Garfield	23
#28	Richard Nixon	9
#29	Martin Van Buren	32
#30	Gerald Ford	16
#31	Rutherford B. Hayes	21
#32	Calvin Coolidge	15
#33	Chester A. Arthur	11
#34	Benjamin Harrison	22
#35	George W. Bush	27
#36	Zachary Taylor	20
#37	Herbert Hoover	14
#38	Millard Fillmore	29
#39	John Tyler	31
#40	William Henry Harrison	24
#41	Franklin Pierce	45
#42	Warren G. Harding	28
#43	Donald Trump	10
#44	James Buchanan	44
#45	Andrew Johnson	30

Table 14-5   Comparison of Latest Siena (2022) to This Ranking

Terry L. Koglin

For Republicans, WSJ did not rank anyone higher than This Ranking did. Nineteen presidents were ranked by WSJ within five points of This Ranking. Only seven presidents had rankings by WSJ that varied by twenty or more points from the This Ranking; six are Democrats: James Madison, Franklin Roosevelt, Andrew Jackson, Harry Truman, John Kennedy, and Lyndon Johnson; and one Republican, Richard Nixon.

APSA RANKING	PRESIDENT	APSA RATING	THIS RANKING & RATING (modified to match APSA's numerology)	
#1	Abraham Lincoln	95.03	2	90.8
#2	George Washington	92.59	1	91.6
#3	Franklin D. Roosevelt	89.09	34	32.0
#4	Theodore Roosevelt	81.39	7	75.6
#5	Thomas Jefferson	79.54	4	80.4
#6	Harry Truman	75.15	35	30.4
#7	Dwight Eisenhower	74.03	8	71.6
#8	Barrack Obama	71.13	40	13.2
#9	Ronald Reagan	69.29	3	86.8
#10	Lyndon Johnson	69.06	41	9.2
#11	Woodrow Wilson	67.40	39	16.8
#12	James Madison	64.48	38	17.6
#13	Bill Clinton	64.25	36	25.6
#14	John Adams	63.24	5	78.8
#15	Andrew Jackson	62.16	42	6.0
#16	John Fitzgerald Kennedy	61.86	37	18.0
#17	George H. W. Bush	60.90	18	56.0
#18	James Monroe	60.74	17	58.8
#19	William McKinley	55.49	12	64.8
#20	James K. Polk	54.09	6	77.2
#21	Ulysses S. Grant	52.88	26	48.0
#22	William H. Taft	51.86	13	63.2
#23	John Quincy Adams	51.9	19	54.8

#24	Grover Cleveland	51.01	25	49.2
(Cleveland is rated once for both terms)				
#25	Gerald Ford	47.28	16	59.6
#26	Jimmy Carter	45.04	33	33.6
#27	Martin Van Buren	44.27	32	34.0
#28	Calvin Coolidge	42.23	15	61.2
#29	Rutherford B. Hayes	41.50	21	53.2
#30	George W. Bush	40.42	27	46.0
#31	Chester A. Arthur	39.9	11	66.0
#32	Benjamin Harrison	37.63	22	50.0
#33	Richard Nixon	37.18	9	70.8
#34	James A. Garfield	36.64	23	50.0
#35	Zachary Taylor	33.34	20	54.0
#36	Herbert Hoover	33.27	14	61.6
#37	John Tyler	31.46	31	37.2
#38	Millard Fillmore	27.71	29	42.8
#39	Warren G. Harding	25.26	28	45.2
#40	Andrew Johnson	24.91	30	42.0
#41	Franklin Pierce	23.25	44	-2.0
#42	William Henry Harrison	19.02	24	50.0
#43	James Buchanan	15.09	43	4.0
#44	Donald Trump	12.0+	10	67.6

Joseph Biden had not yet been sworn in as president.

Table 14-6   Comparison of APSA Ratings and Rankings to This Rating and Ranking

Wall Street Journal 2005 for the Federalist Society by James Lindgren of Northwestern University Law School
Times of London 2008 ranked 42 presidents
University of London, Iwan Morgan, United States Presidency Centre 2011
American Political Science Association 2015, 2018 (see Newsweek/APSA above)

Other presidential poll sources:
Potus.com/presidential-facts/historical-ratings
Reddit.com/r/AskHistory/comments
Google.com/site/thepoliticsteacherorg

An aggregate ranking for all the presidents can be based on the "mainstream" rankings in Appendix E, totaling twenty-one—some are updates of earlier rankings also included in the aggregate. Some of the surveys making up the aggregate exclude more recent presidents because the surveys were conducted before that president took office or completed his term. Several rankings ignored William Henry Harrison and James Abram Garfield because their terms were brief. These dismissals are not entirely valid, as both William Henry Harrison and James Abram Garfield campaigned with certain cabinet members in mind and in place while they were president; many of these persons remained to do valuable, or at least significant, work under the presidential successor who might not have appointed them if the successor had been elected as president. Nevertheless, comparing this mainstream aggregate or composite ranking with the ranking developed here can be informative (see table 14-7).

As can be seen in table 14-7, this ranking rated twenty-six presidents higher than the mainstream aggregate average. Only two of these were Democrats: Thomas Jefferson and James K. Polk. Both men were given extra credit by this ranking for having greatly increased the geographical size of the United States, by the Louisiana Purchase and the Mexican Cession, respectively. A third Democrat, John Tyler, was also ranked higher by this ranking, but he ran as a Whig for vice president with William Henry Harrison, only returning to his Democrat political stance after assuming the office of president. Tyler also helped increase the size of the United States by encouraging the admission of Texas, formerly independent, as the twenty-eighth state.

The Crime of the Democrats

President	Mainstream Ranking[18]	This Ranking	Difference (M-T)
Trump	46 (3 votes)	10	36
Nixon	38 (19 votes)	9	29
Hoover	34	14	20
Arthur	30	11	19
Taylor	37	20	17
William Henry Harrison	41 (13 votes)	24	17
Coolidge	31	15	16
Harding	44	29	15
Reagan	17 (17 votes)	3	14
Ford	29 (19 votes)	16	13
Andrew Johnson	43	31	12
Taft	24	13	11
Benjamin Harrison	33	22	11
Fillmore	40	30	10
Adams	15	5	10
Garfield	32 (13 votes)	23	9
Grant	35	27	8
George W. Bush	36 (10 votes)	28	8
Tyler	39	32	7
George H. W. Bush	25 (16 votes)	18	7
Polk	12	6	6
Hayes	27	21	6
McKinley	18	12	6
John Quincy Adams	23	19	4
Washington	3	1	2
Jefferson	5	4	1
Buchanan	45	45	0
Eisenhower	8 (20 votes)	8	0
Monroe	16	17	-1
Lincoln	1	2	-1
Theodore Roosevelt	4	7	-3

---

[18] Twenty-one ranking entities but not all evaluated all forty-six presidents.

Pierce	42	46	-4
Cleveland (1st Term)	21[19]	25	-4
Cleveland (2nd Term)	21[20]	26	-5
Carter	28 (19 votes)	34	-6
Van Buren	26	33	-7
Clinton	19 (15 votes)	37	-18
Biden	20 (1 vote)	42	-22
Madison	14	39	-25
Kennedy	11 (19 votes)	38	-27
Truman	6 (20 votes)	36	-30
Lyndon Johnson	13 (19 votes)	43	-30
Obama	10 (6 votes)	41	-31
Wilson	7	40	-33
Franklin Roosevelt	2	35	-33
Jackson	9	44	-35

Table 14-7   Aggregate Mainstream Presidential Ranking vs. This Ranking

The mainstream aggregate average ranking was higher than this ranking for eighteen presidents. Sixteen of these were Democrats, and only two were Republicans: Abraham Lincoln and Theodore Roosevelt. The aggregate was quite close to this ranking for both Republicans. Both were extreme activists as president and were responsible for substantial changes in the United States.

The aggregate ranking is the same as this ranking for two presidents: Buchanan and Eisenhower. The aggregate ranking is within five points of this ranking for eleven presidents and differs by more than twenty points for eleven presidents. Of these, this ranking ranks eight Democrats lower by twenty points or more and ranks three Republicans higher. This ranking placed four Democrats higher than the aggregate: Jefferson, Tyler, Polk, and Andrew Johnson. This rank-

---

[19] Combined ranking by all participants.
[20] Combined ranking by all participants.

ing ranked two Republicans lower than the aggregate: Lincoln and Theodore Roosevelt.

For the thirty presidents that were ranked by all twenty-one systems, from Washington to Franklin Roosevelt and excluding William Henry Harrison and James A. Garfield, who were rated by only thirteen entities, Lincoln's composite average was the highest ranking, followed by Franklin Roosevelt, Washington, Theodore Roosevelt, Jefferson, Wilson, Jackson, Polk, Madison and John Adams (tied), Monroe, McKinley, Cleveland (one rating), and John Quincy Adams in order. The lowest composite average of the thirty was for Buchanan, below Harding, Andrew Johnson, Pierce, Fillmore, Tyler, Taylor, Hoover and Grant (tied), Benjamin Harrison, Coolidge, Arthur, Hayes, Van Buren, and Taft. Not surprisingly, the four presidents leading up to the Civil War, all of whom failed to provide sufficient leadership to prevent it, are among the worst-rated presidents per the aggregate.

The twenty-one mainstream rankings tabulated in Appendix E can be evaluated by looking at the range between the lowest and highest ranking by that group for each president, with rankings numbered from best = #1 to worst = #45 (see table 14-8). Exact comparison between all presidents is not possible due to the different numbers of rankings for different presidents. All presidents through Franklin Roosevelt, except for William Henry Harrison and Garfield, were in twenty-one different rankings, while more recent presidents were in fewer; Biden is only included in one ranking and Trump in three.

Not considering Biden, who was only ranked once, there is near consensus on seventeen presidents, with ranking ranges of twelve or less; most of these presidents can be considered activists, who expanded the role of the presidency beyond its strict constitutional limits. Fourteen are early presidents with the same number of rankings, so that there are no adjustments necessary. On the contrary, nine presidents have rankings that vary by eighteen or more; these were Republicans or pre-progressive Democrat presidents; only two, Reagan and George W. Bush, have less than the full complement of twenty-one rankings, so that adjustment issues do not come into significant account.

President	Lowest Ranking	Highest Ranking	Range	Range Order (T = tie)
Washington	4	1	3	4(T2)
John Adams	19	8	11	16(T2)
Jefferson	7	3	4	6(T3)
Madison	20	8	12	18(T4)
Monroe	18	8	10	14(T2)
John Quincy Adams	25	11	14	24(T5)
Jackson	23	5	18	37(T4)
Van Buren	34	15	19	41(T2)
William Henry Harrison	42	25	17	33(T3)
Tyler	39	22	17	33(T3)
Polk	20	8	12	18(T4)
Taylor	36	24	12	18(T4)
Fillmore	38	24	14	24(T5)
Pierce	42	27	15	29(T2)
Buchanan	43	26	17	33(T3)
Lincoln	3	1	2	2(T2)
Andrew Johnson	45	19	26	44
Grant	38	20	18	37(T4)
Hayes	33	13	20	42(T3)
Garfield	34	25	9	10(T4)
Arthur	35	17	18	37(T4)
Cleveland	26	8	18	37(T4)
Benjamin Harrison	34	20	14	24(T5)
McKinley	22	11	11	16(T2)
Theodore Roosevelt	7	3	4	6(T3)
Taft	25	16	9	10(T4)
Wilson	13	4	9	10(T4)
Harding	42	29	13	22(T2)
Coolidge	36	23	13	22(T2)
Hoover	38	19	19	33(T2)

Franklin Delano Roosevelt	3	1	2	2(T2)
Truman	9	5	4	6(T3)
Eisenhower	21	5	16	31(T2)
Kennedy	18	6	12	18(T4)
Lyndon Johnson	18	10	8	9
Nixon	37	23	14	24(T5)
Ford	32	23	9	10(T4)
Carter	34	19	15	29(T2)
Reagan	26	6	20	42(T3)
George H. W. Bush	31	17	14	24(T5)
Clinton	24	8	16	31(T2)
George W. Bush	39	19	20	42(T3)
Obama	18	8	10	14(T2)
Trump	44	41	3	4(T2)
Biden	19	19	0	1

Table 14-8   Rank Value Ranges - Mainstream Presidential Rankings

Interestingly, Republicans seem to improve more with time in the composite rankings, but for true comparison, it is necessary to evaluate each president's passage through time equally. Very few evaluations include rating score data, so rankings must be used. The ranking numbers change with the number of presidents being evaluated, making comparisons most informative when evaluations rank the same presidents. Forty-two presidents were evaluated by five polls between 1994 and 2000. In this field, thirteen Republican presidents improved over time in the rankings, while only five Democrats, including Andrew Johnson, did so. The number of presidents who declined in the rankings over time was almost the reverse, nine Democrats and five Republicans. The greatest improvement was by six Republicans, with Coolidge up eleven places, Grant up six places, and Harding up four places. The best improvement by Democrats was Cleveland, up seven places, and Jackson, up five. This provides a different look at this issue. Both C-Span and Siena have periodically repeated their surveys, allowing changes in ranking over time to be observed. C-Span's surveys for 2000, 2009, 2017, and 2021 are shown in table 14-9.

Ivan Eland in Recarving Rushmore (2014) rated 41 presidents from the Libertarian point of view: "promoting prosperity, liberty, non-interventionism, and executive roles." A few of his conclusions from his evaluations include the following: Washington as the only one deserving to be on Mount Rushmore, Teddy Roosevelt as over-rated, Lincoln as having provoked a civil war that did not achieve much, Jefferson as a hypocrite, Harding as better, and Truman as worse than usually ranked.

There are noticeable differences in the mainstream rankings, this ranking, and the Eland (Libertarian) ranking. As shown in Appendix D2, the mainstream composite favors strong presidents and dislikes moderate and weak ones, while Eland (Libertarian) favors moderate and weak presidents and has a strong dislike for strong ones. The ranking developed on these pages has less partiality to strong or weak presidents than the mainstream composite, while disagreeing with Eland on strong and weak presidents and is neutral on moderate presidents. Reflecting its liberal bias, the Wikipedia mainstream composite mentions Eland but does not include his ranking in its table of rankings.

The World Almanac and Book of Facts, in their 2019 edition, provides a ranking of the presidents based on a survey conducted by C-Span in 2017 of 91 "historians and other presidential observers," C-SPAN's Historians Survey(s) on Presidential Leadership (and also from C-Span 2000, 2009, and 2021; table 14-9).

As can be seen, the only presidents who have maintained a constant ranking in this latest composite are Lincoln, Theodore Roosevelt, Jefferson, Pierce, Andrew Johnson, and Buchanan: three universally ranked as among the best and three considered by nearly all to be among the worst. Among the others, some have increased in ranking over time, others have decreased, and a few seem to fluctuate with the barometer.

The Crime of the Democrats

2021	2017	PRESIDENT	2009	2000
1	1	Lincoln	1	1
2	2	Washington	2	3
3	3	F. D. Roosevelt	3	2
4	4	T. Roosevelt	4	4
5	5	Eisenhower	8	9
6	6	Truman	5	6
7	7	Jefferson	7	7
8	8	Kennedy	6	8
9	9	Reagan	10	11
10	12	Obama	-	-
11	10	L. Johnson	11	10
12	13	Monroe	14	14
13	11	Wilson	9	6
14	16	McKinley	16	15
15	19	J. Adams	17	16
16	17	Madison	20	18
17	21	J. Q. Adams	19	19
18	14	Polk	12	12
19	15	Clinton	15	21
20	22	Grant	23	33
21	20	G. H. W. Bush	18	20
22	18	Jackson	13	13
23	24	Taft	24	24
24	27	Coolidge	26	27
25	23	Cleveland (1 ranking)	21	17
26	26	Carter	25	22
27	29	Garfield	28	29
28	25	Ford	22	23
29	33	G. W. Bush	36	-
30	35	Arthur	32	32

31	28	Nixon	27	25
32	30	B. Harrison	30	31
33	32	Hayes	33	26
34	34	Van Buren	31	30
35	31	Taylor	29	28
36	36	Hoover	34	34
37	40	Harding	38	38
38	37	Fillmore	37	35
39	39	Tyler	35	36
40	38	W. H. Harrison	39	37
41	-	Trump	-	-
42	41	Pierce	40	39
43	42	A. Johnson	41	40
44	43	Buchanan	42	41

Biden was not included in the above rankings and Cleveland's two separate terms were combined.

Table 14-9   Presidential Rankings by C-Span 2021, 2017 2009 2000

The greatest improvement was by U. S. Grant, who moved from thirty-third to twenty-third to twenty-second to twentieth. The worst drop was by Cleveland by eight slots and Hayes by seven, the same as Wilson. See also page 154.

What do the people say? According to a Gallup poll conducted in 2011, which asked 1,015 adults in the United States, "Who do you regard as the greatest United States president?" Response was as follows (table 14-10):

Ronald Reagan	19%
Abraham Lincoln	14%
Bill Clinton	13%

John F. Kennedy	11%
George Washington	10%
Franklin Roosevelt	8%
Barrack Obama	5%
Theodore Roosevelt	3%
Harry Truman	3%
George W. Bush	2%
Thomas Jefferson	2%
Jimmy Carter	1%
Dwight Eisenhower	1%
George H. W. Bush	1%
Andrew Jackson	<0.5%
Lyndon B. Johnson	<0.5%
Richard Nixon	<0.5%

Table 14-10   Gallup Poll Presidential Rankings 2011

Personal memory apparently plays a significant role in popularity contests; only three of the presidents on the above list are from before the Civil War (out of a total of fifteen), while eleven are from after World War II (out of a total of twelve to 2011). The total accounts for less than 94.5% of the votes, apparently with fifty-five or so votes scattered among other presidents. Eight of the top ten presidents according to this ranking are on the above list, as are nine of the top ten presidents from the average of the mainstream rankings, but only three of the Libertarian top ten are included. Seven of the top ten according to the APSA 2018 poll are the top ten of this list, though not in the same order. The apparent flaws in public opinion polls are evident, with only three presidents from the first fifteen included; only two from the second fifteen, while six of the last six presidents made the cut. The only president since the Depression of the 1930s not on the list is Gerald Ford, who happens to be the only completely unelected president (the poll was conducted before the presidencies of Trump and Biden). Of the top ten listed, nine can be considered popular personalities, both during their presidencies and in retrospect. Gallup conducted another poll in 2022 asking the approval ratings of thirteen presidents (excluding Biden) who have been in office since World War II:

President	Approval Percentage
Kennedy	70.1
Eisenhower	65.0
George H. W. Bush	60.9
Clinton	55.1
Lyndon Johnson	55.1
Reagan	52.8
George W. Bush	49.4
Nixon	49.0
Obama	47.9
Ford	47.2
Carter	45.5
Truman	45.4
Trump	41.1
(Biden not included)	

Table 14-11   Approval Ratings of Recent Presidents as of 2022

As can be seen in table 14-11, the top three include two Republicans and one Democrat, while the bottom three consist of two Democrats and one Republican. Presidential rankings may or may not correlate with the quality of government provided to Americans. Over time, minor infractions can be forgotten, and well-polished images can be maintained. Some delay is necessary in evaluating a president's performance, and that of Congress, to more accurately assess the impact of policies, but the amount of time required to arrive at a true picture is debatable.

Finally, we have a quote from the late Charles S. Roberts, author and publisher from Baltimore, Maryland: "The Republican

Party was in absolute control of the nation from the start of the Civil War until the onset of the Great Depression. The Republican Party, however, was not a monolith and was quite capable of progressive mutation. It was a coalition at its beginning in 1854 and has always had a populist liberality growing in its soul. In reality, then and today [1997], it is the party of the little guy and devoted to maximum freedom for the individual."[21]

---

[21] From *Triumph I: Altoona to Pitcairn 1846–1996* by Charles S. Roberts, assisted by Gary W. Schlerf, Baltimore, 1997 (p. 148).

The Real Ranking of the Presidents

APPENDIX A

RANKINGS FOR EACH PRESIDENT - RATINGS BASED ON FOUR CRITERIA

NOMINAL "NEUTRAL" RATING = 0.0   MINIMUM RATING = -36.0   MAXIMUM RATING = 36.0

PRESIDENT	RANKING	ENHANCING AMERICAN GREATNESS VALUE	PCT	IMPROVE QUALITY OF LIFE VALUE	PCT	MEET CRISES VALUE	PCT	OVERCOME OPPOSITION VALUE	PCT	TOTAL RATING
Washington		10	80%	8	60%	10	80%	8	0%	20.8
Lincoln	1	10	80%	8	10%	10	100%	8	20%	20.4
Reagan	2	10	60%	8	60%	10	60%	8	20%	18.4
Jefferson	3	10	100%	8	40%	10	20%	8	0%	15.2
J Adams	4	10	40%	8	40%	10	40%	8	40%	14.4
Polk	5	10	80%	8	20%	10	40%	8	0%	13.6
T Roosevelt	6	10	60%	8	60%	10	20%	8	0%	12.8
Eisenhower	7	10	40%	8	60%	10	20%	8	0%	10.8
Nixon	8	10	40%	8	60%	10	0%	8	20%	10.4
Trump	9	10	80%	8	50%	10	0%	8	-40%	8.8
Arthur	10	10	40%	8	10%	10	0%	8	40%	8.0
McKinley	11	10	40%	8	30%	10	10%	8	0%	7.4
Taft	12	10	50%	8	40%	10	0%	8	-20%	6.6
Hoover	13	10	0%	8	-30%	10	50%	8	40%	5.8
Coolidge	14	10	40%	8	40%	10	0%	8	-20%	5.6
Ford	15	10	30%	8	30%	10	10%	8	-20%	4.8
Monroe	16	10	20%	8	30%	10	0%	8	0%	4.4
G H W Bush	17	10	10%	8	10%	10	20%	8	-10%	3.0
J Q Adams	18	10	0%	8	30%	10	0%	8	0%	2.4
Taylor	19	10	20%	8	20%	10	0%	8	-20%	2.0
Hayes	20	10	0%	8	0%	10	0%	8	20%	1.6
B Harrison	21	10	0%	8	10%	10	0%	8	-10%	0.0
Garfield	22	10	0%	8	0%	10	0%	8	0%	0.0
W H Harrison	23	10	0%	8	0%	10	0%	8	0%	0.0
Cleveland(1)	24	10	-20%	8	-20%	10	20%	8	20%	0.0
Cleveland(2)	25	10	-20%	8	-30%	10	20%	8	20%	-0.8
Grant	26	10	0%	8	0%	10	-10%	8	0%	-1.0
G W Bush	27	10	0%	8	0%	10	-20%	8	0%	-2.0
Harding	28	10	20%	8	20%	10	-60%	8	0%	-2.4
Fillmore	29	10	-10%	8	0%	10	-10%	8	-20%	-3.6
A Johnson	30	10	0%	8	0%	10	-80%	8	50%	-4.0
Tyler	31	10	-20%	8	-10%	10	-20%	8	-20%	-6.4
Van Buren	32	10	-20%	8	-30%	10	-20%	8	-20%	-8.0
Carter	33	10	-20%	8	-30%	10	-30%	8	-10%	-8.2
F D Roosevelt	34	10	-40%	8	-40%	10	-10%	8	-10%	-9.0
Truman	35	10	-20%	8	-50%	10	-30%	8	-10%	-9.8
Clinton	36	10	-40%	8	-40%	10	-50%	8	0%	-12.2
Kennedy	37	10	-40%	8	-20%	10	-80%	8	-30%	-16.0
Madison	38	10	-50%	8	-20%	10	-80%	8	-20%	-16.2
Wilson	39	10	-50%	8	-50%	10	-20%	8	-70%	-16.6
Obama	40	10	-80%	8	-60%	10	-40%	8	-20%	-18.4
Biden	41	10	-80%	8	-50%	10	50%	8	-40%	-20.2
L Johnson	42	10	-60%	8	-40%	10	-80%	8	-40%	-20.4
Jackson	43	10	-40%	8	-70%	10	-60%	8	-60%	-20.4
Buchanan	44	10	-50%	8	-90%	10	-60%	8	-60%	-23.0
Pierce	45	10	-60%	8	-80%	10	-80%	8	-70%	-26.0
	46						AVERAGE RATING =			-1.03

155

Copyrght 2023 Terry L Koglin   CODrrpappA20231231   December 31, 2023

APPENDIX B PAGE 1 OF 2
POPULAR VOTE FOR PRESIDENT 1788-2020

YEAR	WINNER	VOTE	PERCENT	LOSER(S) (max 3 highest)	TOTAL VOTE	VOTE
1788	Washington	69	100.0%	J Adams	69	ELECTORAL
1792	Washington	132	100.0%	J Adams, G Clinton	132	ELECTORAL
1796	J Adams	71	51.1%	Jefferson	139	ELECTORAL
1800	Jefferson	73	50.0%	Burr, J Adams, Pinckney	146	ELECTORAL
1804	Jefferson	162	92.0%	Pinckney	176	ELECTORAL
1808	Madison	122	72.2%	Pinckney, G Clinton	169	ELECTORAL
1812	Madison	128	59.0%	D W Clinton	217	ELECTORAL
1816	Monroe	183	84.3%	King	217	ELECTORAL
1820	Monroe	231	99.6%	J Q Adams	232	ELECTORAL
1824	J Q Adams	113,122	31.8%	Jackson, Crawford, Clay	355,242	POPULAR
1828	Jackson	647,231	56.0%	J Q Adams	1,156,328	POPULAR
1832	Jackson	687,502	56.5%	Clay, Floyd, Wirt	1,217,691	POPULAR
1836	Van Buren	762,678	58.2%	W H Harrison, White, Webster	1,310,685	POPULAR
1840	W H Harrison	1,275,017	53.1%	Van Buren, Birney	2,403,089	POPULAR
1844	Polk	1,337,243	50.7%	Clay, Birney	2,636,311	POPULAR
1848	Taylor	1,361,393	47.3%	Cass, Van Buren	2,876,354	POPULAR
1852	Pierce	1,601,474	53.6%	Scott, Hale	2,988,052	POPULAR
1856	Buchanan	1,836,072	45.3%	Fremont, Fillmore	4,051,480	POPULAR
1860	Lincoln	1,865,908	45.0%	Douglas, Breckinridge, Bell	4,149,271	POPULAR
1864	Lincoln	2,216,066	55.1%	McClellan	4,024,791	POPULAR
1868	Grant	3,015,071	52.7%	Seymour	5,724,686	POPULAR
1872	Grant	3,597,070	55.9%	Greeley	6,431,149	POPULAR
1876	Hayes	4,034,311	48.5%	Tilden	8,322,857	POPULAR
1880	Garfield	4,449,053	50.0%	Hancock	8,891,683	POPULAR
1884	Cleveland	4,911,017	50.3%	Blaine	9,759,351	POPULAR
1888	B Harrison	5,443,892	49.6%	Cleveland	10,978,380	POPULAR
1892	Cleveland	5,551,883	47.2%	B Harrison, Weaver	11,758,456	POPULAR
1896	McKinley	7,035,638	52.1%	Bryan	13,503,584	POPULAR
1900	McKinley	7,219,530	53.2%	Bryan	13,577,601	POPULAR
1904	T Roosevelt	7,828,834	60.6%	Parker, Debs	12,913,325	POPULAR
1908	Taft	7,679,005	54.5%	Bryan, Debs	14,088,111	POPULAR
1912	Wilson	6,293,152	45.3%	Taft, T Roosevelt, Debs	13,896,281	POPULAR
1916	Wilson	9,129,606	51.7%	Hughes, Benson	17,667,827	POPULAR
1920	Harding	16,152,200	63.8%	Cox, Debs	25,299,553	POPULAR
1924	Coolidge	15,725,018	54.3%	Davis, La Follette	28,933,460	POPULAR
1928	Hoover	21,392,190	58.8%	Smith, Thomas	36,408,632	POPULAR
1932	F D Roosevelt	54,281,858	59.2%	Hoover, Thomas	91,739,076	POPULAR
1936	F D Roosevelt	27,751,597	62.5%	Landon, Lemke	44,431,180	POPULAR
1940	F D Roosevelt	27,243,466	55.0%	Wilkie	49,548,221	POPULAR
1944	F D Roosevelt	25,602,505	53.8%	Dewey	47,608,783	POPULAR
1948	Truman	24,179,345	49.9%	Dewey, Thurmond, HA Wallace	48,496,829	POPULAR
1952	Eisenhower	33,938,252	55.4%	Stevenson	61,253,244	POPULAR
1956	Eisenhower	35,585,316	57.8%	Stevenson	61,616,638	POPULAR
1960	Kennedy	34,227,096	50.1%	Nixon, Byrd	68,333,642	POPULAR
1964	L Johnson	43,126,506	61.3%	Goldwater	70,303,305	POPULAR
1968	Nixon	31,785,480	43.6%	Humphrey, George Wallace	72,967,119	POPULAR
1972	Nixon	47,165,234	61.8%	McGovern	76,336,008	POPULAR
1976	Carter	40,828,929	51.1%	Ford	79,977,869	POPULAR
1980	Reagan	43,899,246	51.6%	Carter, Anderson	85,100,118	POPULAR
1984	Reagan	54,281,858	59.2%	Mondale	91,739,076	POPULAR
1988	G H W Bush	48,881,921	53.9%	Dukakis	90,687,343	POPULAR
1992	W Clinton	44,908,254	43.3%	G H W Bush, Perot	103,751,662	POPULAR
1996	W Clinton	47,401,185	50.1%	Dole, Perot	94,683,948	POPULAR
2000	G W Bush	50,459,211	48.4%	Gore, Nader	104,297,515	POPULAR
2004	G W Bush	62,040,610	51.2%	Gore	121,069,054	POPULAR
2008	Obama	69,456,897	53.7%	McCain	129,391,711	POPULAR
2012	Obama	65,915,795	52.0%	Romney	126,849,299	POPULAR
2016	Trump	61,192,764	47.1%	H Clinton, Johnson, Stein	130,040,527	POPULAR
2020	Biden	80,951,601	50.97%	Trump	158,829,047	POPULAR

156

APPENDIX B PAGE 2 OF 2
RANKED BY PERCENTAGE OF VOTE - ELECTORAL VOTE ONLY PRIOR TO 1824

RANKING	WIN VOTE	TOTAL VOTE	WINNER PERCENTAGE		
1	1	69	69	100.0% WASHINGTON 1ST	
2	1	132	132	100.0% WASHINGTON 2ND	
3	17	231	232	99.6% MONROE 2ND	
4	4	162	176	92.0% JEFFERSON 2ND	
5	17	183	217	84.3% MONROE 1ST	
6	39	122	169	72.2% MADISON 1ST	
7	29	16,152,200	25,299,553	63.8% HARDING	
8	35	27,751,597	44,431,180	62.5% F D ROOSEVELT 2ND	
9	9	47,165,234	76,336,008	61.8% NIXON 2ND	
10	42	43,126,506	70,303,305	61.3% L JOHNSON	
11	7	7,828,834	12,913,325	60.6% T ROOSEVELT	
12	3	54,281,858	91,739,076	59.2% REAGAN 2ND	
13	35	22,821,857	38,583,698	59.1% F D ROOSEVELT 1ST	
14	39	128	217	59.0% MADISON'S 2ND	
15	14	21,392,190	36,408,632	58.8% HOOVER	
16	33	762,678	1,310,685	58.2% VAN BUREN	
17	8	35,585,316	61,616,638	57.8% EISENHOWER 2ND	
18	43	687,502	1,217,691	56.5% JACKSON 2ND	
19	43	647,231	1,156,328	56.0% JACKSON 1ST	
20	28	3,597,070	6,431,149	55.9% GRANT 2ND	
21	8	33,938,252	61,253,244	55.4% EISENHOWER 1ST	
22	2	2,216,066	4,024,791	55.1% LINCOLN 2	
23	35	27,243,466	49,548,221	55.0% F D ROOSEVELT 3RD	
24	13	7,679,005	14,088,111	54.5% TAFT	
25	15	15,725,018	28,933,460	54.3% COOLIDGE	3-man race
26	10	48,881,921	90,687,343	53.9% G H W BUSH	
27	35	25,602,505	47,608,783	53.8% F D ROOSEVELT 4TH	
28	41	69,456,897	129,391,711	53.7% OBAMA 1ST	
29	45	1,601,474	2,988,052	53.6% PIERCE (30)	
30	12	7,219,530	13,577,601	53.2% MCKINLEY 2ND	
31	24	1,275,017	2,403,089	53.1% W H HARRISON	
32	28	3,015,071	5,724,686	52.7% GRANT 1ST (31)	
33	12	7,035,638	13,503,584	52.1% MCKINLEY 1ST	
34	41	65,915,795	126,849,299	52.0% OBAMA 2ND	
35	40	9,129,606	17,667,827	51.7% WILSON 2ND	
36	3	43,899,246	85,100,118	51.6% REAGAN 1ST	3 man race
37	27	62,040,610	121,069,054	51.2% G W BUSH 2ND	
38	5	71	139	51.079% J ADAMS	
39	34	40,828,929	79,977,869	51.050% CARTER (16)	
40	42	80,951,601	158,829,047	50.97% BIDEN	
41	6	1,337,243	2,636,312	50.7% POLK (32)	
42	25	4,911,017	9,759,351	50.3% CLEVELAND 1ST (11)	
43	38	34,227,096	68,333,642	50.1% KENNEDY	
44	37	47,401,185	94,683,948	50.1% CLINTON 2ND	3 man race
45	22	4,449,053	8,891,683	50.036% GARFIELD	
46	4	73	146	50.0% JEFFERSON 1ST	
47	36	24,179,345	48,496,829	49.9% TRUMAN	
48	21	5,443,892	10,978,380	49.6% B HARRISON	
49	23	61,192,764	123,696,802	49.5% TRUMP-CLINTON	ONLY
50	20	4,034,311	8,322,857	48.5% HAYES	
51	27	50,459,211	104,297,515	48.4% G W BUSH 1ST	
52	19	1,361,393	2,876,354	47.3% TAYLOR	3-man race
53	26	5,551,883	11,758,456	47.2% CLEVELAND 2ND	3 man race
54	44	1,836,072	4,051,480	45.319% BUCHANAN	3-man race
55	40	6,293,152	13,896,281	45.287% WILSON 1ST	3-man race
56	2	1,865,908	4,149,271	45.0% LINCOLN 1ST	4 man race
57	9	31,785,480	72,967,119	43.6% NIXON 1ST	3-man race
58	37	44,908,254	103,751,662	43.3% CLINTON 1ST	3 man race
59	18	113,122	355,242	31.8% J Q ADAMS	4-man race

11 NO ELECTION (ARTHUR)
16 LOST ATTEMPT TO RETAIN PRESIDENCY (FORD)
30 NO ELECTION EXCEPT LATER 3RD PARTY (FILLMORE)
31 NO ELECTION (A JOHNSON)
32 NO ELECTION (TYLER)

The Crime of the Democrats

APPENDIX C   PAGE 1 OF 2

CONTROL OF THE GOVERNMENT - PRESIDENTS AND CONGRESS 1789-2022
PARTY: R=REPUBLICAN, WHIG, NATIONAL REPUBLICAN, FEDERALIST, WASHINGTON
M=MIXED
D=DEMOCRAT, ANTIFEDERALIST, DEMOCRATIC REPUBLICAN, "REPUBLICAN" (pre 1854), JACKSONIAN

CONGRESS	HOUSE PARTY OF SPEAKER	DATE START	SENATE MAJORITY LEADER OFFICIAL - 1919	CONGRESS	PRESIDENT		GOVT			
1	WASH	1789	WASH	R	WASHINGTON	WA	R	GOVERNMENT		
2	F	1791	AF, F	M	WASHINGTON	WA	M	FROM 1789 TO 1801		
3	AF	1793	F, AF	M	WASHINGTON	WA	M			
4	F	1795	DR, F	M	WASHINGTON	WA	M	CONGRESS		
5	F	1797	F	R	J ADAMS	F	R			
6	F	1799	F	R	J ADAMS	F	R	REP	3	50.0%
7	DR	1801	"REP"	D	JEFFERSON	D	D	MIX	3	50.0%
8	DR	1803	"REP"	D	JEFFERSON	D	D	DEM	0	0.0%
9	DR	1805	"REP"	D	JEFFERSON	D	D			
10	DR	1807	"REP"	D	JEFFERSON	D	D	PRESIDENT		
11	DR	1809	"REP"	D	MADISON	D	D			
12	DR	1811	"REP"	D	MADISON	D	D	REP	6	100.0%
13	DR	1813	"REP"	D	MADISON	D	D	MIX	0	0.0%
14	DR	1815	"REP"	D	MADISON	D	D	DEM	0	0.0%
15	DR	1817	"REP"	D	MONROE	D	D			
16	DR	1819	"REP"	D	MONROE	D	D	LONGEST STRETCH		
17	"REP"	1821	"REP"	D	MONROE	D	D			
18	DR	1823	"REP"	D	MONROE	D	D	"REPUBLICAN' I E DEMOCRAT		
19	"REP"	1825	JACK	D	JQ ADAMS	NR	M	FROM 1801 TO 1825 = 24 YEARS		
20	JACK	1827	JACK	D	JQ ADAMS	NR	M			
21	JACK	1829	JACK	D	JACKSON	D	D	IF J Q ADAMS IS "REPUBLICAN"		
22	JACK	1831	JACK	D	JACKSON	D	D	FROM 1801-1841 = 40 YEARS		
23	JACK	1833	JACK	D	JACKSON	D	D			
24	DEM	1835	JACK	D	JACKSON	D	D	GOVERNMENT		
25	DEM	1837	DEM	D	VAN BUREN	D	D	FROM 1801 TO 1861		
26	DEM	1839	DEM	D	VAN BUREN	D	D			
27	WHIG	1841	DEM-WHIG	M	W H HARRISON	W	M	CONGRESS		
28	DEM	1843	WHIG	M	TYLER	W	M			
29	DEM	1845	DEM	D	POLK	D	D	REPUBLICAN	0	0.0%
30	WHIG	1847	DEM	M	POLK	D	M	MIX	9	30.0%
31	DEM	1849	DEM	D	TAYLOR	W	M	DEMOCRAT	21	70.0%
32	DEM	1851	DEM	D	FILLMORE	W	M			
33	DEM	1853	DEM	D	PIERCE	D	D	PRESIDENT		
34	AMER	1855	DEM	M	PIERCE	D	M			
35	DEM	1857	DEM	D	BUCHANAN	D	D	REPUBLICAN	6	20.0%
36	REP	1859	DEM-REP	M	BUCHANAN	D	M	MIX	0	0.0%
37	REP	1861	REP	R	LINCOLN	R	R	DEMOCRAT	24	80.0%
38	REP	1863	REP	R	LINCOLN	R	R			
39	REP	1865	REP	R	LINCOLN	R	R			
40	REP	1867	REP	R	A JOHNSON	D	M			
41	REP	1869	REP	R	GRANT	R	R			
42	REP	1871	REP	R	GRANT	R	R			
43	REP	1873	REP	R	GRANT	R	R			
44	DEM	1875	REP	M	GRANT	R	M			
45	DEM	1877	REP	M	HAYES	R	M			
46	DEM	1879	REP	D	HAYES	R	M	GOVERNMENT		
47	REP	1881	DEM-IND-REP	M	GARFIELD	R	M	FROM 1861 TO 1931		
48	DEM	1883	REP	M	ARTHUR	R	M			
49	DEM	1885	REP	M	CLEVELAND	D	M	CONGRESS		
50	DEM	1887	REP	M	CLEVELAND	D	M			
51	REP	1889	REP	R	B HARRISON	R	R	REPUBLICAN	19	54.3%
52	REP	1891	REP	M	B HARRISON	R	M	MIX	13	37.1%
53	DEM	1893	REP-DEM	M	CLEVELAND	D	M	DEMOCRAT	3	8.6%
54	REP	1895	REP	R	CLEVELAND	D	M			
55	REP	1897	REP	R	MCKINLEY	R	R	PRESIDENT		
56	REP	1899	REP	R	MCKINLEY	R	R			
57	REP	1901	REP	R	MCKINLEY	R	R	REPUBLICAN	26	74.3%
58	REP	1903	REP	R	T ROOSEVELT	R	R	MIX	0	0.0%
59	REP	1905	REP	R	T ROOSEVELT	R	R	DEMOCRAT	9	25.7%
60	REP	1907	REP	R	T ROOSEVELT	R	R			
61	REP	1909	REP	R	TAFT	R	R			
62	DEM	1911	REP-DEM	M	TAFT	R	M	NO MORE MIDTERM CHANGE		
63	DEM	1913	DEM	D	WILSON	D	D	APRIL 8 1913 17TH AMENDMENT		
64	DEM	1915	DEM	D	WILSON	D	D	DIRECT ELECTION OF SENATORS		
65	DEM	1917	DEM	D	WILSON	D	D			
66	REP	1919	DEM	R	WILSON	D	M			
67	REP	1921	REP	R	HARDING	R	R			
68	REP	1923	REP	R	HARDING	R	R			
69	REP	1925	REP	R	COOLIDGE	R	R			
70	REP	1927	REP	R	COOLIDGE	R	R			
71	REP	1929	REP	R	HOOVER	R	R			

158

APPENDIX C   PAGE 2 OF 2
CONTROL OF THE GOVERNMENT - PRESIDENTS AND CONGRESS 1789-2023

PARTY:
R=REPUBLICAN, WHIG, FEDERALIST, WASHINGTON
M=MIXED
D=DEMOCRAT, ANTIFEDERALIST, DEMOCRATIC REPUBLICAN, "REPUBLICAN", JACKSONIAN

CONGRESS	HOUSE PARTY OF SPEAKER	DATE START	SENATE MAJORITY LEADER OFFICIAL - 1919	CONGRESS	PRESIDENT		GOVT			
72	DEM	1931	REP	M	HOOVER	R	M			
73	DEM	1933	DEM	D	F D ROOSEVELT	D	D			
74	DEM	1935	DEM	D	F D ROOSEVELT	D	D			
75	DEM	1937	DEM	D	F D ROOSEVELT	D	D			
76	DEM	1939	DEM	D	F D ROOSEVELT	D	D			
77	DEM	1941	DEM	D	F D ROOSEVELT	D	D			
78	DEM	1943	DEM	D	F D ROOSEVELT	D	D			
79	DEM	1945	DEM	D	F D ROOSEVELT	D	D			
80	REP	1947	REP	R	TRUMAN	D	M	GOVERNMENT		
81	DEM	1949	DEM	D	TRUMAN	D	D	FROM 1931 TO 1981		
82	DEM	1951	DEM	D	TRUMAN	D	D			
83	REP	1953	REP	R	EISENHOWER	R	R	CONGRESS		
84	DEM	1955	DEM	D	EISENHOWER	R	M			
85	DEM	1957	DEM	D	EISENHOWER	R	M	REPUBLICAN	1	4.0%
86	DEM	1959	DEM	D	EISENHOWER	R	M	MIX	9	36.0%
87	DEM	1961	DEM	D	KENNEDY	D	D	DEMOCRAT	15	60.0%
88	DEM	1963	DEM	D	KENNEDY	D	D			
89	DEM	1965	DEM	D	L JOHNSON	D	D	PRESIDENT		
90	DEM	1967	DEM	D	L JOHNSON	D	D			
91	DEM	1969	DEM	D	NIXON	R	M	REPUBLICAN	9	36.0%
92	DEM	1971	DEM	D	NIXON	R	M	MIX	0	0.0%
93	DEM	1973	DEM	D	NIXON	R	M	DEMOCRAT	16	64.0%
94	DEM	1975	DEM	D	FORD	R	M			
95	DEM	1977	DEM	D	CARTER	D	D			
96	DEM	1979	DEM	D	CARTER	D	D	GOVERNMENT		
97	DEM	1981	REP	M	REAGAN	R	M	FROM 1981 TO 2024		
98	DEM	1983	REP	M	REAGAN	R	M			
99	DEM	1985	REP	M	REAGAN	R	M	CONGRESS		
100	DEM	1987	DEM	D	REAGAN	R	M			
101	DEM	1989	DEM	D	GHW BUSH	R	M	REPUBLICAN	3	13.6%
102	DEM	1991	DEM	D	GHW BUSH	R	M	MIX	17	77.3%
103	DEM	1993	DEM	D	CLINTON	D	D	DEMOCRAT	2	9.1%
104	REP	1995	REP	R	CLINTON	D	M			
105	REP	1997	REP	R	CLINTON	D	M	PRESIDENT		
106	REP	1999	REP	R	CLINTON	D	M			
107	DEM	2001	DEM	M	GW BUSH	R	M	REPUBLICAN	11	52.4%
108	REP	2003	REP	R	GW BUSH	R	R	MIX	0	0.0%
109	REP	2005	REP	R	GW BUSH	R	R	DEMOCRAT	10	47.6%
110	DEM	2007	DEM	D	GW BUSH	R	M			
111	DEM	2009	DEM	D	OBAMA	D	D			
112	REP	2011	DEM	M	OBAMA	D	M			
113	REP	2013	DEM	M	OBAMA	D	M			
114	REP	2015	REP	R	OBAMA	D	M			
115	REP	2017	REP	R	TRUMP	R	R			
116	DEM	2019	REP	M	TRUMP	R	M			
117	DEM	2021	MIX	M	BIDEN	D	M			
118	REP	2023	DEM	M	BIDEN	D	M			

159

APPENDIX D1
RANKINGS FOR EACH PRESIDENT- RATINGS COMPARED TO OTHERS

PRESIDENT	THIS RANKING	LIBERTARIAN ELAND	MAINSTREAM HIGH	MAINSTREAM LOW	RANGE THIS - LIBERT	RANGE MAIN H-L	INSIDE MAINSTR THIS RANKING	INSIDE MAINSTR LIBERTARIAN	IN MAIN TO WITHIN 5 THIS	IN MAIN TO WITHIN 5 LIBERTARIAN	+20 TO MAINSTR THIS	+20 TO MAINSTR LIBERTARIAN
Washington	1	7	1	4	6	3 Y	N	Y	Y			
Lincoln	2	29	1	3	27	2 Y	N	Y	N		Y	
Reagan	3	35	6	26	32	20 N	N	Y	N			
Jefferson	4	26	2	7	22	5 Y	N	Y	N			
J Adams	5	22	9	19	17	10 N	N	Y	Y			
Polk	6	38	9	20	32	11 N	N	Y	N			
T Roosevelt	7	21	2	7	14	5 N	N	Y	N			
Eisenhower	8	9	5	21	1	16 Y	Y	Y	Y			
Nixon	9	30	23	36	21	13 N	Y	N	Y			
Trump	10	-	41	44	-	3 N	-	N	-	N	-
Arthur	11	5	17	35	6	18 N	N	N	N			
McKinley	12	39	11	21	27	10 Y	N	Y	N			
Taft	13	20	16	25	7	9 N	Y	Y	Y			
Hoover	14	18	19	38	4	19 N	N	Y	Y			
Coolidge	15	10	23	36	5	13 N	N	N	N			
Ford	16	16	23	32	0	9 N	N	N	N			
Monroe	17	25	7	18	8	11 Y	N	Y	N			
G H W Bush	18	33	17	31	23	14 N	N	N	Y			
J Q Adams	19	12	11	25	6	14 Y	Y	Y	Y			
Taylor	20	13	24	35	6	11 N	N	Y	N			
Hayes	21	4	13	33	16	20 Y	N	Y	N			
B Harrison	22	15	19	34	6	15 Y	N	Y	Y			
Garfield	23 NR		25	34 XX		9 N	XX	Y	XX		XX	
W H Harrison	24 NR		26	42 XX		16 N	XX	Y	XX		XX	
Cleveland (1)	25	2	8	24	23	16 N	N	Y	N			
Cleveland (2)	26	2	8	24	24	16 N	N	Y	N			
G W Bush	27	37	19	39	10	20 Y	Y	Y	Y			
Grant	28	19	21	38	9	17 Y	N	Y	Y			
Harding	29	6	29	42	23	13 Y	N	Y	N		Y	
Fillmore	30	14	24	38	16	14 Y	N	Y	N			
A Johnson	31	17	19	42	14	23 Y	N	Y	Y			
Tyler	32	1	22	39	31	17 Y	N	Y	N		Y	
Van Buren	33	3	15	34	30	19 Y	N	Y	N			
Carter	34	8	18	34	26	16 Y	N	Y	N			
F D Roosevelt	35	31	1	3	4	2 N	N	N	N	Y	Y
Truman	36	40	5	9	4	4 N	N	N	N	Y	Y
Clinton	37	11	8	24	26	16 N	Y	N	Y			
Kennedy	38	36	8	16	2	8 N	N	N	N	Y	Y
Madison	39	28	8	20	11	12 N	N	N	N			
Wilson	40	41	4	11	1	7 N	N	N	N	Y	Y
Obama	41	34	8	18	7	10 N	N	N	N	Y	
Biden	42	-	19	19	-	0 N	-	N	-	N	-
L Johnson	43	32	10	17	10	7 N	N	N	N	Y	
Jackson	44	27	5	18	16	13 N	N	N	N	Y	
Buchanan	45	23	26	43	21	17 N	N	Y	Y			
Pierce	46	24	27	41	21	14 N	N	Y	Y			
				YES TOTAL			17	6	30		15	8	7
				NO TOTAL			28	36	15		27		

160

APPENDIX D2 — rankings adjusted for W H Harrison, Garfield, Cleveland

THIS RANKING	PRESIDENT	WEAK	MOD	STRONG	THIS (W)	LIBERT (W)	MAIN (W)	THIS (M)	LIBERTARIAN (M)	MAIN (M)	THIS (S)	LIBERT (S)	MAIN (S)	MAINSTREAM AVERAGE	ADJUSTED LIBERTARIAN
1	Washington			Y							1	8	3	3	8
2	Lincoln			Y							2	33	1	1	33
3	Reagan			Y							3	39	16	15	39
4	Jefferson			Y							4	30	5	5	30
5	J Adams			Y							5	26	15	13	26
6	Polk			Y							6	42	12	13	42
7	T Roosevelt			Y							7	25	4	5	25
8	Eisenhower			Y							8	10	8	9	10
9	Nixon			Y							9	34	34	30	34
10	Trump			Y							10 nr		41	43 nr	
11	Arthur		Y					11	6	29				28	6
12	McKinley	Y			12	43	19							17	43
13	Taft		Y					13	24	24				21	24
14	Hoover		Y					14	22	35				30	22
15	Coolidge		Y					15	11	31				28	11
16	Ford	Y			16	20	27							26	20
17	Monroe		Y					17	29	17				14	29
18	G H W Bush	Y			10	37	23							21	37
19	J Q Adams		Y					18	13	22				18	13
20	Taylor		Y					19	14	36				31	14
21	Hayes		Y					20	5	26				26	5
22	B Harrison	Y			21	16	32							29	16
23	Garfield	Y			22	17	30							27	17
24	W H Harrison	Y			24	19	39							34	19
25	Cleveland 1		Y					25	2	20				18	2
26	Cleveland 2		Y					26	2	20				18	2
27	G W Bush		Y					27	41	33				31	41
28	Grant	Y			28	23	37							30	23
29	Harding	Y			29	7	43							38	7
30	Fillmore	Y			30	15	40							34	15
31	A Johnson		Y					31	21	42				37	21
32	Tyler		Y					32	1	38				34	1
33	Van Buren	Y			33	4	25							24	4
34	Carter	Y			34	9	28							26	9
35	F D Roosevelt			Y							35	35	2	2	35
36	Truman			Y							36	44	6	7	44
37	Clinton	Y			37	12	18							17	12
38	Kennedy	Y			38	40	10							12	40
39	Madison	Y			39	32	14							13	32
40	Wilson			Y							40	45	7	8	45
41	Obama		Y					41	38	11				12	38
42	Biden	Y			42 nr		19							19	-
43	L Johnson			Y							42	36	13	13	36
44	Jackson			Y							43	31	9	11	31
45	Buchanan	Y			44	27	44							39	27
46	Pierce			Y				45	28	41				37	28

The Crime of the Democrats

APPENDIX E

#	President	SCHLESINGER SR 1948	SCHLESINGER 1962	M-B 1982	CHICAGO TRIBUNE 1982	SIENA 1982	SIENA 1990	SIENA 1994	RIDINGS & MCIVER 1996	SCHLESINGER 1996	C-SPAN 2000	WALL STREET JRNL 2000	SIENA 2002	WALL STREET JRNL 2005	C-SPAN 2009	SIENA 2010	USPC 2011	AMER POL SCI ASSN 2015	C-SPAN 2017	AMER POL SCI ASSN 2018	C-Span 2021	SIENA 2022	IVAN ELAND 2014	THIS RANKING	AGGREGATE MAINSTREAM RANKING	INTEGRAL RANKING
1	WASHINGTON	2	2	3	2	4	4	4	3	3	2	1	4	1	2	4	3	2	2	2	2	3	7	1	2.619	3
2	ADAMS	9	10	14	15	8	14	14	14	14	16	13	12	13	17	17	12	19	19	14	15	16	22	5	13.381	14
3	JEFFERSON	5	5	4	5	5	4	4	4	4	7	4	5	4	7	5	7	5	7	5	7	5	26	4	4.905	5
4	MADISON	14	14	14	11	17	9	10	10	9	18	15	9	17	20	6	17	13	17	12	16	10	28	39	13.381	14
5	MONROE	12	12	18	16	16	15	15	13	15	14	16	15	25	14	14	16	17	16	18	12	12	25	17	13.857	16
6	J Q ADAMS	11	13	17	17	16	11	11	18	18	19	20	16	26	25	19	20	17	21	15	22	17	12	22	18.333	19
7	JACKSON	6	6	7	9	13	13	9	8	5	13	6	10	13	10	13	9	18	18	15	22	23	27	9	11.095	11
8	VAN BUREN	15	17	20	21	19	22	21	21	22	30	23	25	27	27	20	21	25	27	23	22	34	3	26	24.333	24
9	W H HARRISON	NR	NR	NR	NR	NR	NR	35	36	37	NR	38	37	35	39	30	39	39	39	42	40	40	1	39	33.500	33
10	TYLER	22	25	28	24	28	34	34	35	35	37	34	36	36	35	37	35	37	38	37	37	39	38	17	33.810	34
11	POLK	10	8	12	13	10	13	11	11	11	12	9	11	NR	9	12	9	14	14	20	18	15	13	44	12.667	13
12	TAYLOR	25	24	27	26	28	35	35	29	29	33	34	31	33	33	31	29	34	29	35	38	36	14	32	30.952	37
13	FILLMORE	24	26	29	30	32	32	32	36	35	37	39	36	38	37	38	35	38	37	38	38	38	14	40	34.095	41
14	PIERCE	27	28	31	33	35	36	36	38	36	39	41	38	41	40	40	38	40	40	42	42	41	23	44	36.857	42
15	BUCHANAN	26	29	33	34	36	38	39	40	40	41	39	41	42	42	44	40	43	43	44	44	43	29	45	38.952	45
16	LINCOLN	1	1	2	1	3	2	2	1	1	1	2	1	2	1	3	2	1	1	1	1	1	17	43	1.429	1
17	A JOHNSON	19	23	32	32	30	36	37	39	38	40	42	36	37	37	36	33	42	41	40	43	45	19	24	37.238	43
18	GRANT	28	30	35	35	36	38	38	33	32	33	32	33	29	28	26	23	28	22	21	20	21	7	25	29.952	34
19	HAYES	13	14	22	22	22	26	25	25	23	25	30	24	30	33	32	29	33	29	29	25	21	4	37	25.762	27
20	GARFIELD	NR	NR	NR	NR	NR	30	29	NR	30	NR	33	28	NR	29	30	32	29	29	31	27	27	5	27	26.714	30
21	ARTHUR	17	21	24	24	28	25	26	32	30	27	25	26	32	32	31	26	25	25	31	21	25	15	23	27.571	31
22	CLEVELAND 1	8	11	13	17	13	17	16	13	16	17	13	12	25	21	21	17	17	23	24	25	21	2	11	17.762	20
23	B HARRISON	21	20	26	25	28	29	27	31	31	30	31	29	34	30	34	30	32	30	33	32	34	15	25	28.810	33
24	CLEVELAND 2	8	11	13	17	13	17	16	13	16	17	13	12	25	21	21	17	17	23	24	25	21	2	22	17.095	20
25	MCKINLEY	18	15	18	18	19	18	19	18	16	15	14	15	19	18	16	15	16	16	19	14	19	39	26	17.095	18
26	T ROOSEVELT	7	7	5	4	5	2	5	6	6	4	4	4	5	4	2	7	4	4	4	4	4	21	12	4.524	4
27	TAFT	16	16	19	20	20	21	24	22	20	24	20	22	20	11	24	20	21	22	22	23	25	9	40	7.905	25
28	WILSON	4	4	6	6	6	4	6	6	11	6	6	11	8	11	9	10	11	10	11	11	13	41	29	38.286	7
29	HARDING	29	31	36	36	39	40	41	41	39	38	37	38	40	38	42	40	42	42	39	37	42	6	15	28.476	44
30	COOLIDGE	23	27	30	29	33	36	36	33	25	27	29	27	34	29	26	31	27	29	28	24	18	8	14	29.952	32
31	HOOVER	20	19	21	24	24	29	24	24	24	31	31	24	29	34	34	36	38	36	36	36	20	10	35	14.529	28
32	F D ROOSEVELT	3	3	8	8	2	1	1	2	2	1	3	2	3	1	1	4	3	3	3	3	2	31	36	21.063	17
33	TRUMAN	NR	8	9	8	7	7	7	7	7	5	7	5	7	9	6	6	6	6	6	6	6	40	6	6.900	24
34	EISENHOWER	NR	21	11	10	9	12	8	9	10	9	9	8	10	8	10	8	5	5	7	5	8	9	8	9.200	19
35	KENNEDY			13	14	14	10	11	15	12	8	14	15	11	15	11	8	8	8	11	8	9	36	10	12.053	38
36	L JOHNSON			10	12	12	13	12	10	11	12	15	18	16	18	16	10	11	12	10	11	14	32	12	12.632	11
37	NIXON			34	35	34	35	33	32	33	25	33	28	32	23	28	26	27	28	33	30	30	30	36	30.053	36
38	FORD			24	23	24	24	23	27	27	23	24	28	22	24	25	25	26	25	24	28	24	6	29	26.263	29
39	CARTER			22	24	25	27	32	19	19	30	27	27	34	25	25	33	28	25	26	26	18	8	28	25.895	28
40	REAGAN			NR	NR	NR	20	20	26	25	11	17	6	16	18	22	11	9	9	8	11	7	35	17	14.529	17
41	G H W BUSH				16		18	22	22	24	20	21	20	24	19	22	17	20	20	18	21	19	33	24	21.063	24
42	CLINTON								23		21	24	18	22	22	13	15	8	13	13	19	14	11	19	17.400	19
43	G W BUSH													23	36	39	30	35	30	33	29	35	37	38	31.000	38
44	OBAMA															15		18	17	8	13	10	28	11	12.333	11
45	TRUMP																				41	43	41	46	42.667	46
46	BIDEN																					19	34	10	19.000	23

201

APPENDIX F

UNITED STATES SUPREME COURT

PRESIDENT	CHIEF JUSTICE	ASSOCIATE JUSTICES								APPOINTED DEM REP
		1	2	3	4	5	6	7	8	9	10	

```
WASHINGTON,            1789
GEORGE          JAY, JOHN  WILSON, JAMES                                              2
                        1789   1789  RUTLEDG CUSHING IREDELL  BLAIR,
"FEDERALIST"            F      F      1790    1790    1790    1790                    6
APPOINTED                             1791 F          F       F
     10          10                   JOHNSON, THOMAS                                 6
                                      1792 AF
                                      1793
                                      PATERSON, WILLIAM
                                      1793 AF

* SENATE REJECTED     1795 AF?                              1795
RUTLEDGE AS CHIEF     RUTLEDGE, JOHN*                                                 6
JUSTICE               1795 AF
                      ELLSWORTH, OLIVER                CHASE, SAMUEL                  6
                      1796                             1796
ADAMS,                1797
JOHN                           1798

FEDERALIST            1800  WASHINGTON, BUSHROD                                       6
APPOINTED                    F           F        1799
     3            3                               MOORE, ALFRED                       6
                                                  1800
                      MARSHALL, JOHN                                                  6
                      1801


JEFFERSON,                     1801
THOMAS                 F        F       F        F       F
                                                 1804
"REPUBLICAN"                                     JOHNSON, WILLIAM                  1   5
APPOINTED                                        1804
                                       1806            AF
     3            3                    LIVINGSTON, HENRY     TODD, THOMAS          3   4
                                       1807                  1807
                               F        F       "R"    F     "R"    F     "R"
                                                AF                        AF
MADISON,                       1809
JAMES                                           1810
"REPUBLICAN"                                    DUVALL, GABRIEL                    4   3
APPOINTED                                       1811
     2            2                             AF                                 1
                               F        F       "R"    "R"    "R"    F     "R"
                                                                     1811
                                                                     STORY, JOSEPH  5   2
                                                                     1812
                                                                     AF
MONROE,                        1817
JAMES
"REPUBLICAN"                            1823
APPOINTED                               THOMPSON, SMITH
     1            1                     1823                                       5   2
                               F        F       "R"    "R"    "R"    F     "R"
                                                AF
ADAMS,                         1825
JOHN Q.
DEM-NATL REPUB                                                1826
APPOINTED                                                     TRIMBLE, ROBERT      4   3
     1            1                                           1826
                               F        F       "R"    "R"    "R"    F     AF
JACKSON,                       1829
ANDREW                                 1829
DEMOCRAT                               MCLEAN, JOHN           BALDWIN, HENRY       6   1
APPOINTED                              1830                   1830
                               F        D       "R"    "R"    "R"    D
     6            6                                     1834
                                                        WAYNE, JAMES               6   1
                                       1835             1835    1835
                                       TANEY, ROGER    BARBOUR, PHILIP             7   0
                                       1836            1836           CATRON, JOHN 8   0
                                       D                                      1837
                               D        D       "R"    D       D      F       D
                                                        163
```

APPENDIX F

VAN BUREN, MARTIN DEMOCRAT APPOINTED 1		1837							MCKINLEY, JOHN 1838 D	1 9	0
HARRISON, WILLIAM H. WHIG		1841			1841						
TYLER, JOHN WHIG-DEMOCRAT APPOINTED 1 1		1841		DANIEL, PETER 1842 1843 D						9 8 7	0 0 0
POLK, JAMES DEMOCRAT APPOINTED 3 3	D	1845 D	VACANT D GRIER, ROBERT 1846	D	F WOODBURY, LEVI 1845	1844 VACANT D 1845 NELSON, SAMUEL 1845	D			8 9	0 0
TAYLOR, ZACHARY WHIG	0	1849									
FILLMORE, MILLARD WHIG APPOINTED 1 1		1850				1851 CURTIS, BENJAMIN 1851 D				8	1
PIERCE, FRANKLIN DEMOCRAT APPOINTED 1	D	D 1853	D	D	D	W	D	D	1852 VACANT CAMPBELL, JOHN 1853	8	1
BUCHANAN, JAMES DEMOCRAT APPOINTED 1 1	D	D 1857	D	D	D	W 1857 CLIFFORD, NATHAN 1858 1860 D	D	D	D	8	1

LINCOLN, ABRAHAM REPUBLICAN APPOINTED 5 6D, 3R	J (D)	1861 1861 MILLER, SAMUEL 1862 L (R) R 1864 CHASE, SALMON 1864	P (R)	SWAYNE, NOAH 1862 L (R)	J (D)	B (D)	P (D)	J (D)	1861 DAVIS, DAVID 1862 L (R) R FIELD, R 1863	6 6 5	3 4 5
YEARS 5D, 5R											
JOHNSON, ANDREW DEMOCRAT APPOINTED NONE 3D, 5R	0	L (R) R 1865 L (R)	P (D) D	L (R) R	J (D) D 1867 NO JUDGE 3 YEARS	B (D) D B (D)	P (D) D P (D)	J (D) D	L (R) R 1865 NO JUDGE 5 YEARS L (R)	L (R) R L (R)	4 3	5 5
GRANT, ULYSSES REPUBLICAN APPOINTED 4 1D, 8R	4	1869 1873 WAITE, MORRISON 1874 G (R) R	1870 POSITION VACATED SEE FIELD, STEPHEN 1863 L (R)	R NO JUSTIC L (R)	BRADLEY, JOSEPH 1870 G (R)	B (D)	1872 R HUNT, WARD 1873 R G (R)	STRONG, WILLIAM 1870 G (R)	L (R)	L (R)	2 1	7 8

164

Prepared by terry koglin 2/14/2024

APPENDIX F

President										
HAYES, RURTHERFORD REPUBLICAN APPOINTED 1	1877 1						1877 HARLAN, JOHN 1877 1880 R		1	8
GARFIELD, JAMES REPUBLICAN	1881			1881	1881					
ARTHUR, CHESTER REPUBLICAN APPOINTED 4	1881 4			WOODS, WILLIAM 1881 R	MATTHEWS, STANLEY 1881 R		GRAY, HORACE 1882 BLATCHFORD, SAMUEL 1882	1882	0 0 0	9 9 9 1
	R	R	VACANT	R	R	R	R	R	R	
CLEVELAND, GROVER DEMOCRAT APPOINTED 2	1885 2			1887 LAMAR, LUCIUS					1 2	8 7
		1888 FULLER, MELVILLE 1888		1888 R						
HARRISON, BENJAMIN REPUBLICAN APPOINTED 3	1889 D 3	R 1890 BROWN, HENRY 1891 R	VACANT	D R	R 1889 BREWER, DAVID 1890 R 1892 SHIRAS, GEORGE 1892 R	R	R	R	2 2 2	7 7 7
CLEVELAND, GROVER DEMOCRAT APPOINTED 3	1893 3			1893 WHITE, EDWARD 1894 D	1893 JACKSON, HOWELL 1893 R 1895 PECKHAM, RUFUS 1896				2 2 3	7 7 6
	D	R	VACANT	D R	R	D R	R	R		
MCKINLEY, WILLIAM REPUBLICAN APPOINTED 1	1897 1							1897 MCKENNA, 1898	3	6
ROOSEVELT, THEODORE REPUBLICAN APPOINTED 3	D 3	1901 R	VACANT VACANT	D	R	D	R 1902 HOLMES, OLIVER W. 1902	R	3	6
					1903 DAY, WILLIAM 1903 R				3	6
		1906 MOODY, WILLIAM 1906 R							3	6
TAFT, WILLIAM REPUBLICAN APPOINTED 6	1909 6 WHITE, 1910 R	1910 LURTON, HORACE 1910		1910 PITNEY, MAHLON 1912	1910 HUGHES, CHARLES E. 1910 VAN DEVANTER, WILLIS 1911 R			1911 LAMAR, JOSEPH 1911	2 0 0 0	7 8 9 9
ALL REPUBLICAN JUSTICES	R	R	VACANT	R	R	R	R	R		

165

Prepared by terry koglin 2/14/2024

APPENDIX F

President									
WILSON, T. WOODROW DEMOCRAT APPOINTED 3	1913 3		1914 MCREYNOLDS, JAMES 1914 D				1916 BRANDEIS, LOUIS 1916 D	1916 CLARKE, JOHN 1916 D	1 8 3 6
		1921		VACANT					
HARDING, WARREN REPUBLICAN APPOINTED 4		1921 TAFT, WILLIAM 1921 R			1922 1922 SUTHERLAND, GEORGE 1922 BUTLER, PIERCE R 1923			1922 SANFORD, EDWARD 1923 R	3 6 3 6 2 7
COOLIDGE, CALVIN REPUBLICAN APPOINTED 1	1923 1		VACANT					1925 STONE,	2 7
HOOVER, HERBERT REPUBLICAN APPOINTED 3	1929 1930 HUGHES, CHARLES 1930 3 R		1929				1930 ROBERTS, OWEN 1930 1932 R CARDOZO, BENJAMIN 1932	1925 R	2 7 2 7
	R	D	VACANT R	R	R	D	R	R	
ROOSEVELT, FRANKLIN DEMOCRAT APPOINTED 9 TURNED COURT 1939 DEMOCRAT	1933 9 R	D	VACANT D	1938 REED, STANLEY 1938 D R 1939 FRANKFURTER, FELIX 1939 D	1937 BLACK, HUGO 1937 D D	1938 D 1939 D DOUGLAS, WILLIAM 1939	R MURPHY, 1940		3 6 4 5 5 4 6 3 6 3
*NOTE: STONE APPOINTED BY COOLIDGE AS ASSOCIATE JUSTICE 1925		1941 STONE, 1941 D	1941 BYRNES, JAMES 1941 D 1942 RUTLEDGE, WILEY 1943 D					1941 JACKSON, 1941 D	8 1 8 1
TRUMAN, HARRY DEMOCRAT APPOINTED 4	1945 D 1946 VINSON, FRED 1946 4 D	D CLARK, TOM 7 YRS, D	VACANT D 1949 1949 D	D	D VACANT D	D 1949 MINTON, SHERMAN 1949 D	D 1945 D BURTON, HAROLD 1945 D D		9 0 9 0 9 0 9 0
EISENHOWER, DWIGHT REPUBLICAN APPOINTED 5	1953 R WAREN, EARL 1953 5 R			19 YRS, R 1957 WHITTAKER, CHARLES 1957	7 YRS, R 1956 D	1956 BRENNAN, WILLIAM 1956 D	13 YRS, R 1958 STEWART, POTTER 1958	13 YRS, D 1954 HARLAN, 1954	8 1 7 2 6 3 5 4 4 5
TURNED COURT 1958 REPUBLICAN	R	D	VACANT R	D	D	R	D	R	

166

APPENDIX F

President										
KENNEDY, JOHN DEMOCRAT APPOINTED 2 TURNED COURT 1962	1961			1962 WHITE, 1962 D	1962 GOLDBERG, ARTHUR 1962 D				5	4
DEMOCRAT	R	D 1963	VACANT D	D	D	R	D	R R		
JOHNSON, LYNDON DEMOCRAT APPOINTED 2 2					1965 FORTAS, ABE 1965 D				5	4
		1967 MARSHALL, THURGOOD 1967 D							5	4
	R	D	VACANT D	D	1969 D	R	D	R R		
NIXON, RICHARD REPUBLICAN TURNED COURT 1970		1969 BURGER, WARREN 1969 D			BLACKMUN, HARRY 1970				5 4	4 5
APPOINTED 4	R 4	D	VACANT D	R	D 1971 POWELL, LEWIS 1972	R	D	R 1971 REHNQUIS 1972	3	6
FORD, GERALD REPUBLICAN APPOINTED 1	1974 1						1975 STEVENS, JOHN 1975		2	7
CARTER, JAMES E. DEMOCRAT	0	1977								
REAGAN, RONALD REPUBLICAN APPOINTED 4		1981	VACANT				1981 O'CONNOR, SANDRA 1981 R		2	7
	4	1986 REHNQUIST, WILLIAM 1986 R						1986 SCALIA, 1986 R	2	7
					1987 KENNEDY, ANTHONY 1988				2	7
BUSH, GEORGE H.W. REPUBLICAN APPOINTED 2	1989 2					1990 SOUTER, DAVID 1990			2	7
		1991 THOMAS, CLARENCE 1991							1	8
	R	R	VACANT D	R	R	R	R	R		
CLINTON, WILLIAM DEMOCRAT APPOINTED 2 2	1993 D REPUBLIC. REPUBLICAN B			1993 GINSBUR 1993 D DEMOCRA	1994 BREYER, STEPHEN 1994 DEMOCRA REPUBLIC.	REPUBLIC. D	REPUBLIC.	REPUBLIC. REPUBLICAN R	2	7
BUSH, GEORGE W. REPUBLICAN APPOINTED 2	2001 2005 2 ROBERTS, JOHN 2005 R								2	7
							2006 ALITO, SAMUEL 2006 R		2	7

167

Prepared by terry koglin 2/14/2024

APPENDIX F

OBAMA, BARRACK DEMOCRAT APPOINTED 2		2009				2009 SOTOMAYOR, SONIA 2009 KAGAN, ELENA 2010		3 4	6 5
TRUMP, DONALD REPUBLICAN APPOINTED 3	R 2017	R	VACANT	D (GINSBURG) BORN 1933 86 DIED SEPT 18, 2020	D	R	D 2018 KAVANAUGH, BRETT 2018	D 2010	R	R 2016 GORSUCH 2017 R	4 3	5 5
			VACANT	BARRETT AMY 2020	R				3	6
BIDEN, JOSEPH DEMOCRAT APPOINTED 1		2021			JACKSON, K B 2022				3	6

CURRENT COURT AS OF FEBRUARY 2024

APPOINTED BY:	REPUBLICAN	REPUBLICAN	VACANT	REPUBLICAN	DEMOCRAT	REPUBLICAN	DEMOCRAT	DEMOCRAT	REPUBLICAN	REPUBLICAN
PRESIDENT:	BUSH G W	BUSH G H W		TRUMP	BIDEN	TRUMP	OBAMA	OBAMA	BUSH G W	TRUMP
DATE:	2005	1991		2020	2022	2018	2009	2010	2006	2017
NAME:	ROBERTS	THOMAS	VACANT	BARRETT	JACKSON	KAVANAUGH	SOTOMAYOR	KAGAN	ALITO	GORSUCH
BORN:	1955	1948		1973	1970	1965	1954	1960	1950	1967
AGE IN 2024:	69	76		51	54	59	70	64	74	57

TOTAL AVERAGE AGE IN: 2024 63.8

DEMOCRAT 49 APPOINTMENTS COURT AS OF 2024 6 REPUBLICAN APPOINTMENTS
REPUBLICAN 71 APPOINTMENTS   3 DEMOCRAT APPOINTMENTS

Prepared by terry koglin 2/14/2024

About the Author

Terry L. Koglin has been a political activist nearly his entire life, dating from his first experience as a toddler accompanying his parents to vote at the local town hall. He organized mock elections at his elementary school and elevated his political activity upon attending the University of Wisconsin at Madison. His professional career involved interactions with politicians and media personnel, sometimes necessitating adept handling of sensitive issues. His mother was a Republican, and his father was a Democrat, but he also has had friends and relatives with more exotic political perspectives.